MW01101020

AN
IDOLATROUS
REVOLUTION

The Movies of ELVIS PRESLEY
and The Politics of Rock & Roll

Mark Jaskela

An Idolatrous Revolution
Copyright © 2020 by Mark Jaskela

All rights reserved. No part of this publication may
be reproduced, distributed, or transmitted in any
form or by any means, including photocopying,
recording, or other electronic or mechanical
methods, without the prior written permission of
the author, except in the case of brief quotations
embodied in critical reviews and certain other non-
commercial uses permitted by copyright law.

Tellwell Talent
www.tellwell.ca

ISBN
978-0-2288-3109-9 (Hardcover)
978-0-2288-3108-2 (Paperback)
978-0-2288-3110-5 (eBook)

To my dear friend
and patron Nancy Kier,
May this book bless you
with enjoyment and
insight.
                    Love,
            Mark Jarstfer

In memory of my parents,
Eric and Edith, who loved reading.

"Truth is like the sun. You can shut it out for a time, but it ain't going away."

A handwritten note inside Elvis Presley's Bible

TABLE OF CONTENTS

Acknowledgments

Special thanks are due to my friend Graeme Hiebert, whose technological expertise and help with rounding up research materials proved indispensable. Michael Barnholden's editing of an earlier, less revolutionary version of what follows here was also invaluable. Thanks also to Letitia Henville for her editing a late draft of this book.

INTRODUCTION

Elvis Aron Presley's entire show business career was circumscribed by the Cold War, that battle for hearts and minds of those rarely given credit for having much of either. Alongside whatever else they may have been, Presley's movies were propaganda tools for a nation that departing president Dwight D. Eisenhower warned to "beware the military-industrial complex." Presented here is a series of critiques of all 31 movies that Presley acted and sang in.[1] These critiques demonstrate how popular culture of the 1950s and 1960s, including the Presley movies, harmonize with the aims of a government within a government, one wrought through wars that in turn sponsors more wars.

Presley's first four movies, all produced and released in the 1950s, not only capitalized on the craze surrounding rock & roll and Presley himself. They were also informed by efforts to normalize the new musical movement, to promote its most auspicious emissary, and to aid in establishing a culture of distraction, maintaining and advancing political stability both within and beyond U.S. borders. That this effort was undertaken, despite the 1950s films function as light entertainment, with noticeably higher production standards than the Presley movies

---

[1]   In 1969's *Charro!* Presley sings the theme song, although his on-screen character does not sing.

of the 1960s, indicates that initially more care was exercised in selling the public on the star and on the legitimacy of rock & roll. Later, after his 1958–60 military service, most of Presley's movies reflect the idea that capitalist democracy is the highest form of social, economic and political organization because it's the most fun.

On the liner notes of an early Bob Dylan record, Johnny Cash wrote: "To imitate the dead is mockery." If that's the case, Presley holds the distinction of being the most widely and wildly mocked entertainer who ever lived. According to a BBC documentary, as of 2002 over 80,000 U.S. citizens reported to the Internal Revenue Service that their primary source of income was being an Elvis impersonator (or "tribute artist," as it's now more pretentiously being called). There are at least three basic kinds of Elvis impersonators. The first kind exhibits a brand of kitsch sentimentalism that, even at its most raucous, seems oriented toward giving audiences a living sense of both Presley and the 1950s. The second kind produces renditions of his hugely successful, black-leather-pants-and-jacket-clad 1968 Comeback Special. The third kind of Presley impersonator is often based on the perception of the man as a clown, one drawn from his more flamboyantly attired Las Vegas period.

The latter of the three varieties of impersonators suggests resentment toward a king who disappointed his subjects, one who dissipated and died due to obesity and a legendary prescription drug addiction. The quality of his acting, mostly in shoddy movies even by their late star's estimation, probably perpetuated that resentment too. Revealingly, out of Presley's entire movie career, one resulting in passably entertaining pictures in the 1950s and largely poorly crafted ones in the 1960s, no one has appeared interested in impersonating his big screen roles of the latter decade. While in most instances the Presley movies of the 1960s rarely rise to the level of mediocrity as cinema in their own right, for politically and historically minded critics, they're rich in terms of what they say about the times of their production and the nature of the industry that spawned them. With the inclusion of a lesser known theory developed, in part, by another, still controversial luminary of the twentieth century, Sigmund Freud, and his use of the concept of "thraldom" (explained below), I've sought to unravel the mystery of the mania that dogged Presley for most of his life.

At this point some might object, asking, "why not go back further, before Presley, to the Frank Sinatra craze among the bobby-soxers?" One can always find precedents. When it comes to popular culture, originality is a non-entity. That Elvis Presley was a phenomenally talented performer is not at issue, but to what ends the man and his talent were used. Of particular interest in this discussion is how Presley the movie star, whose first few movies showed real promise, would soon be placed in the servitude of churning out rubbish, rubbish that both reflected and failed to reflect on the times in which it was produced. The biographical details of this discussion have been kept to a minimum, details already well-covered by a host of others. Perhaps somehow this book might defend Presley *despite* his movie career. Viewed from the standpoint of his screen career, the picture that emerges is of a catastrophic waste of their star's abilities and potential.

Catastrophic too was the commercial success of most of those movies, something that only accelerated the downward spiral of the star and his product. Paradoxically, it was alleged by members of Presley's own inner circle, the Memphis Mafia, that his movie contract sustained his life. They claimed that Presley's making movies and accompanying soundtrack albums at a rate of two or more per year required that he maintain his personal discipline, discipline that kept the pronounced excesses of his ongoing drug abuse at bay. Speculation from Presley's gravy train riders aside, drug addiction is invariably progressive. Without treatment, dying due to a drug addiction is commonplace—even for a king.

In response to the threat of global communist revolution, American popular culture seemed to deem it necessary to generate a surrogate or counterfeit revolution. That counterfeit revolution was rock & roll. I've no interest in speculating on the extent to which rock & roll must therefore be looked upon as some sort of consciously engineered cultural plot, although that ought not be ruled out entirely either. That rock & roll was, and to some extent remains, a counterfeit revolution only reflects a recognition of the basic dialectical truth that emergent phenomena give rise to their opposites. Thesis, in this case the Communist Revolution, plus antithesis, in this case postwar liberal democracy, results in synthesis, a hedonistically heady cultural response to Marxist austerity. It was the forward-looking but grievously flawed idealism of a communist revolution that eventually gave rise to the juggernaut of societal regression called rock & roll. Perhaps one of the most blatant tip-offs as to the counterfeit nature of rock & roll as a revolutionary movement was in Presley's coming to be regarded as its king. This configuration ironically illuminates the subjugation of Presley fans in relation to their idol: whoever heard of a revolution being led by a king?

That Presley would go to Hollywood to embark on a movie career was not unprecedented. As Steve Pond observes in his *Elvis in Hollywood* (1990), singing stars Rudy Vallee, Bing Crosby and Frank Sinatra had all trod that same path before him. More noteworthy was the fact that Presley's move to movies marked an accelerated cinematic instrumentalization of rock & roll. Within the brief span of the making of *Love Me Tender* (1956) to *Loving You* (1957), and *Jailhouse Rock* (1957) to *King Creole* (1958), Presley's early big screen presence cashed in on and promoted the new music, arguably doing so toward pointedly political ends. His 1958–60 service in the army effectively cooled him off as artificial revolutionary figurehead. Subsequently, the 1960s cycle of Presley movies stand apart for their exceptionally forgettable, throwaway quality. In most, if not all cases, they manifest a ravenous capitalizing on his monetary and propaganda potential. Presley's manager, the infamous 'Colonel' Tom Parker, himself an ex-convict and ex-carnival man, had effectively mass-marketed Presley as something of a sideshow attraction. Nowhere is a revisiting of those facets of Presley's past more evident than in the celluloid travesties *Girls! Girls! Girls!* (1962), *Kissin' Cousins* (1964) and *Harum Scarum* (1965) from among a host of others made during that decade.

The reader may notice that I use the terms 'popular culture,' 'mass culture' and 'the culture industry' interchangeably. Admittedly, this was a tactical decision on my behalf for the purpose of acclimatizing the reader to my style of analysis. Popular culture is serviceable, but problematic because it implies that that which it addresses is by definition likable. Still, the term is useful because of a general understanding that the term refers to the mixed media bag of movies, television, radio, recorded music, bestselling publications and other, more recently developed forms of mass communication.

"Mass culture," a term employed by New York's *Partisan Review* contributors from 1934–2003, bespeaks a more critical orientation to its objects of study. Yet it too is problematic implies something produced by and for the masses. In fact, mass culture is most often a seemingly apolitical entertainment phenomenon that postures at being for everyone while belonging to no one. Moreover, mass culture is a term that suggests something that emerges spontaneously from the masses. Such claims are at a distant remove from the truth.

"The culture industry" is a seemingly more concise term, one coined by Frankfurt School philosophers Max Horkheimer and T.W. Adorno. It is a designation that acknowledges that what the public consumes as their 'popular culture' is, in fact, culture at the point where culture becomes ideology. The ensuing result, presumably, is that what mass audiences look to for their entertainment is also their indoctrination into forms of social and political control. It's an effective, but politically leftist-tainted approach to culture criticism.

Additionally, to speak of a culture industry invokes the accurate recognition that the culture it produces is not so much created or crafted as it is calculated and engineered, just as it aims at advancing a generalized, homogeneous consciousness among its audiences. In his introduction to Peter Burger's *Theory of the Avant-Garde,* Jochen Schulte-Sasse goes so far as to refer to it as 'the consciousness industry.' However, the term "culture industry" is problematic too because of its neo-Marxist ideological baggage and the often all-too-bleak conclusions that the application of its theoretical application, 'Critical Theory', yields. In using all three terms judiciously, popular culture, mass culture and the culture industry, I hope to have achieved a balanced understanding of the matters at hand.

This isn't just a study of Presley's movies and Presley the movie star. It's an attempt to make clear what a broad, interdisciplinary range of approaches look like when applied to mainstream history, without resorting to the all-too-common practice of over-simplification. The reader will encounter facets of the American novel, semiotics (the science of understanding systems of signification), psychology, feminism, economics, theology, Friedrich Nietzsche, Karl Marx, Russian literary philosopher Mikhail Bakhtin, and a few other stray cats. Accusations of postmodernism might be levelled against the intellectual eclecticism. That charge is handily refuted by the constancy of the glue that holds the entirety of this discussion together: Elvis Presley himself.

An Idolatrous
Revolution

"Thou shalt have no other gods before Me."
Exodus 20:3.

"Thou shalt not bow down thyself to them,
nor serve them, for I the LORD thy God am a
jealous God, visiting the iniquity of the fathers
upon the children unto the third and fourth
generation of them that hate Me,"
Exodus 20:5.

El: one of the oldest names of a monotheistic god, dating back
as early as 2,300 BC on Syrian stone tablets.

vis: n; p. vi res [L] force; power; strength; vigor, energy; kinetic
energy.

Although not at first in an overly aggressive manner, rock
& roll and Elvis Presley's first few movies served, in part,
as advertisements promoting the acceptability and normality of
the new music. In turn, that promotion was, in some instances,
implicitly defined in contrast against traditional Judeo-Christian
values. That Elvis Presley, brought up in an itinerant, Pentecostal,
Assembly of God spiritual culture, would become one of show

business's biggest idols is an irony that greatly supersedes the allusion to deity in his first name. By extension, being a fan, an abbreviation of 'fanatic,' might in many instances be a condition derived from displaced religious impulses. Seventeenth-century theologian, philosopher, mathematician and scientist Blaise Pascal wrote about what he called the God-shaped vacuum in each of us, an infinite need that can only be adequately met by an infinite God. Unprecedented masses of North American youth tacitly but ravenously embraced the proposition that, in each of them, there resided an Elvis Presley-shaped vacuum.

revolution: a. A complete or drastic change of any kind;

b. overthrow of a government, form of government, or social system, with another its taking its place.

Webster's Twentieth-Century Dictionary

Modernity not only made for strange bedfellows, it elicited vast, new conflicts. Although not as all-determining as Karl Marx and Friedrich Engels claimed, class struggle, conflicts emerging due to inequalities in the distribution of wealth, has had a major bearing on the affairs of this world. Marx and Engels' designs for revolution owed much to the Bible, too, insofar as they liberally pilfered biblical concepts, retooling them within the rhetoric of their own dialectical materialism and attacks on religion. Looking back on rock & roll's beginnings, it was as if American liberal democracy and its popular culture, in addition to the lucrativeness of the new music, perceived in that music an alternative to the promises of communist revolution. Part of the political shrewdness of capitalism was in its appropriating the principles of class struggle, then redefining that conflict not as materialist but as a conflict between generations.

The redefinition of the struggle between haves and have-nots was a matter of shifting the attention to differences between young and old. This form of conflict could be easily understood by the film's young audience, and could as well be easily wrapped up in cinematic happy endings, far more so than mass, armed insurrection. Hollywood reconfigured the terrain of the revolution within the confines of the middle class, the American family or the orphaned or semi-orphaned Presley protagonist. From this vantage point, as a form of political expression, rock & roll took its cues from Hollywood celebrity-making. Young audiences were offered a steady succession of musical idols as the king shifted more of his time and energy from making records into making movies.

Almost since its inception, rock & roll has emulated the outward qualities of a broadly-based political movement. With stadiums as a favored location for its presentation, a favored delivery system, dictating fashions as its own variation on the uniform, riots and near riots, an acceptable accompanying measure of violence and a cast of millions, rock & roll has forwarded perhaps the most stunning display ever of the revolutionary without being a revolution in any traditional, political sense. The most politically significant achievement of these theatrics has been entirely counter-revolutionary. It has done much to cement the perpetuation of the existing order. Rock & roll has been a triumph of marketing and, simultaneously, an age-targeting agency for the polarization and ensuing dis-empowerment of the public. For America and, by extension, what had been termed the free world, the central ingredients in putting this deception across were race and sex. As for any meaningful political impact wrought through rock & roll, the Rolling Stones might just as well have played square dance music; Jimi Hendrix might just as well been a master of the accordion; and Led Zepplin achieved their notoriety by doing cover versions of Bing Crosby songs.

In his insightful, at times gratuitously coarse *Last Train to Memphis: The Rise of Elvis Presley* (1994), Peter Guralnick intersperses his narrative of Presley's early career with familiar references to Black America's influence on the young performer. As is typical of most historical distortion on the subject, however, Guralnick refrains from venturing to articulate the emergent correlations. The sensationalism of Presley's arrival on the cultural scene was not just that of a young, White man who brazenly appropriated Black music. To whatever extent it registered consciously among White Americans, the most genuinely revolutionary element of Presley as a performer was his culturally incorporating racial integration into his stage persona. Guralnick chronicles how Presley's early stage performances were far more sexually suggestive than surviving film and television records indicate. What Guralnick overlooks is that along with the introducing the aesthetics of Black America to White America, Presley's stage choreography was a near caricature of asserting overcharged, male sexual vigor.

As foremost ambassador for rock & roll, Presley introduced an entire generation of comparatively repressed adolescent girls to an embodiment of raw, youthful, masculine sexual energy. For many of them, Presley was the purveyor of a quasi-sexual experience. To explore the dynamics of that experience, consider Sigmund Freud's possible explanation of the fundamental hysteria which Presley was often greeted with, both in concert and on screen. Freud employed Von Kraft Ebing's concept of sexual thraldom, an expression used

> to denote the fact that one person may develop an unusually high degree of dependence and *helplessness* towards another with whom he [or she] has a sexual relationship ... Kraft-Ebing derives the origin of sexual thraldom from the conjunction of '*an unusual degree of development*

of love and weakness of character'[2] *in one partner with unbounded egoism in the other* ... *the decisive factor is the strength of sexual resistances that are surmounted* together with the extent to which this conquest is concentrated in one single act and carried out once and for all ... *sexual thraldom is incomparably more frequent and more intense in women.*[3] [my emphasis]

The sexual relationship between Presley and his maniacally adoring fans was a largely symbolic, unconsummated one. Yet the hysterical response to Presley, as per the theory of thralldom, was a kind of helplessness. In terms of cultural likes and dislikes, most mass culture doesn't encourage audiences to mature psychologically past adolescence. Much mass culture offers an escapism into idealized love relationships that many have either missed or been cynical about. Musical quality and Presley's renowned offstage humility aside, a musical performance by the Presley of the 1950s might be looked upon as a manifestation of *"unbounded egoism."* His intentions can only be speculated on. All that is known of his singularly Presleyan stage choreography is that they was a kind of physical ad lib evoking mass mania. After he stumbled upon the moves, those backstage told him to keep doing them. In terms of psychological effect promoting thraldom, the result was, at least metaphorically, evocative of a mass cultural breaking down of a generalized climate of libidinal restraint.

---

[2]   Von Kraft-Ebing, 'Bemarkungen uber "geschlectliche Horigkeit" und Masochismus' quoted by Sigmund Freud (1918) *On Creativity and the Unconscious,* (New York, Harper and Row, 1958) 188.

[3]   Sigmund Freud, *Contributions to the Psychology of Love,* "The Taboo of Virginity" (1918), reprinted in *On Creativity and the Unconscious* by Sigmund Freud, (New York, Harper and Row, 1958) 188.

Von Kraft-Ebing's explanation of thraldom, by way of Freud, demystifies Presley's effect on teenage girls. At the same time, the English homonym, "thralldom," goes some way toward describing the kind of relationship that existed between the idol and his fans, that it was one of bondage and servitude of the fan to the idol. But how does one begin to account for his popularity among adolescent boys? According to Guralnick, many male youths were jealous of the attention and adoration that Presley received from girls. Yet Presley was a culture hero for male youth who cared to accept him as such, including no lesser youths than Bob Dylan and John Lennon. Concurrent with the aforementioned climate of libidinal restraint, Presley was the manifestation of a young, masculine and *unmarried* sexual identity. Suddenly, with all the force that the popular culture of the day was capable of mustering, Presley was in society's face, a society that had long denied what he was the convulsive, hyperbolic embodiment of. He affirmed young, single maleness as a legitimate, dynamic sexual identity. He was the locus of attention through which popular culture found a new way to vent its power by using him as a stimulus to hasten and heighten female sexual awakenings.

From a present day perspective, the rock & roll revolution that began in the 1950s set the stage for the erroneously named sexual revolution of the 1960s and 1970s. In a summer 2013 CBC Radio interview, musician and painter Joni Mitchell recalled the "Free Love" movement of the 1960s and seeing through it immediately. Mitchell pointed out that, prior to that time, it was difficult "for men to get laid." Women had nothing to gain from the new sexual freedoms, she observed. Rock & roll's contribution to increasing sexual permissiveness was that of a new entertainment genre's promoting something intrinsically quite primitive. That in addition to targeting what was civil sexuality, the conventional family and education were at the top of rock & roll's hit list ought not be surprising. In the cumulative, moral backwardness of it all, the continuity of these developments was ideal for inventing and promoting idols "And Introducing Elvis Presley".

"And Introducing Elvis Presley"

The western was a cinematic commonplace when Presley made his big screen debut in 1956's *Love Me Tender*. There seemed little else remarkable about slotting him in such a vehicle, one set somewhere in the American South at the end of the Civil War. More noteworthy about this feature is how it deploys Presley as a countering force to international communism. If, as Marx and Engels began *The Communist Manifesto* (1848), "All history is the history of class struggle," Hollywood resolved that the way to eradicate class struggle was to simply eradicate history.

Love Me Tender opens with the displacement of history. It is April 10, 1865, the day the American Confederacy surrendered to the American Union. Like a Shakespearean tragedy, a band of Confederate soldiers, unaware that the war has ended, rob a payroll from a Union train as a military action. For the hero and his followers, time is out of joint. For most of the movie, Vance (Richard Egan) the leader of this Confederate band, stands on the principle that the stolen loot is "the spoils of war." Vance's unapologetic adherence to that creed suggests he's in denial about the South having lost the war. To the investigating government agents and Union soldiers, he will heroically lie his face off.

The theme of historical displacement, of what becomes of men whose existence has extended beyond the era that shaped them, has made for some compelling westerns. It's an integral to the westerns *Shane* (1953), *The Great Northfield Minnesota Raid* (1972), and *Tom Horn* (1980). In the case of *Love Me Tender,* the plot element that inexorably leads to the killing of Vance's younger brother Clint Reno (Presley), is Vance's unwillingness to forget the war. Vance is hardly a tragic hero, but by movie's end, it's seems things would have gone better for all concerned if he were an amnesiac. Typical of much popular culture, memory is treated disdainfully.

Thought dead by his family, Vance returns to his homestead to learn that his sweetheart Cathy (Deborah Paget) has married his brother Clint. The opening shot of Presley as Clint is fleeting but revealing. He's introduced as hard at work plowing the family farm. He is a trope for the working class, what communism deemed the subject and object of all history.

Initially, relations between the Reno brothers are mutually affectionate. When an almost apologetic Clint tells his brother of his marriage to Cathy, as with the South itself, Vance shows himself to be a gracious loser. After dinner, the reunited Reno family, including Ma Reno (Mildred Dunnock), are treated to a porch-top musical performance by Clint. The tune "We're Gonna Move" might sound plausible as an 1860's song. However, Presley's accompanying bopping and shimmying is emblematic of a much later era. That's followed by a 45 rpm recording–perfect rendition of the title track, sung by Clint first to Ma Reno, then to wife Cathy. Here is illuminated a sanitizing of Presley's sexuality. His character's attachment to his wife, it's intimated, is but a newly-established graduation from love of mother to love of spouse. His musical product is wholesomely oedipal.

Later that night, Cathy awakens crying, and not because she sleeps in a separate bed from her husband (which she does), but because she's had a bad dream, the particulars of which aren't specified. Clint comforts her in this foreshadowing of impending conflict. The following day, after Vance turns down some of the stolen loot by his army buddies, two gratuitous Presley musical numbers are thrown in at a visit to the county fair. He lets loose with the unrestrained "Let Me" and "Po' Boy."

Presley idolization is naturalized as his rock & roll gyrations are greeted with glee by squealing teenage girls, supposedly in the nineteenth century. The Idolatrous Revolution is thereby implied again. All history, it would seem, is the history of rock & roll.

After a clandestine meeting between thwarted lovers Vance and Cathy, both of them wanting to behave honourably, Clint senses something's wrong but can't articulate it, a typical male adolescent posture. Vance lies effortlessly to government agents seeking the stolen payroll, doing so despite assurances that they only want the money back and have no interest in punishing him. Refusing to admit to the theft to investigating officials, Vance is arrested. Ex-Confederate soldier Mike Gavin (Neville Brand) and his cronies persuade Clint to join their quest to spring Vance. Unknown to Clint, they're after the stolen cash. Apparently, at least until the money is returned, the war isn't over. If the war isn't over, Black people haven't been freed from slavery in America. If Black people haven't been freed from slavery in America, the relevance of the young, White southerner who exploded on the mass cultural scene with the Black American sound is seriously endangered.

Richard Egan's portrayal of Vance is strange too. Introduced as a leader and man of action, decent in being family-oriented, gallant in his fraternal and gentlemanly acceptance that his brother has married his true love, his heroism is co-mingled with ongoing dishonesty. Whether it was a directorial decision or Egan's limitations as an actor, Vance shows no difference in behavioral nuances between when he's telling the truth or lying. It's a characterization evocative of the political rhetoric of warfare. Recall Republican California Senator Hiram Johnson's (1866–1945) succinct aphorism, "The first casualty, when war comes, is truth."

While the term 'martial law' isn't mentioned in *Love Me Tender,* that's what's put into effect by government soldiers occupying the Reno farm in expectation of the fugitive Vance's return. Cathy successfully flees from them to rendezvous with Vance, only to be inexplicably informed that he's going to return the money to the government. He tells Cathy of his intention to leave the Reno family farm. "It won't help, Vance," she emotes; "you and I will never forget each other." This is what the movie presents as the problem: not love itself, but memory.

Meanwhile, Mike Gavin emerges as a latter-day Iago in a very shorthanded appropriation of *Othello*. Motivated by greed, he manipulates Clint into a rage, insinuating that his brother Vance is planning to keep the money and steal his wife. That development is relayed by a member of Mike's gang, who tell Cathy that Clint is "half-crazy now." Moments later, another says, "He's out of his mind with jealousy." That's a pretty quick trip from over-the-top familial devotion to half-crazy to out of his mind. All the better to help the audience sympathize with Clint when, at Mike's urging, he shoots Vance in the shoulder. The wounding occurs as the older brother attempts to calm Clint down by telling him the money will be returned and everyone will "have clean hands." There'll be a happy, hygenic ending. Unfortunately, in a last-minute moment of nobility, Clint screams at Mike and his henchman as they storm Vance. Clint's insanity was indeed temporary, very temporary. Mike shoots Clint and is shot himself when Union soldiers arrive. Presley's Clint is a casualty of the Postwar Reconstruction, though not before a melodramatic death scene with Vance and Cathy comforting him. Fraternity is restored between the brothers just before Clint dies. Either Clint's death was completely preventable, or perhaps his life was oddly redundant. This is how modernity does tragedy. Sadder than the loss of human life is the grief over waste. Vance is reestablished in his proper historical moment through the martyrdom of his younger brother, one who's premature passing facilitates another reconstruction, that of his relationship with Cathy. Order is restored.

Responding to reactions from audiences of early screenings of the movie who found the death of their idol too much to take, the studio had a giant specter of Presley, guitar in hand, superimposed over the final shot of Ma Reno and kin leaving Clint's grave. The monumentally beatified Presley reprises the title song, smiling gently just before the concluding fade-out, thereby reassuring anyone worried that he might have really died or, possibly, leaving audiences with a sense of Presley as a gargantuan martyr as a grand gesture of idolatrous hubris.

By putting the premier figure of rock & roll in movies, Hollywood knew they knew they were attempting something subversive. Having had more commercial success with rock & roll than anyone else in the 1950s, it's possible that the responsibility fell to Presley to propagandize for further public acceptance of the new music. As his follow-up pictures of that decade illustrate, and as the improbable successor to James Dean who'd perished only a year earlier, Presley the movie star posited the next stage in Hollywood's construct of American male youth. In 1955's *Rebel Without A Cause,* it was Dean's Jim Stark who shrieked at his parents, "You're tearing me apart!" Presley's Clint Reno is also torn apart, not by parents, but by family nevertheless. *Love Me Tender* contains most of the main ingredients of rock & roll's idolatrous revolution: disillusionment with family, and radical skepticism toward marriage as an institution capable of meeting either the emotional or sexual needs of the young, as per Clint and Cathy's separate beds. The irony of the cinematic introduction of a young White singer with a Black sound in a movie conspicuous for a total absence of Black people ought not be overlooked, one who gets shot only to be reconstituted as a giant apparition of his former self.

DAMAGE CONTROL

F ar more than the black and white production of *Love
Me Tender,* Presley's 1957 full-color follow-up feature,
Loving You, stresses his character's working class origins. In
many ways it's a standard Hollywood tale of a young singer's
ascent to stardom, only with rock & roll and Presley plugged
into it. The two new elements are disarmingly advanced
through an otherwise familiar showbiz yarn wherein didactic
assurances abound, an insistence really, that the stir generated
by Presley's Deke Rivers and his new music aren't really new.
As ideology, *Loving You* glorifies the rise of the leisure industry.
Simultaneously, it asserts, albeit in a different way, a cynicism
toward the family comparable to what *Love Me Tender* depicted.
By contrast, *Loving You* is a largely joyful expression of a young
performer's journey to becoming a cultural commodity. In her
account of the movie in *The Films of Elvis Presley* (1991), Susan
Doll notes, "Since Elvis was so maligned in the press as a figure
of controversy and rebellion, the people in charge of his career
took on the task of remolding his image." By 1957, Presley
was big business and, after adverse publicity stemming from a
punch-up with a gas station attendant, it was deemed necessary
to do damage control.

Loving You opens at a gubernatorial campaign rally for an
incumbent guber and southern huckster who's shown doing

business with Glenda Markle (Elizabeth Scott), the manager for the country and western band playing at the event. Presley's Deke Rivers arrives in a hot rod to deliver crates of beer, the working man's drink. In mentioning the characters Presley played, notably, despite whatever strengths he might have been said to possess as an actor, those characters tended to be not so much rounded, complex characterizations as they are a set of circumstances in which to situate Elvis Presley, the screen construct. This was hardly unique to Presley's film career. It's been the stock and trade of many other big movie stars throughout most of commercial American cinematic history, and is very much with us to this day. Despite their prolific film careers, Humphrey Bogart and James Cagney rarely ventured far from their tough guy personas. More recently, how often have Sylvester Stallone, Jean-Claude Van Damme or Arnold Schwarzenegger demonstrated that, as actors, they're great bodybuilders?

The otherwise banal occasion livens up when, in conjunction with his having brought the liquid fun, a co-worker tells Glenda that Deke sings. After being cajoled by Glenda and under protest, Deke takes to the stage. Deke launches into the exuberantly rocking "Got a Lot o' Livin' to Do." Lyrically, the song is a simple declaration of the self-evident: he's young. Deke's hostile prelude to performing invokes the cliché of the reluctant hero. It's an archetype traceable to at least as far back as the initial unwillingness of Moses to lead the Israelites out of bondage to Egypt at the behest of God. Rather than exhibiting the humility of Moses, however, Deke asserts a more commonplace angry grumbling. His reluctance is a nod to the idea that, despite all appearances to the contrary, there's nothing self-seeking about what he does on stage. It's a sacrifice of sorts. His disdain for his own performing suggests that he recognizes that there's something undignified, even vulgar, about his performing. This cagey strategy externalizes the resistances of movie audience members not yet enthralled by Presley or in danger of falling out of thraldom with him. Deke Rivers identifies with those who resent his rock & roll persona. In part, the ensuing narrative is the story of how he learns to love that persona and, by example, instructs us to do likewise.

Following a crowd-pleasing performance, Glenda gloms on to Deke. "Deke … short for Deacon?" she asks. "I guess," he replies. Whereas Glenda's question situates him within a context of Christian legitimacy, his answer suggests he doesn't know who he is at this point. The term 'deke' can also be traced back to 1950s hockey, a fake or a feint used to deceive a defensive player. Deke refuses Glenda's invitation to join her and the band on the road, telling her he wants to keep his delivery job and buy a farm. Foundational here is the evocation of the qualities of a reluctant hero, which form the basis for the laundering of Presley's image. Not many audience members were likely to have wondered at this point if they were going to watch Presley deliver beer for another eighty minutes, although many might have happily subjected themselves to doing so. Deke's farming aspirations re-emphasize his essentially decent, working-class identity and identification with the land. After he leaves, the affably devious Glenda phones in a false complaint to his employer that will result in his getting fired. The next morning, Deke joins up with Glenda and band leader Walter 'Tex' Glannon (Wendell Corey) and the rest of the band—thirty minutes late, another nod to his reluctance—and they all go out on the road.

Glenda has told Tex that he needs a "gimmick" (a deke?), and that Deke is it. In so saying, it's indicated that what Deke does on stage can be seen as a kind of deception. On the road, Deke again sings "Whole Lot o' Livin' To Do." That's followed by a condensed presentation of him at various venues, county fairs, a Lion's Club hall meeting, and so on, performing the lively "Let's Have A Party," "Hot Dog" and the major hit "Teddy Bear."

The tunes are all musically peppy, lyrically pleasure-oriented and conspicuous for their brevity. It's not until Deke sings the morose ballad "Lonesome Cowboy" that there is any sign that this rock & roll performer has any place whatsoever in a country and western band, except for his donning a flashy silk cowboy shirt. His attractiveness to adolescent girls is stressed. During the rock & roll numbers, his precision-mussed hair visually resonates with the jiggling of his body. As with the new music that he expediates, he is *electric*.

Offstage action digresses into romance as Deke dates the band's female vocalist, Susan Jessup (Delores Hart) and wins a caged budgie for her by knocking over some milk bottles at a fairground contest. They return to their hotel lodgings, where Tex and company are playing poker. The incidentals are telling. They augur the rise of the leisure industry in North America and the Western world at large. Everyone in the movie is constantly engaged in some facet of entertainment or other boredom-killing pastime. Even the production designers of *Love Me Tender* took recourse to having Presley perform at a county fair. Existence co-mingled with or otherwise at the periphery of various forms of amusement is established as a determining context in almost every Presley movie. Success in Presley's movies is frequently equated with his character's experience of pleasure, whether through singing or some other means. Conflict or drama emerge when someone or something interferes with his having a good time.

The girlfriend to a young tough makes it known she wants Deke to perform. He obliges by singing the roaring "Mean Woman Blues." The song initiates a brawl. The brutal episode concludes with Deke landing a punch that sends his opponent crashing into a juke box, knocking him out in the process. The interconnectedness between Presley, his music and the thrill of violent, young male competition is clear.

Deke and his jiggling hair return to a theater gig for another rendition of "Teddy Bear." Subsequently, an amorous female fan invades his dressing room, then presses him into kissing her. She unconscionably resorts to calling him that most abominable of names, the one that compelled James Dean go berserk in *Rebel Without a Cause:* chicken. Like Dean before him, Deke rises to the challenge but, before they get carried away, they're interrupted by Glenda and a photographer, who captures the incriminating moment on film. Deke and rock & roll now face the threat of being revealed for what's been widely suspected of all along: being completely concerned with sex. His heroic status is further undermined in that, unlike the classic hero, it may now be imputed that he isn't chaste. After accommodating a gaggle of squealing female fans by signing autographs, Deke is told by Tex, "You're the kind of boy a man would be proud to have as a son." Tex then volunteers to serve as Deke's manager. It's nowhere suggested that there's anything untoward in this intertwining of surrogate fatherhood with profit motives. Deke declines the offer on the grounds that Glenda is already his manager.

In a car overlooking Susan's family's farm the next day, Deke chats with her about his own agricultural desires. Meanwhile, Glenda and Tex have an adult, 1957-Hollywood-movie discussion about sex and how it's used to sell everything. The contrast between the discussions of the two couples heightens the contrast in the purity of Deke and Susan. Deke's fantasy life doesn't extend beyond the desire to own a farm. An imminent lip lock between him and Susan is preempted by someone turning up to ask him to sing. He obliges with a performance of the movie's title ballad, "Loving You." Erotic gratification has been stymied and channeled into the song. Narrative advancement is momentarily discarded to allow Presley to perform a musical commercial for the movie and himself. He performs gently in a wholesome farm environment. The sequence is capped off by the arrival of Glenda and Tex in a brand spanking new white convertible for Deke. "I'll be here. I'll always be here," his eternal farm girl sweetheart promises.

Deke's receiving the car is followed by a heart-to-heart with Glenda. Reception of the luxury vehicle prompts a self-unmasking. Apparently, still waters do run Deke. He admits he's not really "Deke" at all, but Jimmy Tompkins, an orphan who appropriated his *nom de deke* from a tombstone after fleeing his burning foster home. No word if he set the fire. "Ever since then, I bin runnin'," Jimmy Deke Presley confesses to Glenda. The twist at once suggests the evocation of pity and empathy for his having grown up without a family, pointing to a hazy explanation for why Jimmy does what he does as Deke on stage.

Developments resemble more of an ideological expression when Deke's next gig at a civic hall in *Free*gate, Texas, is threatened with being closed by city hall. A throng of young fans in front of the hall fails to have any impact. Glenda tells reporters, "This is a freedom of speech" issue. Deke's heroism comes into sharper relief here. He and rock & roll must be allowed to continue unfettered, not because they advance free speech itself, but because preventing Deke from performing would be interfere with America's cherished First Amendment right. But precisely what is Deke's music at the level of freedom of speech? That he has A Whole Lot o' Livin' To Do? That he wants to Have a Party? Hot Dog, Hot Dog Uber Alles?

Glenda makes the case for Deke and rock & roll at a city hall meeting. She observes that jazz caused quite a commotion at first, that the works of Debussy and Stravinsky sparked riots upon their debuts. The rock & roll revolution is no revolution at all. The sound and the fury it generates are natural and therefore, like nature itself, irrefutable. The ideological contradiction here, the ideology of rock & roll as presented in *Loving You,* is that rock & roll is a novelty that isn't novel.

Glenda triumphs making the case for deke & roll before city hall, though not before a disillusioned Deke flees as the time of his national TV debut draws near. Tex show up for the telecast drunk, but it's okay because he's only a musician. He chews out Glenda for letting Deke kiss her, then lets the *in vino veritas* cat out of the bag in that he, Tex, and Glenda had married and divorced. Combined with Tex's paternalism toward Deke, oedipal undercurrents in Deke's relationship with Glenda resound. That is to say, by Freudian standards, there's at least one thing normal about Deke.

The live TV broadcast of Deke's scheduled national debut opens with a shot of a map of America, followed by testimonials from fresh-faced teens bearing witness to Deke's decency, their pride in him, and his lack of "any [bad] influence." Even the amorous gal photographed kissing him in his dressing room explains it was just a stunt, "a shop-off kind of thing." Here, cinema defers to the power of television where, in real life, Presley had shot to national prominence. Television is the site of his character's vindication. Throughout most of his movie career, there's an ongoing blurring of distinctions between Presley and his movie roles. In this instance, the new medium of television provides his unassailable vindication.

Glenda intercepts the angry Deke, who's acting out his generic, youthful frustration by driving recklessly. As his surrogate mother-figure, she gives him a rousing pep talk, advising him, "You've got fifteen minutes to get on that stage and find out if you've even got a future." Television is posited as his opportunity for redemption: redemption from being orphaned, redemption from self-hatred and, perhaps, redemption from needing to try to go back to delivering crates of beer for a living.

Arriving at the TV studio just in time to be introduced with the words, "America, judge for yourselves," Deke humbly states, "Ladies and gentlemen, I don't even know if I'm worth listening to, but I'm grateful for the chance." He reprises the movie's title ballad. Despite wearing a tough-looking jean jacket with upturned collar and work shirt, a reiteration of Elvis the Worker, he melodically restates an identity rooted in the American pastoral idealism of his girlfriend's family farm. This identity is the "You'" in "Loving You" that Deke and Presley might be thought to love. Having so ingratiated himself, it's then safe for him to reprise "Whole Lot o' Livin' To Do." As was the case among those in attendance when he rattled off "Mean Woman Blues," the prelude to beating up the youth who'd coerced him into first singing it in the restaurant, the entire studio audience immediately breaks into perfectly synchronized, rhythmic clapping. In his essay "Some of the Social Implications of Modern Technology" (1941), philosopher Herbert Marcuse theorized that one such social implication is the overtaking of sexual fetishism by a fetish for efficiency. The new, electric music notably exemplified by "Mean Woman Blues" and "Whole Lot o' Livin' To Do" is shown to cause audiences to instantly behave like machines. Here, mass enjoyment of rock & roll is acceptable because, as with much standardized production in capitalist society, it is the metaphorical reduction of humanity to all but completely superfluous appendages to the means of production.

The crowning musical climax merges the song "Loving You," first sung in an idealized farm setting, together with the straight ahead, violent rock & roll number, "Mean Woman Blues." Interweaving ballads with hard rock songs, as is the case here, is a standard presentation of rock & roll. Such exercises in the fine art of keeping audiences off balance insures a higher likelihood that listeners will hear something they like while providing a sonic bulwark against boredom.

Reunited with girlfriend Susan backstage after performing, an elated Deke tells Glenda, "You and Tex and Susan are all that I've been looking for." In the land of self-reinvention, the alienated youth has reinvented his own family. Deke the orphan has been amalgamated into a surrogate family, signified and sealed by the romantic reunification of Glenda and Tex as they kiss each other. An agent herds Deke over to sign a contract, but he tarries to kiss Susan. Yet clearly, he's made the big time and is a hit with America. As for Jimmy Tomkins, it might be just as well that he's forgotten amid all this excitement. The failure of the conventional nuclear family is remedied through its being surpassed by the formation of a super-family, one incomparably more lucrative than the traditional family, with fame and fortune thrown in to boot. Deke kisses Susan as the happy ending is sealed in the context of an impending contract signing. A common convention of business is aesthetically canonized. Everything is circumscribed by the deal.

Loving You exemplifies the capacity of Hollywood propaganda's appeal to simple-minded psychology to advance political and business aims. Deke's stage persona and, by implication, Presley's, are characterized as an outgrowth of a dysfunctional upbringing. Surely no one given a decent family upbringing would act out in such a way, it's implied. Through his homelessness, consigned to a life of ceaseless wandering after his foster home burned down, the event he confesses to Glenda that he hadn't stopped running from since, his function as rock & roll star begrudgingly affirms the need for family. There's also a cynicism toward family made plain, in that it's caricatured as a series of at times manipulative, economically-based relationships, a backhanded acknowledgement, perhaps, of The Holy Family by Marx and Engels. Through his servitude to the progeny of the nuclear family, Presley's predominantly submissive Deke Rivers forwards a configuration of consolation, a re-articulation of the master-slave relationship for those distressed by rock & roll and Presley. *Loving You* provides the assurance that the young, White man with the Black sound will, like the Blacks from whom he appropriated his sound, continue being subjugated to the White world. As another antidote to the problem of class struggle, a working-class Elvis is redeemed by a new, seemingly superior reconfiguration of the middle-class family and its newest member: television.

REBELLION INC.

Among the early, exotic deceptions in the marketing of Elvis Presley was that the rock & roll movement he fronted was constituted, in part, by a kind of domesticated criminality. The first genuine rock & roll movie, *The Girl Can't Help It,* preceded Presley's 1957 turn in *Jailhouse Rock* by a year, expressing an identical theme. Initially, Presley's songs weren't deemed rebellion, but hillbilly music. Insofar as it pertained to his career origins, Presley's was a musical aesthetic that wasn't so much a transgression against law, but a transgression against class. Hillbilly music was making a big-time incursion into the more respectable echelons of the cultural mainstream. With its over-determined emphasis on the significance of class struggle and, more significantly, it's century-plus history of consistent failure, Marxism is a well-proven failure as a political solution. Arguably, though, it does constitute a counterpoint from which some social and economic problems can be identified.

Willingness amid popular culture to trade in cultural goods of a quasi-criminal nature was a smokescreen for bigger problems. Rock & roll and Elvis Presley were a calculated cultural risk, a risk that society could withstand the popularization of a measure of chaos and disorder for societal sustenance and advancement. With that in mind, *Jailhouse Rock* presents rock & roll as sanitized, processed rebellion. Cinematically, as someone who championed American ideals over and above that of the red menace, Presley's sympathetically-portrayed, young anti-heroes with working-class tendencies seemed well-able to overpower their ideological rival, if only by virtue of sheer sensationalism.

From Nazism to Ronald McDonald, those claiming the youth of a nation as their own also claim every tomorrow as their own. In redefining youth by way of the likes of Marlon Brando in *The Wild One* (1953), the possibly homicidal Montgomery Clift in *A Place in the Sun* (1951), the alienated James Dean in both *East of Eden* (1955) and *Rebel Without a Cause* (1955), as well each of the four Presley movies of the 1950s, there was hidden the anxious heart of existing realities. The very real threats of a world-wide communist revolution, of a nuclear war, of the wealth in the Western world undergoing a radical redistribution all loomed large, at least among those most conspicuously possessive of money and power. Even among those without such privilege, enforced political godlessness was understandably unappealing to a then-predominantly Christian America. Presley's class-specific identity as a performer of hillbilly music was good fodder for movie roles about troubled youths, orphans and juvenile delinquents. As Vince Everett in *Jailhouse Rock,* Presley inhabits an amalgam of all three. In fact, nowhere does *Jailhouse Rock* make any reference to Presley's character as having had any family background whatsoever, orphaned or otherwise. He just sort of *is.*

On one level, Presley's first appearance in the musical melodrama suggests an unintentional parody of Soviet socialist realism. A vigorous-looking Vince Everett drives up in a bulldozer to collect his paycheck. In this, the third of Presley's movies, he's again introduced in the mode of Elvis-as-worker. After cheerfully springing for drinks because he lost a bet arm wrestling, Vince proves his masculinity through the more manly exhibition of belting another bar patron to death. Reiterating shades of *Loving You,* the fatal blow is struck when Vince sends the loutish provocateur crashing into a bar room juke box. The sovereign figurehead of the new musical movement is here asserted to be a lethal force. Triggering the brawl was Vince rescuing the lout's girlfriend, who'd made a pass at him and, not insignificantly, the lout insulting Vince's hairstyle.

Sentenced to one to ten years for manslaughter, Vince becomes cellmate to seasoned convict and entrepreneur Hunk Houghton (Mickey Shaugnessy), who gradually shows him how to get along in stir. In his DVD commentary to *Jailhouse Rock: Elvis in Hollywood* (19XX), author Steve Pond observes that rock & roll was under attack when this movie was being made, citing *Blackboard Jungle* (1955) and *The Wild One* (1953) as exemplary of anti–rock & roll sentiment. In *The Wild One,* however, it's actually jazz that's indicted as the dangerous catalytic element. Pond quips, "There were people out there who thought Elvis in jail was a pretty good idea." Thematically, there's a duality at work. *Jailhouse Rock* not only registers recognition of an anti-Presley sentiment: it also affiliates rock & roll with homicide. The contradiction of Hollywood making movies both for and against rock & roll is hardly peculiar. It demonstrated their eagerness to try appealing to every possible market, even trying to invent markets where none existed.

Cellblock troubadour Hunk Houghton sings fellow prisoners to sleep with an ersatz Negro spiritual, "One More Day," a pseudo–"Swing Low, Sweet Chariot" ballad. He inspires Vince to try his own musical luck. Vince's star rises rapidly during his incarceration, eventually landing him a TV appearance telecast from prison. He gives a polished performance of the effective ballad "Young and Beautiful." Again, as per *Loving You,* the pivotal role of television in the star-making process is acknowledged. Also during his character's incarceration, Presley doffs his shirt in three scenes, twice while shoveling coal, once when flogged for his role in an obligatory prison riot. In addition to whatever sex appeal was to be conveyed through repeatedly showing him shirtless, including for a flogging, Presley's boyish physique is an anatomical downplaying of his dangerousness.

Upon his release, Vince gives a passing indication to the warden that his youthful arrogance is intact, suggesting that prison hasn't reformed him. He receives stacks of fan mail that his envious cellmate Hunk had hidden from him. As a kind of anti-Bildungsroman, an anti-growth of character story, *Jailhouse Rock* champions ignorance as a virtue. In effect, Vince is shown to be rewarded with career and other success for remaining impenitent after his term of incarceration and other punishment.

After showing his amusement upon reading a sexually suggestive fan letter from a fifteen-year-old girl who saw his prison broadcast, Vince obtains an acoustic guitar from a pawn shop. Unrepentantly, he makes his way to a burlesque bar where he meets record promoter Peggy Van Alden (Judy Tyler). In his borderline lewdness to Peggy, it's difficult to tell if Vince is tipsy or just reasserting his surliness, a possible consequence of Presley letting his hairstyle do much of his acting for him. Trying to prove himself as a performer with an unsolicited rendition of "Young and Beautiful," he's ignored by the bar patrons. The disruptive laughter of a drunk moves Vince to rush off the stage and smash his guitar on the drunk's table. Again, as per the brawl in his previous movie *Loving You,* Presley-the-singer is one with Presley-the-violent-rebel.

Despite the poor response to Vince's singing, Peggy takes an interest in him. She takes him to a recording studio where, with a band backing him, he delivers a colorless version of a pop tune, "Don't Leave Me Now." Expressing astonishment at how bad he thinks he sounds when he hears the playback, Peggy coaches him to sing "Like how you feel. Put your own emotions into the song. Make it fit you." Assimilating these few vague recommendations, Vince does the song again in a sultry, bluesy manner, the backing band instantaneously doing a different, corresponding arrangement.

Vince and Peggy visit a slick record executive in an attempt to market Vince's audio wares. The opulently attired executive accepts the recording, but expresses disinterest at the prospect of another vocalist with "a distinctive sound." Commenting on Vince's ingratitude for her help and the executive's consideration, Peggy asks, "Vince, don't you know the meaning of the word 'courtesy'?," to which he replies, "We don't use it much in the backwoods." This is what Presley-the-myth brought to rock & roll: an absence of manners, a lack of refinement, a hillbilly uncouthness that was a cipher for everything about civil society that the new music and its heroes were rebelling against.

Vince's discourtesy is drawn into even sharper relief when he attends a party at the home of Peggy's liberal, intellectual parents. They appear entirely accepting of Vince being an ex-convict. Generic-sounding jazz plays on their Hi-Fi as a coterie of pretentious-sounding musical aesthetes discuss atonality. Given an opportunity to join in the conversation, Vince functions as the righteously profane voice of resentment toward their snobbish privilege. "Lady, I dunno what the hell you're talkin' about," he says and walks out of the party. This is the rock & roll identity: angry, coarse, profane, rude, unreflective and unable to engage in conceptual or linguistic abstractions. Vince hasn't been ostracized from respectable society. Rather, he rejects it. Hardly coincidental is the inclusion of jazz as the soundtrack to that against which Vince expresses his hostility. For whatever shortcomings jazz might be said to have, much of it is of far greater complexity, range and depth than the stylistically narrower genre of rock & roll.

That Presley and his Vince Everett character are completely motivated by sex is implicated in Peggy's innuendo-laden reprimand, "You finally got your sensation. I hope you're satisfied." To her indignation, he says, "I ain't gonna let you hate me," and forces a kiss on her. To Peggy's enraged protestation, "How dare you think such tactics could work on me!" he casually replies, "That ain't tactics. It's just the beast in me." Denying that he actually thinks about the instincts he acts on, Presley's character plays on what he was being denounced from some American pulpits at the time as being: "the beast," an antichrist. The following day Vince reconciles with Peggy by offering a simulacrum of an apology without really saying he's sorry. As per rock & roll's false emancipation of rudeness, Vince's inability to communicate regret parallels the idea that rock & roll is a form of communication for those who can't or won't express themselves linguistically. Alternatively, rock & roll robs individuals of language with which to communicate or make sense of life.

Upon learning that the record executive he'd approached with Peggy for a recording contract stole his song and gave it to another singer, Vince cusses out the executive and slaps him silly. Vince's reaction is understandable. Yet he still acts like an unreformed criminal. His disillusionment becomes the mother of invention when he announces to Peggy that they'll start their own record company. Together with her, they enlist the services of a lawyer, without any apparent idea about how they'll secure or finance the means of manufacturing or distribution. Such details can readily be discarded when the American Dream is involved. There's a litigious, utopian element revealed therein as well. The most essential component to succeed in America, it's suggested, is to have a good attorney.

Musically appealing to the myth of the self-made man is reinforced by Vince's ability to dictate what he, as product, offers his female fans when he then records "(If You Really Want My Lovin') Treat Me Nice." He and Peggy package copies of the single, make the rounds to distribute it and face much rejection. Humour is interjected when the single receives radio airplay accompanying a commercial for horse meat. Therein is related a truth about what has become of aesthetic experience under modernity: aesthetic experience can be bought and sold, just like horse meat. A deluge of requests from listeners motivate the radio station to play "Treat Me Nice" without the accompanying advertising. Another popular culture formula is reiterated, something basically market-driven is posited as a feature of democracy. From Presley's loose-as-a-goose performance of "Treat Me Nice" in the recording studio, to its establishment as a hit tune, the genealogy and rise of a hit song, and its singer, are abbreviated almost beyond recognition.

Highlights of Vince's rise to success are shown in his successfully negotiating 51 percent of the profits for his records, acquiring fancy cuff links, a white Cadillac, as well as some passionate, closed mouth lip-pressing with Peggy. Further romantic developments don't occur until some time later. Commenting on how Vince now seems only interested in money, she exercises her non-exclusivity by going out with Teddy Talbot (Dean Jones), the horsemeat baron and deejay who launched Vince's hit single. Without responding to Peggy's criticism, Vince allegedly goes from being completely sexually motivated to completely monetarily motivated. Nevertheless, Peggy catches him cavorting with another woman at one of his parties. Evidently his change in character has not yet been fully realized. When a recently released Hunk Houghton turns up at the party, Vince offers no resistance to granting Hunk a comfortable place on his gravy train.

Reintroducing Hunk immediately foreshadows the main production number, "Jailhouse Rock," which Vince performs on a TV broadcast wherein he acts as his own emcee. The inmate-dancers then return obediently to their mock cells, Hunk being too fat to be among them. In 1957, this centerpiece of the movie, this production number remains blithely free of entanglements with homoerotica, succeeding in this regard amid two dozen men dancing with each of and lyrics such as

"You're the cutest jailbird I ever did see / C'mon and do the jailhouse rock with me."

Hunk tries, unsuccessfully, to get a spot on the same show to reprise his "One More Day." It's determined in the TV control room to cut his "hillbilly number." Apparently, America wasn't yet ready for the Incredible Hunk. Animosities erupt between him and Vince when Vince ditches the contract he had drawn up for Hunk. Vince downsizes Hunk's earnings by ten percent. In another cinematic parallel with Presley's real life, Vince goes to Hollywood to embark on a movie career at Climax Studios, a studio name that, in more recent years, might cause audiences to wonder what kind of movies he was going to make.

Vince goes on a publicity junket with his indifferent blond siren of a leading lady, Sherry Wilson (Jennifer Holden). The two go panning for gold at an amusement park, shoot at targets for kewpie dolls, have novelty photos taken of themselves, attend hot rod races and go on a tour of the homes of the stars. Again and even more than in *Loving You,* Presley's life is equivocal with the pursuit of fun—or, at least, fun that can be purchased in the marketplace. Success and glamor are equated with engagement in a life of perpetual pleasure-seeking.

Commencing a real romance with the bored Sherry after filming a love scene that spills over into his getting her engine started for real, a digression into 1950s Hollywood-style eroticism transpires between Vince and Sherry in a swimming pool. Their lip merger becomes the occasion for Vince to exclaim, "I want to throw a party to celebrate!" And he does so, leisure on top of more leisure. At his poolside party, Vince performs "(You're So Square) Baby I Don't Care," a rollicking actual rock & roll song, the likes of which will be largely absent from his movies of the following decade. Afterward, one bathing suit–clad debutante swoons, "Gee Vince, when you sing, it's real gonesville." He's the uppermost height of musical fashion, it's stated, evoking and informing superlatives in the adolescent vernacular of the day. That neither the song lyrics nor the vernacular really say anything aside from an amorphous affirmation of Vince is another matter.

A disgruntled Hunk, now seeing Vince as someone less than gonesville, comments bitterly on how Vince has walked over people to get to where he is. Peggy arrives as the swell-headed idol is kissing Sherry. Peggy reminds him that he must go back to making records, something he grudgingly acknowledges. It's soon established that Vince has become an overnight movie star and, according to Hunk, an overnight heel too. Vince's manager tells him a major record company wants to buy out his and Peggy's label. This framing of Vince's transformation shortens the narrative, probably making things easier for Presley the actor as well.

Hunk and Peggy's observations on the decline in Vince's character are further verified when Vince breaks his remaining contract with Hunk and orders him to walk the dogs. In fairness to Vince, by this point the pleasure of hearing Hunk singing "One More Day" at bedtime was probably wearing pretty thin. Nothing to do but surrender to unbridled greed. Vince tells Peggy he's sold their record company, to which she sobs, "Dollars! Dollars! Is there no emotion left in you but the lust for money?" Apparently she misses the old Vince who, although a beast, was only completely concerned with sex. Not one to be a wallflower and somewhat liquored up, the hefty Hunk joins in to punch Vince four times in the head and once in the throat. He's then shocked to discover that Vince has been hurt.

The movie's conclusion is quite a feat of condensation. Vince is hospitalized and receives an emergency tracheotomy. He's instantly reconciled with an apologetic Hunk and with Peggy. She commends Vince for not hitting back. It's not clear, though, if he's being commended for turning the other cheek, or just mindlessly submitting to a brutal beating. The attending physician warns Peggy and Hunk that the violent episode could have turned Vince into a psychological mute. Perplexing too is that Hunk isn't shown punching Vince in his psychology. The remaining happy ending is tacked on when Vince returns home to cautiously and successfully reprise "Young and Beautiful." Hunk looks on happily as Vince takes Peggy to his side. Has Vince learned something about love and humility, or only the fear of being violently beaten into submission?

A MAGNUM ELVUS

Adapting the risque 1952 Harold Robbins novel *A Stone for Danny Fisher* into the 1958 Elvis Presley feature *King Creole* required more than a little retooling. As with every Presley movie of the 1950s, *King Creole* presents its own myth as to how he developed his musical talent. Though mythical, King Creole is the most poetic and, symbolically, closest to the truth. In *Love Me Tender,* it's suggested that becoming an Elvis-type performer is an outgrowth of entertaining a nineteenth-century homesteading family on the porch after supper, something natural and naturally American. In *Loving You,* the unusual performing abilities of Presley's Deke Rivers is the by-product of his orphaned childhood. Destroying families is good, the reasoning seems to be, if it yields performers of Presley's caliber. Deke Rivers exemplifies how the absence of a traditional upbringing results in a superior adolescent. Hence, simultaneous with this glorification of youth is the implication that family is a redundant encumbrance. In *Jailhouse Rock,* it's as if Presley's talent is something he simply picked up during a prison stretch, or maybe caught from hearing nighttime serenades by Hunk Houghton. It's also intimated that the penal system is a determining factor in turning him into a sensational, greater-than-standard–garden-variety adolescent.

Compared with his earlier movies, *King Creole* opens with a more honest plot device to showcase Presley's singing. He joins voices from his apartment window, singing an a cappella ode to gumbo with two Black women on the street below. Brief and mildly sexually suggestive though it is, this is nearest any Presley movie ever got to acknowledging his indebtedness to Black American music. While the term "Creole" can apply loosely to anyone from Louisiana, it can also pertain to someone interracially both Black and Creole. The veiled reference to racial co-mingling also suggests another cinematic attempt to cash in on one of the most the more intriguing questions raised by the popular culture of the era: how do you explain Elvis Presley as a musical performer? Concomitant with the need to address that question was an even bigger question: what is rock & roll? *Loving You* and *Jailhouse Rock* provided a straightforward answer: rock & roll is *product*—unfamiliar, seemingly untamed, but essentially product nevertheless and, as such, no cause for alarm.

Following his morning song, he dresses, his hair jiggling, and is propositioned by two neighborhood prostitutes. "You'd have to pay me," he cheerily replies in possibly the most adult moment in a Presley movie up that time. Identifying his character of Danny Fisher as sexually precocious, the fleeting scene introduces the theme of prostitution. Later, the young hero will fall in love with a prostitute. During breakfast with his older sister Mimi (Jan Shepard), it's established that it's the day before his high school graduation, his second shot at it, and that their mother is deceased. Arriving at the nightclub where he works as a busboy, Ronnie, a woman of easy virtue (Carolyn Jones), is winding down an all-night drinking session with two gangsters. When one of the tipsy goons makes a more pointed comment about her profession, Ronnie cynically quotes Shakespeare's Polonius: "To thine own self be true." The hint of elevated literacy suggests she's that more than a common prostitute.

After slapping one of her escorts for euphemistically impugning her honour, Danny is coaxed into singing his school song a cappella. The conflict is momentarily alleviated. When the hoods try getting rough with Ronnie, Danny fends them off with improvised weapons, a pair of shard-edged bottlenecks. Gallant, streetwise and dangerous, he again shows his capacity for violence soon thereafter when, after sharing a taxi with Ronnie to go to school and getting razzed by classmates for kissing her goodbye, Danny punches one of the jeering mockers. He's immediately expelled because of the assault. As per his turn in *Loving You,* absence of formal education will be shown to have no bearing on musical career success. Suggested therein is a convergence of the myth of the self-made man with a disdain for formal education typical of rock & roll values.

Reluctantly expelled by a sympathetic but dutiful school principal, Danny denies being a hoodlum. Citing his extensive menial work history, he adds, "but I am a hustler." In part, Danny is a variation on an idealized Protestant work ethic. The idea of Elvis-as-worker is referenced yet again. In his 1950s movies, Presley is presented as someone who, despite his youth, has paid his dues as a blue collar laborer. He's earned the right to be a successful performer, a seemingly effortless profession. It's a necessary formulaic touch that legitimizes him: Presley may be talented, but whatever a rock & roll star does, it certainly ought not be deemed 'work.' Of course, in reality Presley only succeeded because he put much effort and devotion into performing. Ideologically, however, suggesting that his musical development was anything other than pure fun is at odds with everything rock & roll was and is about.

Danny is ambushed by a gang of punks led by Shark (or 'Spit' as he's more endearingly called in the Harold Robbins novel, played by Vic Morrow, who distinguished himself as student most likely to kill his teacher in 1955's *Blackboard Jungle*). The schoolmate Danny punched out that morning was Shark's brother. Deftly resorting to less than Marquis de Queensbury tactics, Danny expediently betters his assailants. Expressing admiration for how Danny handles himself, Shark invites him to join their gang. Danny declines. "Good boy. He fights real dirty," Shark says admiringly.

Expecting to throw a graduation party for his son, complete with ice cream, crepe paper, balloons and everything, Danny's father Mr. Fisher (Dean Jagger) expresses his pride over a graduation he doesn't yet know isn't going to happen. An unemployed pharmacist, Mr. Fisher instructs Danny on how "A profession sets a man apart from the rest of the world." The irony, possibly even the hypocrisy, of these words coming from a character who is, at that point, unemployed, exemplifies what Elvisographer Steve Pond identified as a restatement of the weak, ineffectual father figure. Jim Backus did identical duty as father to James Dean's Jim Stark in *Rebel Without A Cause*. That Mr. Fisher is a pharmacist invokes an interesting dichotomy of the era. In the language of the Beat poets and writers of that period, the dominant social and occupational distinction was said to have been between the Beats, those 1950s hipsters, and the 'pharmacists,' those holding down conventional jobs and leading staid, conformist lifestyles. A further heightening of Mr. Fisher's ineffectuality occurs when Danny chews him out for getting punched in the mouth and his doing nothing about it. Disgusted that his father isn't a man of action, Danny declares, "I'm going out and make a buck!"

In the wake of his anger, Danny joins up with Shark and his gang to pursue ill-gotten gains. He acts as musical decoy while Shark and company do an ambitious daytime shoplifting heist. Brandishing an acoustic guitar, Danny saunters through the store aisles performing the gossamer-thin tune "Lover Doll," featuring the refrain "Let me be your lover boy." Pretty young women shoppers populate the store, instantly enamored by his singing. It's a plausible plot device in this scene. This same manner of musical inclusion will become a staple in later Presley movies. His impromptu singing will invariably transform every young woman into his glassy-eyed love zombie.

Despite how lightweight the tune is, the refrain and context of its presentation implicates another economic principle. In Western society, the culture worker, the *artist,* could be considered symbolically akin to a prostitute. Many creatives and others working in the arts have been known to speak of prostituting their talents. At a practical level, the wares the artist provides are just another fleeting, pleasurable distraction, a decoy in the marketplace to facilitate financially necessary, criminal activities. It's unclear whether or not *King Creole* intentionally critiques the relationship between art and commerce. Yet the parallel between sex, sales, and artistic production persists nonetheless, and from their alignment emerges a trope evident in most of Presley's movies: they're pseudo-fables. M.H. Abrams defines a fable as "a short story that exemplifies a moral thesis or principle of human behavior; usually in its conclusion either the narrator or one of the characters states the moral in the form of an epigram." In part, *King Creole* is Presley's most substantial movie because, as an effective epigram, it cleverly expresses a critical characterization of a relationship between art and commerce, pop music and, by extension, popular culture at large, as a kind of theft.

After singing, Danny converses with Nellie (Delores Hart), a pretty, young soda fountain worker. "You were in on it, weren't you?" she asks him. Her question is met with Danny asking another question: "What time you get through work?" Her immediate consent to date Danny illuminates another moral of the free market. Danny's subservience to criminal enterprise, first when he sings his school song to appease Ronnie's gangster companions, then as he acts as a decoy aiding a heist, dramatizes the prostituting of his talent. In each circumstance, something approximating Danny's sexuality is gratified. By consenting to Danny's proposition, Nellie expresses her own submission to criminal enterprise, portrayed as just another form of business.

Elsewhere in town, Danny's father, Mr. Fisher, is rescued from idleness when a pharmacy owner interrupts an otherwise unsuccessful job interview conducted by his irritable store manager. The owner reprimands his manager for not recognizing the value of Mr. Fisher's experience as an older man. The problem with the business world, it's indicated, is not between manager and employee, but with peevish, petty, middle management, a consequence of what happens when workers get too big for their pharmacy aprons.

Danny returns to blue collar legitimacy, busing tables in his place of work where a Black Dixieland band plays jazz. Shark intrudes to tell him, "We're gonna divvy up [the profits from the thieving that day] later in the alley." In keeping with observations made in the preceding chapter on *Jailhouse Rock,* Presley's identity emerges when he straddles the fence between working class respectability and hoodlum criminality. Gangster and club owner Maxie Fields (Walter Matthau) enters the nightclub, his moll Ronnie in tow, subtly inflicting physical pain on her as part of their normal communications. Upon learning of the morning's violence between Danny and his own men, Fields orders Danny to sing to confirm Ronnie's account. Danny takes to the stage and, in the lone instance in a narrative Elvis Presley movie presenting him performing with Black musicians, he belts out the seductively malevolent song "Trouble," the key refrain to which is "I'm evil, so don't you mess around with me." The context, performing for a gangster and his paid concubine, commences with Presley moving like a well-oiled automaton, extending an aggressively limp wrist as if confronting the audience with the possibility of his sexual ambiguity. As the tempo picks up, he shifts into the dynamically brilliant, physical abandon for which he became famous. The lyrics and the setting restate the marketing of rock & roll as a musical genre thought to offer audiences the thrill of a vicarious experience of criminality.

After performing "Trouble," Danny's boldness is rewarded when Charlie LeGrand (Paul Stewart) owner of the King Creole nightclub down the street, offers him a gig. Danny issues the obligatory nod to the cliché of heroic reluctance by turning him down at first. Why be a nightclub singing star when he can be in a gang and shakedown five-and-dime stores? Joining Shark and the gang to divide the day's ill-gotten gains, Danny insists that a speech-impaired and possibly learning-impaired gang member, "Dummy" (Jack Grinnage), must receive his fair share of the take too. Shark tells Danny there's no room in the gang for him or his ethics, but what Danny has sown into Dummy will result in loyalty benefits he will later reap twice. Dummy struggles to verbalize his thanks to Danny. The moment is an intriguing incursion of Presley's rock & roll idol status external to the movie, inadvertently perhaps, but it's there nevertheless. As with Danny taking a stand for the semi-mute Dummy, Elvis Presley articulated something about male adolescence that many male adolescents couldn't articulate for themselves.

Danny goes to rendez-vous with store clerk Nellie, leading her to a hotel room under the pretense that they'll meet friends there for a party. Unassailable in his confidence, possibly because he's employed the same ruse before, Danny is precociously skilled at seduction. Inexplicably, he has a change of heart, possibly due to concerns over screen decency from the Hays Code, then still in effect. He confesses to Nellie that he gave her a pseudonym. His moral orientation is such that he can accommodate deceiving young women into hotel rooms to do what young, heterosexual couples do alone together in hotel rooms. Nellie confesses to feeling desperate, thinking herself stuck in her job, as well as telling Danny she likes him. This is racy stuff for a 1958 Hollywood youth movie. The presumably virginal young cashier isn't put off by the prospect of a sexually adventurous young man, at least, not if he's Elvis Presley. Initially, he's interested in her is for exclusively sexual purposes. Apparently, Nellie doesn't mind his ruthless readiness to enact that interest. After he walks her home, they kiss goodnight on the lips. Tame by contemporary standards, this too expresses rock & roll generation values, specifically, a greatly accelerated intimacy. As if recognizing that a partial attempt at his own exoneration is in order, Danny tells Nellie, "You played up to me this afternoon. I thought you knew the score." Jargon, the language of criminals, provides a code with which to refer to casual sex. Through jargon, Danny communicates that he thought Nellie was familiar with then-contemporary, pre-fornication formalities.

Danny then encounters Ronnie languishing in a convertible on the neon-festooned Bourbon Street strip. Intimating emerging changes in codes of sexual conduct, he allows her to kiss him. Beyond man-to-woman prostitute relations, the scene asserts the subjugation of females to males and the fan to her idol. To extend the significance of the setting and the symbolic relationship between Danny and Ronny, an evocation of the idol and the temple prostitute might not be far off.

Dropping by his father's workplace to defend him from the intimidating pharmacy manager, Danny pretends to be a customer aided by Mr. Fisher's superior pharmacological expertise. Emboldened, perhaps, by having successfully aided his father, as well as expressing resistance to his father's telling him to find "a profession," Danny goes to Charlie LeGrand and takes him up on his offer to sing at the King Creole. LeGrand tells of how he and Maxie Fields grew up together and of his disdain for Maxie's felonious conduct.

After dinner at the Fishers, Mr. Fisher resolutely declines LeGrand's offer on his son's behalf. Mr. Fisher's refusal hinges on an idea introduced in two earlier Presley's movies—that, whatever Presley's character does as an entertainer, it isn't *real* work. In keeping with the overarching, ideological trajectory of Presley's movies, liberal democracy is the superior political and economic system because it allows for the most pleasure. Central to the path of the Presleyan protagonist is his experience for the pursuit of pleasure.

"Singing is a profession," LeGrand tries explaining to Mr. Fisher, "Alright, so he's starting in a sewer. Sewers can't be ignored. They run under the best cities." In saying as much, LeGrand telegraphs to the audience the salacious context in which Danny will make his official show business debut. Mr. Fisher turns down LeGrand's offer to have a drink with him on the grounds that he's a non-drinker. LeGrand expected as much, he says. Those hostile to rock & roll, in this instance Danny's father, are aligned with the soberly repressive. LeGrand's exit is followed by more disputation between Danny and his father. This conflict, as well as the allusion to LeGrand having said he could be 'a second father' to Danny, restates needs arising from Danny's motherless status. As with the orphaned Deke Rivers in *Loving You*, as well as the unidentified parentage of Vince Everett in *Loving You*, integral to rock & roll is the implied failure of the contemporary family. To his father's plaintive cry of "What do you want?" Danny insolently fires back, "A pink Cadillac!" Itself a possible sign of sexual confusion for a young man.

When LeGrand and Danny's sister Mimi strike up a romance, preliminary mushiness is interrupted by Danny. In turn, Danny strikes up a deal with LeGrand on a handshake to perform at his King Creole nightclub. A parallel is suggested between successful romance and successful business negotiations. Such parallelism will be more evident in many of Presley's later movies, commencing with 1962's extremely profitable *Blue Hawaii*. In the "sewer" of LeGrand's club, an appropriation of the Black American-born singer and dancer Josephine Baker's act occurs. A shapely White Frenchwoman is clad in a see-through body stocking and a few strategically-placed bananas. It's a direct co-opting from Baker, also called the "Creole Goddess." The Baker-inspired chanteuse performs a saucy song about the fruit to which she owes her few shreds of modesty. While the interlude doesn't advance the plot, only emphasizes the tantalizing seediness of where Danny performs and provides eye candy for male viewers, it's ideologically rich too. Many movie-goers might have recognized the scene as having been cribbed from Baker's famous Parisian nightclub act of the 1920s. There's also a possible allusion to American cultural supremacy having superseded French culture, just as was the case with modernist mecca's migration from Paris to postwar New York.

A hostile backstage exchange with a cackling emcee who has no idea what Danny's act is about could be a derogatory caricature of those in and out of the entertainment business who didn't understand what Presley the performer was about. Danny then performs "Dixieland Rock." As per a couple of scenes in *Loving You*, the nightclub audience abandons itself to vigorously clapping to the beat. Director Michael Curtiz finesses the scene to make it more credible than the robotic immediacy of the earlier feature. Recognizing when he sees him a performer who can stir people up, LeGrand instructs an employee to put Danny's name in lights. Danny's romance with Nellie progresses in a seaside, heart-to-heart talk. He cautions her against falling in love with him because "Love means having kids. I don't even know who I am yet." Translation: loves equals procreation. I have to find myself before I can procreate. In a more contemporary context, that would amount to a very counter-cultural creed indeed.

With all the looseness of a well-oiled, bauble-head doll, Danny returns to the King Creole to perform what might be called an easy-listening tune, "Young Dreams," backed up by his trusty Jordanaires. The pop paean to youth is juxtaposed against another scene where Mr. Fisher is chewed out by his manager. Dreams, it's indicated, are the province of the young.

A smartly-attired Shark, now employed by Maxie Fields, persuades Danny to visit his boss. Shark tells Danny that he's working on an angle to get Mr. Fisher out from under the thumb of the drugstore manager. Danny arrives at the home of Maxie Fields to find Fields and Ronnie languishing over drinks. After Fields insists on having Ronnie hike up her skirt to display her prizewinning legs, Danny declines Fields' offers of a drink and the invitation to perform at his club, then leaves. Fields tells Shark he wants him to scheme against Danny, that he "want(s) to be able to twist real hard."

That night, the Jordanaires do double duty as horn section at the King Creole to Danny's rendition of the jazz-blues hybrid "New Orleans." The interlude is pleasant enough, put across well and, unlike a recurring weakness in many other musicals, it's believable. Additionally, the song alleviates a dramatic tension that might otherwise have become too heavy, as seems apparent elsewhere. Director Curtiz is said to have opted for black and white cinematography to convey a film noir theatricality, but the songs rescue the movie from veering into the bleakness that's often typical of that genre.

Jarringly set against the world of music and eroticism inside the King Creole, amid the dark and stormy city outdoors, a pathetic fallacy augurs ill fortune for Mr. Fisher and, subsequently, for Danny. Shark and a crony ambush Fisher the elder, stealing his attache case and leaving him unconscious from a blow to the head. The assault was hatched as an angle through which to bring Danny into submission to Maxie Fields. At the hospital it's made known that, unless Mr. Fisher receives an emergency operation from an expensive brain surgeon, his career as a pharmacist will be seriously compromised. At the behest of Fields, the surgeon is recruited and successfully carries out the task, commenting afterward to Danny on his father's considerable strength. The episode is a form of vindication for Mr. Fisher before his son, who'd previously castigated him for, among other things, his willingness to "crawl."

In his farewell performance at the King Creole, logically enough, Danny sings "King Creole." Once more, the celebratory quality of the music provides a respite from the dramatic tension, but is of relevance to the narrative in name only. Reiterating an effect noticeably displayed in *Loving You,* Presley again invokes his bouncing hairdo moves as a measured, cosmetic wildness. Music functions as a prohibition against the audience's reflecting too long on the gravity of the situation presented.

An Elvis Presley song is accentuated as something providing relief from otherwise hopelessly miserable conditions. Following the song, a crumb of dialog between Danny and Shark communicates that a significant span has elapsed since Mr. Fisher's operation. Shark coerces Danny to go back to the lair of Maxie Fields. Danny deflects advances from Ronnie who, by this time, is tighter than her cocktail dress. Wallowing in equal parts of self-pity and self-loathing, as when Danny first rescued her, Ronnie mentions her having graduated from high school with honors. The idea of the intellectual as prostitute is again invoked. Her admission restates a rock & roll repudiation of the value of formal education, as does Danny's rise to success despite his having twice flunked high school.

There's a lack of clarity in what transpires between Danny and Ronnie in this scene. Ronnie's made it known that she's under orders from Fields to appease Danny sexually, as if a physical consummation is required for Fields to have total ownership of Danny. Ronnie tells Danny she'll be punished if he doesn't stay. The conflict within a conflict, that two people in love might have to make love to each other, works its way up to a kiss between the two. Then contradicting the idea that

Fields is orchestrating a forced intimacy between Danny and Ronnie, the gangster interrupts it from happening. "Now listen to me punk," says Fields, "You're gonna work for me at my club. I can do a lot for ya' and I can do a lot against ya'." He has Danny sign a blank piece of paper, telling him he'll fill in the rest later, a carte blanche for Fields to do with Danny as he pleases. "Now Maxie's got you like he's got me," says a sullen Ronnie. Paralleling his former act as decoy aiding Shark's shoplifting, Danny is again reduced to being a kind of prostitute.

In his swan song at the King Creole, Danny sings "Don't Ask Why." With lyrics such as, "Though you're no good for me, I want you so … It's not the kind of love I dream about, but it's the kind I can't live without." The soul-ish ballad is a homage to lust. After some histrionics from sister Mimi and wistfulness from LeGrand, Danny meets with Nellie in front of a Catholic church. He asks her whether or not she met with Father Franklin. Apparently, the priest is one of the few Catholics at the time who approved of Elvis Presley. Without explanation, however, Danny then breaks off his relationship with Nellie.

Dummy, the speech-impaired youth to whom Danny forced Shark give an equal share of their ill-gotten gains, makes his first installment on repaying Danny's kindness. Dummy gives Danny a note stating that his father has gone to Maxie Fields to break Danny's contract with him. Mr. Fisher is shown explaining something to Fields, not out of concern for Danny, but to insure a steady income for his soon-to-be son-in-law, Charlie LeGrand. At Fields' lair, Mr. Fisher recognizes Shark as the chief assailant responsible for his head injury. Danny approaches the place just in time to be stormed past by his angrily uncommunicative father. Enraged that Fields made known to Mr. Fisher Danny's unwitting participation in the attack, Danny attempts to make good his threat to kill Fields for divulging the matter. While duking it out with Fields,

Danny orders Ronnie to leave. She complies. As per their initial encounter, he's again rescuing her. She's revealed herself as the stereotypical prostitute with a heart of gold who Danny can truly love.

In a dark alley, Shark and a fellow hood try to kill Danny, but Danny prevails, stabbing Shark to death with his own switchblade but getting seriously wounded in one arm during the struggle. Upon staggering home, his father refuses to let him in. Finding Danny, "They're all after you," Ronnie tells him, then rescues him by driving him to her beach house. It's not the family but the prostitute who saves and provides sanctuary. After regaining consciousness one sunny day, Danny gets cozy with Ronnie on the beach house wharf and is treated to her soliloquy about what she calls "girls like me." The digression isn't deep, but she shows more self-knowledge than any other character in the movie. Her revelation of herself is followed by a moment of 1950s Hollywood movie lovemaking. She's then murdered by a gunshot from a vengeful Maxie Fields as he runs toward the amorous, kindred souls along the very long beach house wharf. The moral? Knowing yourself and disclosing as much can be deadly.

Fields continues firing his revolver at Danny from some distance away, but is tackled by Dummy, who drove him there in the first place. It's an odd bit of plotting, this *dummy ex machina* bit—even more intriguing for what it suggests about capitalism. Walter Matthau's Maxie Fields homicidally storming the misbegotten lovers is only shown from a distance here, just close enough for Curtiz to alert the audience that it is, in fact, Maxie Fields. Curtiz seems to have consciously chosen to show Fields in black suit and matching Homburg hat here, not as a specific character, but as a graphic reminder of how early-twentieth-century cartoonists often caricatured capitalists. As per Mario Puzo's *The Godfather* (novel 1969, movie 1972) the Coen Brothers' *Miller's Crossing* (1990), and who knows how many other works relate, murder by gangsters occurs as the logical end of business practices. When Fields kills Ronnie, he's not acting as a jilted lover, but asserting his ownership of her. The intrinsically American glorification of gun violence is manifested when Dummy shoots Fields, thereby expunging this state of affairs of an otherwise incurable evil and asserting a means by which the voiceless can be given a voice.

The movie concludes on a note of restoration, at least partially. Advertising at the entrance to the King Creole proclaims that Danny Fisher is back for a return engagement and "indefinite stay," as if he'll be there happily ever after. Nellie is shown rushing backstage through a crowd of voluptuous showgirls to make her non-stop availability known to Danny. "Not now Nellie, in a little while, maybe when the time is right, but not now," he says somberly. "I'll wait," promises Nellie, "I have time." Given his druthers, it's suggested, desirable male youth will choose the bad girl over the good girl. Of course, here the bad girl isn't so bad in that she's martyred herself for Elvis Presley. As per Susan Jessup in *Loving You,* good girl Nellie is defined by her willingness to wait. And while Nellie waits for Danny to fully recover from the loss of Ronnie, the nightclub environs ensure that he'll have no shortage of bad girls to ease his grieving until he's ready for a good girl.

Danny's closing song at the King Creole, "As Long as I Have You," is a kind of musical summation of his odyssey through violence, heartbreak and a career in show business, a journey that has matured him. As pop ballad and taken as a fact in isolation, the song is a none-too-remarkable expression of romantic love. Yet there's a despairing valor permeating much of it too, musically, lyrically and in terms of Presley's delivery of it. Lyrics such as, "Let the stars fade and fall, and I won't care at all, as long as I have you. Take the love that I bring, then I'll have everything, as long as I have you," make clear that this is a heroic declaration of love. The thing is, Danny no longer has that "you"—Ronnie. For him, she can only live on through his despair, a despair comparable to that which Ronnie exhibited when she was alive.

The tempo of "As Long as I Have You" lifts as Presley marshals increasing vocal strength to put it over. He even manages a flash of a smile as if to reassure us that everything is going to be fine. There's a reaction shot of a tearful sister Mimi in the audience, together with Nellie, who points to Mr. Fisher entering the club. The reaction shot of Mr. Fisher shows he too is transfixed by his son's talent. His facial expression a mixture of affection and pride, the pride in his son that had been thwarted when Danny failed to graduate high school is restored.

These last moments of *King Creole* express the contradiction of rock & roll ideology. Rock & roll both reflected and promoted radical disillusionment with and rejection of parental authority, something dramatically demonstrated by Danny in multiple instances. As this somewhat muted happy ending would have it, parental approval, specifically the approval of one's father, is the greatest consolation and reward. Parents are far from perfect, and obedience to them won't guarantee happiness or success. Yet the value of parental authority can be salvaged. First, parental authority must be destroyed before being valued by it can be enjoyed. As an adaptation of Harold Robbins' *A Stone For Danny Fisher, King Creole* plays exceedingly fast and loose with the narrative that it's purportedly based on. For the Danny Fisher of the novel, his career as a gifted boxer, paralleled in the movie as a career as gifted singer, is but a prelude to his showcasing his true self as an ambitious wheeler-dealer in the cigarette black market of the Second World War. Robbins' Danny is a synthetic legend of the free market economy. One line from the novel is especially instructive in its bearing on the arc of the film translation: of his emerging success as a pugilist, Robbins has Danny, as first-person narrator, state, "If Papa would only realize it was just another way to make a living, everything would be perfect." As the crowning achievement of Elvis Presley's career as a movie actor, the last reaction shot of Dean Jagger establishes that everything *has* been made perfect. In the eyes of his screen dad, he has at finally achieved eternal, immutable legitimacy as Elvis, the successful show-business employee.

ICH BIN EIN TUPELOAN!

During Presley's 1958–60 tour of military service, he was introduced to the wares of the pharmaceutical industry, substances that would have much to do with his personal undoing. He'd have more hit records to ahead, garner more fans and have two hugely successful TV concerts: the 1968 comeback special and the 1973 *Aloha from Hawaii* special. As for later, big-screen roles, especially his accompanying musical performances, Presley was tamer. He'd make more quality musical recordings, occasionally in an authentically rock & roll vein, winning his only Grammy award for one of two powerful gospel albums, and have a successful nightclub and concert career after 1969. The claim that quality gospel music can minister effectively to the needs of its listeners ought not be quickly dismissed. Presley's most culturally impacting influence, in secular terms, however, was of bygone years. He was less a revolutionary figure than the vestige of a revolutionary identity.

The opening credits of Presley's big-screen return stated, "Produced with the full cooperation of the U.S. Army and Department of Defense." Presley was still a gifted performer, as evidenced in *G.I. Blues* (1960). However, he was commencing on a cultural path sharply divergent from rock & roll. Presley's two years of military service in West Germany was the basis for this frothy, romantic musical comedy, heavily emphasizing froth, his most drastic cinematic reinvention.

When Presley reappears after a two-year absence from the public, the opening scene of *G.I. Blues* shows him bundled, head to toe, in infantryman's garb. Huddled atop a tank, he makes a weak joke to his fellow soldiers about the formidably sized artillery shell they're handling. His then recent, real-life, military experience aside, Presley is redefined within the context of West Germany-based army duty, the most overtly militarized theater of the Cold War. The scene encapsulates the grossly irrational polarities of the Cold War: the king of rock & roll handling an apocalyptic military deterrent to the threat of global communism. Concurrently, the screen narrative is a love story between a singing good ol' boy and a gorgeous but stereotypically austere German dancer.

Showing impeccable prowess as a long-range, crack-shot tank gunner, Tulsa MacLean (Presley) goes to the showers with his fellow troops with him, his physique still looking very much adolescent. He doesn't sing, and the dialogue doesn't advance the narrative. Given that nothing specific to a shower scene occurs, no Norman Bates, it could have taken place anywhere else on military grounds. It's a teaser of a scene for the purposes of featuring a semi-nude Presley.

That night, in what professor and writer Jerry Zaslove would call 'the Americanized reality' of the Ratzkeller nightclub, couples jive sedately to instrumental music furnished by Tulsa and his band. Launching into the jaunty title track, "G.I. Blues," Presley's confrontational loose wrist harks back to his *King Creole* stage demeanor, along with another gesture reminiscent of the pre-military Elvis. It's a choreographed hint reminding audiences of an earlier Elvis Presley.

A patron complains, "I wanna hear the real thing!" and has the juke box play Presley's version of the 1950s rock & roll hit single "Blue Suede Shoes." Tulsa belts him and a brawl ensues.

It's a ritualized moment comparable to scenes from *Loving You* and *Jailhouse Rock*. The juke box is evocative of a secular shrine to Presley's screen character, an altar to Presley's music, as well as to physical violence. In *G.I. Blues,* however, the scene is finessed to declare that Presley is no longer identified with rock & roll. He's now in the service of militarily defending democracy.

Wagers made by Tulsa and his army buddies are jeopardized when their platoon Casanova, Dynamite, is shipped out for immoral behavior. Endangered by possible forfeiture is a bet that Dynamite could, within three days, spend an entire night with Lili (Juliet Prowse), an inaccessibly beautiful, famously frosty nightclub dancer. With 300 dollars seed money for a planned nightclub of their own back in the U.S. at stake, Tulsa's buddies are pleased to have him stand in for Dynamite to seduce Lili. The ploy is musically celebrated aboard a train as Tulsa and fellow soldiers jubilantly sing "Frankfurt Special," with apologies to the Frankfurt School. Fawning young women assemble as Tulsa sings "Frankfurt Special's got a special way to go," to the bilingual refrain from his buddies who join in with rousing choruses of "Ja, ja!"

The plot element of wagering on the outcome of an attempted seduction is long in the tooth, going back at least as far as Pierre Choderlos de Laclos's novel *Les Liaisons dangereuses* (1782), eventually adapted to the screen in English as *Dangerous Liaisons* (1988) and *Valmont* (1989). The source material was far more complex and far more sexually frank. Characterizing sexual seduction as a sporting event was part repudiation of the enlightenment era's emphasis on reason, analysis and individualism. *Les Liaisons dangereuses* plays itself out as a hedonistic regression wherein sexuality is destructively abstracted from marital relations. *G.I. Blues* is the stripped-down, sanitized, militarized appropriation of that same reactionary strand in de Laclos's novel. In 1960, the year of *G.I. Blues'* vintage, marriage was still widely recognized as worthwhile, at least for a portion of its God-ordained purpose, the regulating of society and establishing of traditional, nuclear families. Presley, previously public enemy number one to many in terms of what he meant to marriages, among other relationships, would now be made to toe the party line.

Full-color cheesecake pictures of Lili in front of the nightclub merge with live-action footage of her dancing inside it. The dancing, such as it is, expresses not so much a dance aesthetic as a succession of rhythmic postures for the sake of displaying Lili's sparsely attired body. After her performance, she pours a beer over the head of a frisky older male patron, proving, as per a report from one of Tulsa's fellow soldiers, that she's "steamed heat outside, iceberg inside." The reductive psychology is congruent with an Elvis flick.

Lili presents herself as sexually provocative. Provocation is at the core of her theatricality too. She then reacts with indignation when her provocation succeeds. Tulsa doesn't hesitate to sit next to Lili as she elegantly lights up a cigarette. Their meeting is interrupted when Tulsa obediently sings, as requested by an American officer. Absently strumming an inaudible acoustic guitar, Tulsa performs the bland "(I'm Gonna Stop) Shoppin' Around." Following a few aimless narrative garnishes between him, his pal Cookey (Robert Ivers) and Lili, he takes Lili to another club. He instructs a Teutonic trio of local minstrels about rhythm. "The rhythm has to ooze out," Tulsa explains, launching into the syrupy "A Night for Love," with the German musicians joining him in the melodic language. Tulsa and Lili exit the club, clandestinely monitored by three army buddies enthused by his seeming progress with her. The iceberg is thawing. She invites him to her apartment for coffee.

Next follows scenes of amorous attempts by Tulsa's pal Cookey to win a young Italian woman named Tina (Leticia Roman) by empty boasts of how bored he is with the debutantes he dated in the States. She kneels, fawning at his side. It's a weak comic aside. As military propaganda, it's suggested that the life of American G.I.s is such that, even if he's a complete shnook, exotically beautiful women will be scintillated by his every boast of himself.

The following day, Tulsa is alongside a row of tanks in the installment of a running joke. He effortlessly charms his Sargent to let him go on leave from the army base. Soldiering is professional, but military discipline isn't essential. This characterization was a frequent popular culture recruiting enticement, as seen on television's *Hogan's Heroes* (1965–71) and *The Phil Silvers Show* (1955–59) also known as *Sargent Bilko*, a 1996 film remake of which starred Steve Martin, as well as cinema's *The Secret War Of Harry Frigg* (1968) and *Kelly's Heroes* (1970), to name but a few. Having begun liking Lili, Tulsa admits he's conscience-stricken because of his motives. A fellow soldier helps him to rationalize matters. Lili joins Tulsa for a boating tour of Frankfurt am Main. She conducts herself as his *Encyclopedia Germannica* travelogue companion.

On land again, the couple watches a Punch and Judy puppet show. Kitsch is manifested virulently as Tulsa steps into the puppet theater, performing an English and German language rendition of "Wooden Heart," based on the German folk song, "Muss i denn" ("Must I Then"). Presley's pronunciation sounds as if he could have been a native-born speaker of the German language. Childishness aside, the scene presents the militarized subjugation of rock & roll's king into a simple-minded puppet show.

Tulsa and Lili do more sightseeing on a sky ride for two. A sample of Lili's dialogue goes as follows: "Observe the neatness and precision of the grape fields." Talk like that can't help but spark a song from both of them, though mostly from Presley. Together they deliver the lyrically and harmonically bland "Pocketful of Rainbows." Presley and Prowse croon in front of a rear-projected landscape, their voices artificially enhanced by an echo chamber. Within the quasi-monumental setting, they partake of their first kiss.

American military benevolence is highlighted as Cookey drops off Tina at the airport, having magnanimously sprung for her to visit her parents in Italy. Tulsa's conscience kicks in again as he tells Lili in her dressing room, "You see, a guy like me on temporary duty meets a girl like you ... all of a sudden somebody gets hurt. I don't want that to happen." Lili studies her exterior in a makeup mirror. When Tulsa tells Cookey he's calling off the bet, demonstrating typical pal-to-the-protagonist ingenuity, Cookey salvages the wager scheme while en route to Lili. Lili pours Cookey and herself some champagne in her dressing room. It's official: Elvis Presley has driven a woman to drink.

Donning an over-sized, black silk cloak with an elaborate, vampire-like collar, Lili takes to the stage. She discards the cloak to dance, salaciously clad in a black leotard and red sash. Moving through a jazz ballet repertoire of moves, Lili incorporates direct flirtation with an old man in the audience. As per the broader narrative of *G.I. Blues,* Lili's dance conveys a characterization of woman as irrational. Her response to heartbreak is an aesthetic enactment of the contrary, the wholesome fun of exhibitionism. Lili appropriates and puts on a military hat. Her militarized sexuality is a parody of military masculinity. Her gleefully smiling throughout deflects the eroticism of the dance in a wholesome direction.

Babysitting for a fellow soldier and his wife, Tulsa mugs for the baby and the movie audience. Calling the Cafe Europa, he asks Lili to help and, putting aside her hostility, she consents. Lili cajoles Tulsa into singing a lullaby. Could this deployment of Presley be an apologia for rock & roll's antagonism to the nuclear family? Presley's Tulsa and Prowse's Lili reconcile while playing parents by proxy. This is, briefly, possibly one of the reinventions of Presley farthest removed from reality: Elvis as middle-class house hubby.

From the unofficial military surveillance by his fellow soldiers, as well as his having spent the night with Lili, albeit through babysitting, it's determined that Tulsa won the wager. Puzzled, Lili looks on as Tulsa's men collect on the bet from their army competitors. Tulsa's dull Sargent unwittingly discloses what's taken place in front of Lili. Tulsa tries, unsuccessfully, to better explain matters to her. "You underestimate your attraction," she says storming off. Even when he's being spurned by a woman, Presley's attractiveness to women is acknowledged.

The course of true love is soon restored, though. Backstage at an army musical rehearsal, the woman Tulsa babysat for makes it known to Lili that Tulsa was babysitting as a pinch hitter. Moreover, the baby wasn't in on the bet to have Lili stay up all night with Tulsa, or something comparably logical. Before Tulsa asks the big question, she volunteers, "Of course I'll marry you. I love you." And by this point, what woman wouldn't?

Saluting in front of a massive American flag with orchestral accompaniment, Tulsa performs the marching-music-inspired "Didja Ever (Get One of Them Days?)." As with the title track, there's an American military sound, an anthemic quality, to this musical finale. *G.I. Blues* re-situates and redefines of the King of Rock & Roll in a movie musical completely bereft of rock & roll. Between Hollywood and the U.S. army, as a movie star, Presley is reconstructed for a new decade. Musically tamer than his past movies, *G.I. Blues* augers the tone of most of his future movie soundtracks. Presley, proves his effectiveness as a kitsch crooner. He's visibly, physically restrained in his military uniform and military choreography as he performs the milder melodic singing. Over the ensuing years, the shape of rock & roll would be redetermined by performers with other-than-Presleyan innovations.

IDENTITY CRISIS

A recurring tendency is established early in the 1960s filmic marketing of Elvis Presley. In keeping with the market-driven imperative of enslavement to the new, or seemingly new, Presley was being aligned with the pop cultural fashions of the moment. The western genre was wildly popular in American movies and television of the late 1950s and early 1960s. Saddling Presley with a role in a cowboy-and-Indian yarn might have seemed a desirable inevitability. The innovative twist of *Flaming Star* (1960), in addition to its starring Presley, is its presentation of the White rock & roll monarch with Black affinities as both cowboy and Indian. Though distinctly different from the uses he was put to in *G.I. Blues,* Presley is again at a distant remove from his rock & roll self.

Offspring of a Caucasian father and an Indigenous mother, Pacer Burton (Presley) is a continuation of Presley as a rebellious youth, in this instance as a confused youth. Pacer's condition is aggravated by the Old West milieu that is the context for his interracial identity crisis. In the 1950s, Presley's movies implicitly asked *"What* is Elvis Presley?" They either exploited him as a novelty or sought to minimize the cultural trauma of rock & roll—or both. Alternatively, *Flaming Star* is more of a screen personality–oriented motion picture, rather than a singing star–oriented one, forwarding the formulation of

Presley as celebrity, something possibly intuited by pop artist Andy Warhol.

In his 1963 silkscreen *Eight Elvises,* Warhol exalts the movie star celebrity status of the Presley of *Flaming Star* as having taken precedence over his rock & roll status. Philosopher Immanuel Kant's idea of the functionlessness of art resonates in Warhol's work through a glorification of the functionlessness of celebrities. Warhol repeats eight times the same image of Presley cribbed from *Flaming Star,* a full-body depiction of him drawing a six-shooter. As is often the case with Warhol, this work leaves much to puzzle over; while sparse on details, the canvas is large (6.5 feet x 12 feet), and went to an anonymous buyer in 2008 for 100 million dollars. The work references the medium of celluloid projection, as well as Warhol's aesthetic of a simultaneity of the sensational and the repetitious.

Flaming Star commences with Pacer and his older, mixed-race half-brother Clint (Steve Forrest) arriving at a homesteading surprise party for Clint. Those assembled give the fastidiously groomed Pacer what is, for him, a superfluous shaving kit. Pacer wastes no time in picking up a guitar and launching into song, in this instance the folky "A Cane and a High Starched Collar." A hybridizing of musical interludes from 1950s Presley movies occurs. Upon commencing the tune, everyone else does a folk dance with improbable precision. The scene harks back to the comparably robotic response of youths assembling for Presley's restaurant rendition of "Mean Woman Blues" in *Loving You.*

Another component of the hybrid tune, reiterated in most of his subsequent movies, is the effect of Presley's singing on everyone else on screen. As per his deployment as musical decoy aiding a shoplifting scheme in *King Creole,* Presley and his singing enchant and mesmerize. Even in 1968's *Charro!,* the narrative movie in which he didn't sing on screen, singing instead over the opening credits, producers never entirely dispensed with his music. Though *Flaming Star* accords only token acknowledgement to that talent, it's intrinsic to his performative charisma. It's rare that Presley's movie audiences are allowed to long forget that he's a singer. In *Ways of Seeing* (1972), art critic John Berger identifies "glamour" as the quality of being enviable, the preeminent quality among that which advertising uses to sell goods and services. Etymologically, the term "glamour" pertains to enchantment and witchcraft. Disturbingly, both in advertising and popular culture, glamour is often a fundamental ingredient in advertising. Increasingly, Presley's singing would be identified as inherently magical in his movies, regardless of how lightweight that singing might be.

Typically, *Flaming Star* reintroduces Presley by highlighting his singing talent. As in *G.I. Blues,* however, it also suggests a forgetting of his rock & roll persona. The fleeting ditty doesn't provide actual music as much as allude to Presley's cultural authority. His singing overwhelms his young women listeners.

The musical celebration of canes and high starched collars is violently interrupted by an Indian sneak attack, or possibly, by an attack from Hollywood sneaky Indians. That it's a day to live in infamy is characterized by flaming arrows and a tomahawk parting the skull of a homesteader. After a day of grave digging, the Brothers Burton receive post-massacre commentaries from Kiowa chief Buffalo Horn (Rudolf Acosta) and angry racist Angus Pierce (Richard Jaekel). Burton family patriarch Sam Burton (John McIntire), with fierce twelve-step-program determinism, assures his Kiowa wife Neddy (Delores del Rio), "If we have to become a power to ourselves, we'll resist whoever comes against us."

True to an affirmatively forward-thinking 1960s Hollywood is a didactic acceptance of interracial coupling. Racism in *Flaming Star* is another social crisis: one of family survival. Hence, a duality of social agendas is presented. Typical of wobbly though commendable popular culture, in *Flaming Star* there is an evident moralizing attempt to deter racism. The film presents a possible repudiation of collective bigotry. The other agenda, that for which racial conflict is a cypher, centers on family, what philosopher Georg Wilhelm Friedrich Hegel deemed essential for the dissemination of all sound moral and ethical values. Similarly, *Flaming Star* shows that sound moral and ethical values are under siege.

Flaming Star also relates the theme of the survival of the self, specifically Presley's self and, by extension, the survival of an interracial family who society wouldn't tolerate. Pacer's disillusionment accelerates when White vigilantes cause his family's cattle to stampede. Two White saddle tramps barge in on Pacer and his mother Neddy. After repeated racial slurs are slung against him, as well as a failed attempt to violate Neddy, Pacer beats up the outlaws in a savage dust-up. The extremity of the fracas prompts a question that can be asked of much popular culture: is justice being depicted, or has a series of flagrant injustices been depicted for the sake of licensing screen violence?

The next day, Chief Buffalo Horn tells Pacer he'd be valuable as a half-White fighting for the Kiowa; his participation would give the chief "the most powerful magic," Pacer is told. In *Dialectic of Enlightenment* (1947), Max Horkheimer and T.W. Adorno contend that myth was the first form of enlightenment reason. In their critique of Homer's *Odyssey*, Horkheimer and Adorno outline how the hero, Odysseus, consistently overcomes mythical forces through using reason and cunning. In *Flaming Star*, Presley's Pacer Burton, the strongest according to what's posited as traditional Indigenous criteria, will be destroyed, not by reason and cunning, but as a casualty of violent, racist stupidity. Genocide is implicated as a function of Enlightenment reason.

When Pacer and Neddy leave an Indian village where he received Buffalo Horn's invitation to join them, Neddy is shot in an ambush by White vigilantes. The Burton men deliberate over finding a doctor. Their attempts are thwarted by a larger mob of angry White men, and they retreat. Acting on the old adage that, when the going gets tough, the tough take hostages, Pacer grabs the doctor's little girl to force him to treat Neddy. A dying Neddy ventures out alone on a windy night.

Husband Sam cries out after her and, finding her dead in the wilderness, he weeps. At her burial, attended by Clint and Pacer, a fragment of scripture is mentioned by Sam: "'and Adam called his wife Eve because she was the mother of all living.' Neddy, to me, you were the mother of all living."

The ideological theme of America as the new Promised Land is invoked, a promise that hasn't yet been realized, aside from being comparatively much better for many immigrants. This is deep stuff for an Elvis movie, incorporating what Faulkner scholar Jake Brown calls the unifying theme all great American fiction: the tragedy of those who mistakenly believe in their own national mythology. The theme of America as the new Eden is a correlative. Implicitly including these elements in *Flaming Star,* Presley-as-movie-star overshadows Presley-as-rock-&-roll-star. Concomitantly, Presley's performing career, for a time at least, diverges from the ethos of its rock & roll moorings in a movie vehicle championing the virtues of family.

Exploding at the doctor who failed to save his mother's life, Pacer's attempt to attack him with a knife is curtailed by the slightly calmer, Whiter Clint. Pacer rants, "I'm Indian, and I'll never forget they killed her because she was Indian!" In lieu of justice, Pacer's declaration suggests that his memory of an injustice constitutes a form of justice. Clint Burton and buxom lady-friend Roslyn Pierce, sister to red-neck Angus, although their relationship isn't elaborated on, ride into town together. Clint tries and fails to negotiate peace with the hostile White townspeople. His mother's death has intensified Clint's identification with her ethnicity. Pacer joins Chief Buffalo Horn's Kiowa tribe on the condition that his remaining family members, half-brother Clint and father Sam, won't be attacked as White townsfolk. The Kiowa still ambush Sam Burton anyway, downing him with two arrows to the back. Indiginous sneakiness achieves new heights when they gratuitously stampede the Burton family cattle, just as the angry Whites did earlier. When people act in hatred toward each other, it's suggested, one side can act as badly as the other.

In the dark of night, or in day-for-night cinematography, a more extravagant battle erupts in the wake of Sam's death. While the sequence doesn't lack for daring-do and a surfeit of violence, the drama isn't well-served by the cinematography, except symbolically perhaps. Pacer rushes to the aid of Clint, who has sustained a severe arrow wound. Possibly in a directorial effort to alleviate the eventual tedium of the battle sequence, Pacer removes his shirt to reveal the still adolescent-looking Presley physique. After overcoming a Kiowa band member in a prolonged punch-out, Pacer gets Clint on a horse and, as he's sending Clint away, is told by him that the Kiowa killed their father. The uprightness of Pacer's instinctive violence is retroactively vindicated by his being informed of the Kiowa treachery. In that the Kiowa mother is a casualty of racist Whites, and the White father is a casualty of the barbaric Indians, the foundation of the interracial family has been destroyed.

One might fault *Flaming Star* for its omission of how the battle sequence is resolved. Whether by design or not, it's an omission that aligns the movie with stage drama. The next day dawns with the impeccably-groomed Clint awakening in a bed in town, his body precision bandaged, seemingly only to have suffered a flesh wound. He runs to encounter the more gravely wounded Pacer who's outside, atop a horse. "Maybe someday, somewhere, folks will be able to understand folks like us," Pacer opines. Having done his share of punching, stabbing and shooting, he trots away from this mortal coil. His last line is at once corny and insightful. The racist and the mob alike are prone to attacking what they don't comprehend. There's a residue of Presley's earlier big-screen identity appealed to as well, in that Pacer too is incomprehensible.

The nihilism of *Flaming Star,* manifested in Pacer's campaign of revenge, dispels any question about his true allegiances. The Indigenous body-count he accumulates proves he's much Whiter than might have been supposed. Clint beckons to the dying Pacer to come back. "Pacer! Pacer!" he cries repeatedly, in a conclusion reminiscent of little Brandon de Wilde running after Alan Ladd at the end of George Stevens' brilliant 1953 *Shane.*

Approaching *Flaming Star* as a tragedy that takes some of its cues from classical stage drama, omitting a depiction of the final, climactic battle—as per a classic stage drama—invites appraisal of Presley's Pacer as a tragic hero. Ordinarily, part of what makes tragedy tragic is that, despite clues that he might be predestined to suffer great loss, the hero's tragic flaw leading to his death or some other catastrophe is potentially correctable or preventable. That's how tragedy proper is instructive to audiences. Yet Pacer's tragic flaw resides not in his character. In some ways he's rough around the edges, but the purported flaw is completely outside his control: his bi-racial identity. Correspondingly, the tragic flaw resides not with the tragic hero, but with America itself, a Promised Land that has yet to fully live up to its promises. Is this a repudiation of Calvinist predestination through a long-winded, climactic battle sequence that was merely film making incompetence, or a production decision informed by budgetary constraints?

Flaming Star presents a despairing picture of a family that transgresses against societal norms. As such, family also has a kind of tragically heroic status. Whereas in three of his four films of the 1950s, the incomprehensibility of Presley's identity is integral to his ascent to stardom, in *Flaming Star,* it's integral to his destruction and that of his family. Neither the non-conforming family nor their non-conforming progeny can be assimilated by society. Is this Hollywood's indictment of racism in America and destructiveness toward non-conformity? Alternatively, is Flaming *Star* positing the bleaker notion that combating such forces is apt to fail? The specific racism being moralized against in *Flaming Star* relates a possible liberal complicity with misbegotten Puritanism. The epithet of "half-breed" is repeatedly directed against Pacer. Inherent to that epithet isn't just racial hatred and a threat to purported racial purity. There's also an implicit hostility toward sexual intercourse, 'breeding.' The malevolent collective deference to the state over deference to the sanctity of the nuclear family is among the movie's other themes.

Sexual subtexts aside, and as per *G.I. Blues,* in *Flaming Star* Presley is also at a distant remove from rock & roll. In the former, he was used as an overtly militaristic propaganda figure. His turn at being dressed up in a Western would be the heaviest drama he'd ever undertake. Going back to its origins in Ancient Greece, central to tragedy is its presumed capacity to affect catharsis, an emotional cleansing, among audience members. The tragedy of *Flaming Star,* while directing a good finger-wagging at the audience, seems oriented toward making audiences fall more deeply in love with Elvis Presley. Just prior to her demise, Pacer's mother Neddy informs him that, once you see your flaming star, it's time for you to die. By 1960, the White Tennessean with the Black sound hadn't brought America any closer to resolving its racial divide, as the wealth of dramatic clashes pertaining to those problems in the 1960s would obviate. To be fair, affecting such a resolution never belonged to the rock & roll agenda. As allegory, *Flaming Star* echoes a different legacy that the counterfeit revolution of rock & roll was more than a minor player in bringing about: the attack on the nuclear family.

Presley's emerging identity as celebrity-actor here undermines his rock & roll identity. By the 1960s, the heavy toll that Presley and rock & roll had on 1950's normalcy was extensively evident. The increasing erosion in the quality of most of his subsequent movies didn't simply reflect a take-the-money-and-run mentality behind his film projects. The cheapness of the most of the Presley movies of the 1960s doesn't just appear to actively eradicate the memory of his former and greatest significance as a performer. That cheapness also registers the persistence of something Peter Guralnick repeatedly refers to in his Presley biography, *Last Train to Memphis* (1994). Guralnick relates that many of those involved with rock & roll, including Presley, believed that rock & roll would be a short-lived phenomena. That rock & roll was looked upon as transient by many of the people involved in its production and marketing is reflected in the formal properties of its sound and performance. Rock & roll— most of it, anyway—has been characterized by its speed. Rock & roll has largely always been in a hurry to get somewhere, a reflection, perhaps, of the impatience of youth. What often distinguishes Presley's movies of the 1960s, that is, the shoddiness of their production values, might be explained thereby also. To have invested more serious effort into something deemed so transient wouldn't make sense from the viewpoints of either logic or business.

ELVIS PRESLEY: A CASE STUDY

Illustrious playwright Clifford Odets had to earn a living too. Perhaps that's why he was the scribe behind Presley's turn in *Wild in the Country* (1961). Prior to popularization of the term "rock & roll," Presley and others referred to his style of music as "hillbilly music." This feature shows Presley demonstrating a broader range as both actor and hillbilly. Despite Presley's effectively branching out as an actor, he remains situated in the familiar territory of playing yet another troubled youth. Although authority figures are generally deemed antithetical to rock & roll, Presley's status as the king of rock & roll made him a kind of authority figure. With generally good production values, *Wild in the Country* is an intriguing timepiece pitting one implicit authority figure, Presley, against another, psychiatrist Irene Sperry (Hope Lange).

After the obligatory opening theme song sung by Presley, rough-and-ready Glenn Tyler (Presley) is introduced duking it out with his dirty fighter of a brother. The occasion for the brawl is undisclosed, but it culminates in Glenn landing a lethal blow against his lesser than Marquis de Queensbury sibling. A sympathetic court sentences Glenn to live with and be employed by his Uncle Braxton (William Mims). Glenn is also ordered to visit widowed psychiatrist Mrs. Irene Sperry, who is never referred to as "doctor." With a dog named Roosevelt and a modernist painting in her home, it's suggested that she's also a liberal. Hence it's implied that the success or failure of Glenn's rehabilitation will mirror the success or failure of an experiment in American liberalism.

Co-habiting with Uncle Braxton, Glenn is the passionate focus of his cousin Noreen (Tuesday Weld). Aside from Carolyn Jones's Ronnie in *King Creole,* Noreen is the most licentious of Presley's on-screen love interests. Her licentiousness reflects the then-emergent cinematic trend toward promoting sexual permissiveness. A single mother with a two-dollar wedding ring and a fib of her father's, she has an absentee husband 'off at work', Noreen aggressively speaks to Glenn about the joy of inbreeding. Demonstrating his range as an actor, Presley does a credible job of acting drunk. Mrs. Sperry is amused by Glenn's drunken antics in front of her house at night. Glenn's longtime girlfriend Betty Lee (Millie Perkins) rounds out the triad of female attention-givers.

The taboo of incest is suggested when Glenn and Noreen cloister themselves in Uncle Braxton's bathroom together. Presley's modest singing contribution to the movie is plausibly worked into the movie when he serenades an annoyed Betty Lee. He's accompanied by music from the truck radio. Her gradual capitulation as he sings is another assertion of his seductive power. The three Presley songs interwoven into the screen narrative, like the title track, are more mild than wild. Of the widowed Irene Sperry and himself, Glenn tells Noreen, "She thinks she's got a lunatic on her hands ... She thinks I'm lame in the head." Another challenge to the Presley protagonist is suggested therein: he must vindicate his sanity.

Mrs. Sperry dodges overtures from local captain of industry Phil Macy (John Ireland). Phil's drunken lout-about-town son Cliff Macy (Gary Lockwood) has a history of mutual hostility between himself and Glenn. Glenn confesses to Mrs. Sperry that he's "walking around with a cup full of anger," wanting to kill both his father and his brother. He boils over and threatens violence against Cliff. Despite Phil Macy's down-on-his-liver story about son Cliff and his "athletic" heart condition, Irene still refuses to take Cliff on as a patient.

During his evening of binge drinking with Noreen, Glenn finds an acoustic guitar and sings "I'll be True to You in My Way." The musical confessional intimates that, for the Presley protagonist, monogamy is ill-defined and relativistic. Noreen tells Glenn she wants him for "hours and hours of heaven that leads [sic] to hell." Not a good idea. The disparaging view of family presented could possibly be deemed a morally dark apologetic for rock & roll's anti-family sensibility. Despite an absence of rock & roll music in this Presley feature, the same disillusionment with family figures prominently.

After a mildly erotic Sunday afternoon of Glenn and his girlfriend kissing in an idyllic setting, her stiff-necked father scolds Glenn for keeping Betty Lee from church. Family and Christianity, it's suggested, prudishly stifle youthful pleasures. Screenwriter Odets riddles the narrative with snippets of Biblical references, most of them pertaining to idealizing the creative individual. Perhaps Glenn is exempt from church attendance because his writing is synonymous with a spiritual gifting.

During one of their sessions, Irene asks Glenn if he ever thought of writing, because he "turn[s] a phrase a certain way." Though his spelling and grammar are terrible, she says he has the potential to become a great writer. She's shared the story he wrote with a literature professor. After a tiff that erupts because Glenn intended the story for Irene only, they resume seeing each other on a professional basis. They drive to the college together so Glenn can hear the professor's direct endorsement of his writing. The innocence of their trip together is accentuated by their singing a children's song while en route. "For man to discover fire was nothing," an elderly English professor tells the Promethean youth; "for him to learn how to use it was everything." Irene's opinion is validated when the elderly pedagogue says, "He writes exactly as he feels and thinks." For the English professor to honestly make such a claim, he'd have to know exactly how Glenn feels and thinks. Fatigued, Irene nearly crashes the car on the stormy night drive home. They spend the night at a motel and check into separate rooms, reuniting briefly to kiss. Cliff Macy turns up at the same motel with a floozy and spies their names on the motel register. After Cliff casts aspersions on Irene's virtue, Glenn punches Cliff and Cliff dies. Glenn has killed someone again— this time seriously.

Charged with manslaughter, Glenn faces the prospect of his own symbolic crucifixion. A spiteful Phil Macy rebuffs Irene's courtroom attempt to get him to fess up that Cliff had an athletic heart, presumably the true fault for his demise. With Glenn's exoneration a seeming impossibility, Irene goes home to asphyxiate herself in her garage with car exhaust. Having a change of heart of his own, Phil admits to the court that Cliff had a heart condition. Free to enact a rescue, Glenn reaches Irene in the traditional nick of time. Despite mutuality of affection between Glenn and Irene, they agree that, for his own good and that of civilization, he should go to college. The movie ends with a shot of Glenn on campus where, presumably, he'll learn how to spell and conjugate verbs.

As per *Loving You, King Creole* and especially *Jailhouse Rock,* Presley's character's talent is his ticket up and out. Odets used the established template of Presley's character as someone in need of rehabilitation, and talent as the means by which rehabilitation is achieved. In line with Glenn Tyler's readiness for deadly fisticuffs, Presley's own talent is a dangerous quality that must be harnessed. Well-to-do Cliff Macy repeatedly belittles Glenn for being poor. However, belting your oppressor in the face isn't necessarily the most reasonable method of resolving class inequities. As per philosopher Marshall McLuhan's exegesis on the comic book *Superman* in his *The Mechanical Bride,* Hollywood's frequent recourse to depicting physical violence isn't only a means of counteracting boredom. Quick recourse to violence bespeaks the impatience of Americans with the jurisprudence system. Art historian Arnold Hauser's comment that popular culture is about boredom is applicable also. For many, America in general and Hollywood in particular have consistently made the best movies in the world. The frequency of violence in American movies vindicates Hauser's observation. Violence is an antidote to boredom. Simultaneously, movie-makers are ill at ease with allowing audiences opportunities to get contemplative about what they're watching.

Starring in a movie that champions the value of school is thematically at odds with rock & roll, as well the career of its king up to that time. Additionally, polarities presented in *Wild in the Country* exhibit a tendency noted by Christopher Lasch in *The Culture of Narcissism* (1979) that of the usurpation of familial authority by the state. A quasi-orphaned Elvis again functions instructively in another screen vehicle showing another alternative to the nuclear family.

Wild in the Country is also noteworthy as an example identified by Krin and Glen O. Gabbard as the golden age of psychiatry in American cinema (circa 1957–63). Presley's character dismisses as "book talk" Irene's explanation of their mutual attraction being rooted in the psychiatric phenomenon known as transference. Nevertheless, psychotherapy is upheld as the means by which a wayward youth is put on the redemptive road to self-realization, educated refinement and social utility. How is it that a broad range of Hollywood movies made within a six-year span all exhibit this same representational tendency regarding psychiatry? Gabbard and Gabbard speculate that, during this Golden Age, "psychiatrists were authoritative voices of reason, adjustment and well-being. Before this idea became orthodoxy, however, the American cinema began responding to the cultural upheavals of the 1960s."[4] While this hypothesis provides a superficial historical account for the shift away from the cinematic idealization of psychiatrists, it does not explain the single-mindedness with which Hollywood had previously, and would again later, denigrate mental healthcare professionals.

Despite the Gabbards' critical acumen in matters psychoanalytical, their inclusion of *Wild in the Country* in the Golden Age of Psychiatry articulates the situation precisely backwards. It is the patient, Presley's Glenn Tyler, who literally rescues his therapist. In that, the two rescue each other, one rescue for another. Whereas the Gabbards credibly outline the growth of the acceptance of psychiatry in postwar America as being at the root of the Golden Age, neglecting market forces as a determinant of mass culture prohibits a proper assessment of psychiatry's loss of prominence and credibility. Additionally, access to psychiatry entails a measure of economic privilege, a luxury not readily accommodated by American capitalism.

Wild in the Country might be deemed psychiatry's brightest shining moment in Hollywood history. To the extent that *Wild in the Country* might be said to idealize psychiatry, not least among the implications of that idealization is the reduction of thought to a sort of codified fashion. Simultaneously with Presley's Glenn Tyler, the movies other hero is the state. Benevolent, generous and forgiving, it is government that is the greater redemptive overseer amid all of the cinematic goings on. Whereas within a year, Presley's starring in *Follow that Dream* would make plain that Hollywood's honeymoon with psychiatry and psychology was over, the American government would not be comparably dishonored.

---

[4]   Krin and Glen O. Gabbard, *Psychiatry and the Cinema* (Chicago, University of Chicago Press, 1987) p.84.

I AM A FUGITIVE FROM THE GREAT SOUTHERN HAWAIIAN FRUIT COMPANY

Following the somewhat disappointing box office returns from *Wild in the Country,* the runaway success of 1961's *Blue Hawaii* and its hugely successful soundtrack album sales did much to establish the most pervasive aspects of the Presley film formula of the 1960s. If *Wild in the Country* proved anything to those responsible for what he was to star in, it was that, for the most part, mass audiences weren't especially interested in seeing an Elvis Presley with any depth. Arguably, they never would again.

Profit has always been chief behind that which drives popular culture. That's neither surprising nor in itself wrong. However, the lucrativeness of *Blue Hawaii* would be such that its formula would steer much of Presley's subsequent movie career, doing so in projects that were usually little more than naked cash grabs. The drawing power of Presley's unforgotten talent, coupled with the exoticism of the fiftieth state as his backdrop, proved to be an attractive blend for mass audiences. Combining him with glamorous or otherwise spectacular locales became a hallmark of his film products. Increasingly, those products established him as the centerpiece around which were arranged deluges of nubile beauties, stunning real estate, fast cars, and often-invisible musical orchestration. His trusty Jordanaires still backed him up vocally when the scripts demanded that he break out into song, a convention of the standard Hollywood musical which he always regarded as implausible and silly.

As newly discharged ex-soldier Chad Gates returning from an army tour of duty, Presley lands in his screen home of Hawaii to continue romancing his local love Maile, pronounced "my lee", Duval (Joan Blackman), the girl he left behind. The narrative begins with a motorcycle cop, one familiar with Maile's reckless driving, pulling her over for speeding wildly through the Hawaiian streets in her little red Hawaiian convertible. Upon explaining that she's driving that way because Chad's plane is a about to land, the cop immediately waves his duty to ticket her and gives her a motorcycle escort to the airport. The importance of the arrival of Elvis Presley even supersedes the power of conventional law enforcement. As would be standardized in his later movies, his character, in this instance, Chad, is essentially a very thin but somehow necessary pretext for the ceremonial event of a filmed appearance of Elvis Presley.

Introduced disembarking from a plane, then chauffeured by Maile in her sports car, this would typify the majority of Presley's later screen introductions. From this point on, he would ordinarily ride, fly, drive or boat onto his first scene. It's thereby stressed that Presley is someone in near constant motion, active, dynamic and, above all, youthfully active. As the plane door opens, Chad is seen kissing a stewardess. The continual association of Presley with movement is a kind of shorthand acknowledgment of what critic Harold Rosenberg identified as the attractiveness of the American male hero to females and his need to abandon them. More significantly, we see Presley as the irresistible, polygamous locus of female attention. Almost invariably, the Presley protagonist drags the colossus of his rock & roll star aura with him into whatever movie he stars in. Indeed, the man was handsome, but how else are we to account for all the hysteria-inducing fuss he's continually shown generating? His movies of the 1960s won't permit him to inhabit any screen identity other than that of Elvis Presley. It's as if Presley's normal, ongoing state of being is existing in the amorous embrace of one beautiful woman or another.[5] When it's revealed that Chad was only using the stewardess to make Maile jealous, it's suggested that, on a whim, he's able to recruit any woman to do his bidding. That's not

---

[5]   A number of James Bond movies would put a racier spin on the same idea, introducing Bond in some perpetual coital context, the condition to which he returns at the movie's end. It's as if, when not called on to save the world in whole or in part, he exists in a never-ending state of being sexually gratified. The figure of the irresistible polygamous male would soon be established as a staple of representation in the Western mass culture of the 1960s. This tendency in pop culture idealizations of masculinity would appear in nearly all of the Presley movies of the era, throughout the James Bond theatrical releases (beginning in 1962) and in their host of imitators such as the Matt Helm movies (1966–69), the Derek Flint movies (1965 and 1967). Napoleon Solo of television's *Man from U.N.C.L.E.* (1964–68) and Jim West of *The Wild, Wild West* (1965–69), to name only a few. Presley aside, these supermen share a penchant for the finer things in life: they are connoisseurs in the consuming of luxury goods and beautiful women. They stood as the political extension of the answer to the question of what sort of a man reads *Playboy*. They are exemplary of the means, identified by which Christopher Lasch in *The Culture of Narcissism* (1979), as to how the ordinary man is given a taste and an appetite for the extraordinarily expensive.

Never called on to save the world, most of Presley's roles reflect a humbler turn on this same expression of male sexual privilege. T.W. Adorno commented that the one constant lesson of all Clark Gable movies is that Clark Gable is irresistible to women. By the 1960s this formula took on a far more exaggerated tone among leading men. Male movie stars of this kind would no longer simply be enshrined as ideal men. In scenarios vaguely resembling a science fiction gender dystopia, the rarity of the ideal, irresistible masculine identity (such as Presley's) sets in play the panic of an objectified womanhood in a male-dominated economy. Youthful feminine beauty, that which is asserted as the greatest thing a woman might have to offer a man, is shown to be as common as dirt. The gravest danger for women lies in procrastinating respective to her capacity for procreation. As object lessons in sexual relations, these entertainments suggest that women are to be the sexual aggressors while man would do best to remain passive.

something illuminating of the character of Chad Gates. Rather, it reinforces how we're supposed to perceive Elvis Presley. Then, while in Maile's speeding convertible, he fully charms himself back into her good graces by singing "I Was Always Almost True to You", doing so to the childish melody of "Frère Jacques." It's an even more dumbed-down restatement of "I'll be True to You in My Way" from *Wild in the Country*. The song's effectiveness as a ploy to win over Maile identifies her as fundamentally childish.

Chad and Maile visit an idyllic beach together where they engage in wholesome Hawaiian horseplay. They partake of some aimless interacting with two small children, aimless aside from again promoting Presley as someone whose charm can be resisted by no one, regardless of age. There's some tourist-y romantic business as Native canoe enthusiasts perform traditional-sounding Hawaiian tunes for Chad and his sweetheart. He joins in the musicality a couple of times. Yet despite the significant duration of the beach sequence relative to the running time of the movie, not much happens in it, certainly nothing that advances the plot. The incursion of this protracted digression into the non-narrative, something contributing nothing to story development, raises a basic question: what, specifically, is the purpose of the digression?

Roland Barthes' not-entirely-accurate essay on the 1953 Hollywood production of Shakespeare's *Julius Caesar* made uniform use of an archaic Roman hairstyle to convey what Barthes sardonically called "Romanness". Comparably, the rambling tropical paradise digression communicates a sense of Hawaiianness. The digression also presents yet another re-invention of the star: Hawaii is the setting for the re-exoticizing of Presley.

Re-invention is an effective marketing strategy, one impelled by what would inform a prevailing mantra in countless promotions for product innovations: "new and improved." In turn, the re-exoticized Presley is the pitchman not just for Hawaiian tourism but also for the ideological revival of America as the new Promised Land, the result of the Edenic island chain being subsumed as the fiftieth state only two years before the release of *Blue Hawaii*.

Chad rejects a position with his pineapple magnate father's firm in favor of striking out on his own. "The King" accepts charity from no one in any of his movies. This idealizing of the virtue of total self-reliance isolates individuals. The marketplace correlative of this idealization of took hold in the age of enlightenment. It's a myth that divides and undermines much collective human potential that could otherwise destabilize society. Not insignificantly, at a spiritual level, such mythologizing finds its realization in the erroneous embrace of atheism as the pathway to success and personal fulfillment. At the very least, it's in Blue Hawaii that another staple highlighted in most subsequent Presley movies is introduced: Presley as unabashed materialist.

There are multiple levels through which operate an appeal to authenticity apparent in Presley's roles, such as giving him a military background and proficiency in karate, which by this point he had in real life, and by alluding to the impoverished beginnings of his characters, which is absent from *Blue Hawaii* but is featured prominently in several of his other movies. For those fans aware of these continuities between his real life and his screen life, the process at work is one akin to the advertising strategy of blurring distinctions between life on and off screen. Characteristics written into many of Presley's 1960s movie roles, impoverished beginnings, some relation to the military experience, karate, and so on, all relate a pseudo-authenticity. This tailoring isn't something that makes his acting more convincing. Rather, it manifests an attempt to convince those audience members moderately more in the know about him that they're actually experiencing Elvis Presley himself, not his screen likeness. In more recent years, the marketing of what facilitates experience, including prostitution, recreational drug abuse and other, more reputable things, is now being referred to by some Marxist academics as affective capitalism.

In *Blue Hawaii*, originally titled *Beach Boy,* Presley's character isn't of impoverished origins, but he does have a military background. As he'll demonstrate in later movies, he's disdainful of charity, an economic lesson for anyone who might be thinking of going on welfare and implied shaming of those who are. In the tradition of all *real* Americans, Chad aspires to be a self-made man, or at least a self-made beach boy. His Chad Gates spurns an opportunity to have a lofty position with the firm of his opulent fruit czar father, preferring instead to strike out on his own. This unadulterated promotion of American Dream mythology, that a lack of formal education, lack of intellect and lack of support from others is no impediment to success in a capitalist society provided you can carry a tune, goes hand in glove with Presley's implied endorsement of the virtues of military service as America grew ever closer to full-fledged war against Vietnam.

Chad finds employment as a tour guide. He takes on a gaggle of adolescent girls and their female teacher, Miss Abigail Prentice (Nancy Walters). His occupation is entrenched in the leisure industry, his identity synonymous with a prescribed form of marketable fun. When Miss Prentice asks him the most loaded question in Presley film history, "Mr. Gates, do you think you can satisfy a schoolteacher and four girls?" he sheepishly replies, "I'll try." Being in Hawaii with Elvis Presley is a metaphor for polygamous eroticism.

That evening, Chad, smartly-attired in a white blazer, tie and black slacks, drops in on a party at the home of his parents. He breaks out into the festive "Rock-A-Hula." Though noticeably toned down, there are vestiges in Presley's dance moves of his former self. On the whole, however, suiting up him and rock & roll to accompany a mai tai soiree amounts to an uncomfortably surreal self-parody. Presley and rock & roll are now presented as a non-threatening commodity that can be repackaged to suit any occasion.

When first striking out on his own business, a lecherous tourist makes unwanted advances toward Miss Prentice, and Chad punches him out with a combination of karate chops and good old American fisticuffs. Displays of the efficacious use of force belong to the American movie tradition of the classic introduction of the leading man. Individually and collectively, the Presley movies present a different angle on this cliché. With but two exceptions, 1964's *Viva Las Vegas* and 1966's *Spinout,* the Presley character is always called upon at least once per movie to triumphantly think with his fists. As with the American ideological norm, Presley exhibits the *necessity* of violence. Violence in the Presley movies also comes to bespeak a form of paranoia. Circumstances can and always will call for the usually fun-loving hero to protect himself or others or both with physical aggression. Presley is dangerous, yes, but simultaneously he also is someone his fans can imagine feeling safe being with. The all-but-ceaseless, ritualistic inclusion of this element in the Presley film formula comes to signify the notion that violence itself belongs to the domain of pleasure.

In *Blue Hawaii,* Chad's impromptu pugilism lands him in jail just long enough for him to sing the passably enjoyable "I'm in the Can." As is typical of standard American movie musicals, it's a pleasant but superfluous belaboring of the self-evident. Music is employed here as a kind of antithesis to thought, an utterly redundant form of expression in a way comparable to, say, Gene Kelly singing "Singin' in the Rain" while he's singing in the rain in a movie called *Singin' in the Rain* (1952) that otherwise has nothing to do with singing in the rain. Plainly subsidiary to the dance steps of the very agile Mr. Kelly, music, or the semblance of it, is employed to undermine the belief that there might be an actual need for music.

When fired from the tour guide company for his gallantry, without skipping a beat, Chad starts up his own tour guide business. In keeping with an entrepreneurial ethos, as well as capitalism's capacity to thrive on crisis, there are no setbacks, only profitable opportunities, if properly seized upon. The identification of Presley with leisure is thereby driven home all the more forcibly. Chad's striking out on his own is paired with his singing the banal "Hawaii, Island of Lovers."

Miss Prentice and her students are his first clients. He takes her and the girls horseback riding and to a luau where they watch Hawaiian fire dances. One of the girls, Ellie Corbett (Jennie Maxwell), is a spoiled and ill-tempered flirt. The earlier fleeting incursion from a lecherous American aside, despite her relatively brief time on screen, Ellie is the true villain of the piece. Her villainy? She's bored. If, as art historian Arnold Hauser contends, popular culture is about boredom, by culture industry standards, Ellie is desperately wicked. She even goes so far as to contemptuously toss away Chad's offer of a sample of free pineapple that he and the rest of the group enjoy during the tour. Yet if we are to be taught anything by Ellie or by Presley's cinematic oeuvre, it's that not even all the forces of boredom in the universe combined can withstand Elvis Presley. In but a tiny fraction of the time that it took Martin Sheen to find and kill Marlon Brando in *Apocalypse Now* (1979), Chad will terminate Ellie's boredom with extreme prejudice.

Ellie attempts suicide by drowning, presumably the only logical alternative to being entertained. Chad rescues her and brings her into submission by giving her what every woman secretly wants from Elvis Presley: a good spanking. Presley-the-sex-symbol is momentarily transformed into the stern parent, and an allusion to the Electra complex, Jung's hypothesis of feminine sexual attachment to the father figure, is suggested thereby. This is accompanied by Chad giving Ellie a harsh, common-sense-oriented verbal reprimand. Presley is shown to have become the life-saving embodiment of what the music movement he'd fronted in the 1950s was rebelling against. Having had a spiritual awakening as the result of her spanking, the following morning we see a transformed, newly submissive Ellie. She presents a variation on the familiar "thanks, I needed that" device.

Chad's girlfriend Maile gets into another a jealous snit when she peers in on him anxiously fending off and juggling nocturnal hotel visitations from his female clients at the obligatory moment of the maximum seeming compromise of his faithfulness. This scene is a nod to the bedroom farce, but done Presley-style. Origins of the bedroom farce to the plays of the Parisian Georges Feydeau in the 1890s. However, whereas the traditional examples of this genre tend to involve the mischievous recombining of couples punctuated by much door-slamming, what need is there for any additional men when Elvis is around? Yet there's a duality to the would-be comedic anxiousness here, one through which Presley is emasculated. The King of Rock & Roll is here shown being comically uneasy at the prospect of something undermining his sexual virtue.

Chad goes off in hot pursuit of Maile to restore their less-than-skeletal, tacked-on romance. Upon catching up with her, he again demonstrates the ease with which an Elvis kind of guy can win back the girl he wants with little more effort than summoning a yo-yo to return to his palm. The boy-meets-girl, boy-loses-girl, boy-gets-girl-back again structure is given a minor but predictable nod. Just as the movie commenced with an allusion to the arousal of Maile's jealousy, so too does it conclude. This popular circular structure has a nihilistic undercurrent. Logically, audiences of such narratives might be entitled to wonder if they've actually been shown anything. This circularity could be deemed a textbook vindication of poststructuralist philosopher Jean Baudrillard's claim that mass culture is cyclical and ritualistic. After Chad has sung at his own wedding to Maile, the audience is left to return to their own less-than-idyllic lives, perhaps to begin saving up for a trip to Hawaii.

With the conditions for marriage perfected, the restoration of harmonious relations with parents and the requirements for a lucrative business arrangement in place, *Blue Hawaii* ends with a quadruple articulation of an American utopia. The requirements, sexual satisfaction, familial harmony and commercial prosperity on an island paradise, have all been satisfied. As if again forced to enact a cinematic apology for his part in rock & roll, Presley is shown succeeding in the allegedly all-important area of business and finances, the means by which he earns parental approval.

FOLLOW THAT MYTH

Adapted from Richard P. Powell's novel *Pioneer, Go Home!* (1959), 1962's *Follow that Dream* presents Presley as Toby Kwimper, a wholesome backwoods imbecile with superhuman physical strength. Toby bears more than a passing resemblance to Jethro Bodine (Max Baer Jr.) of television's *The Beverly Hillbillies,* which made its debut the same year. Jethro was funnier, but both he and Toby are configurations of a herculean, southern man-child, likewise Will Stockdale (Andy Griffith) of *No Time for Sergeants* (1958). Each of them suggests appropriations of cartoonist Al Capp's *L'il Abner* comics, which first appeared in 1943. The earliest example of the mentally underdeveloped American superman, however, was probably the tragic, depression-era Lenny Small from John Steinbeck's *Of Mice and Men* (1937). Toby Kwimper is an idealized Lenny Small, laundered of his inadvertently homicidal inclinations, endowed with family and gifted with a golden singing voice. Contrasted against *Wild in the Country,* released only a year earlier, the rank animosity with which this feature vilifies psychology as a vocation and a formal discipline exemplifies the readiness with which popular culture willingly changes allegiances to further its ideological aims. Compared to his Blue Hawaiian role as a son of privilege who shows he's capable of earning privilege on his own, the most significant alteration is the shift in Presley's socioeconomic position, from offspring of affluence to impoverished, itinerant son of the soil.

Presley's opening number accompanying the credits is "What a Wonderful Life." As per most simulacrums of the musical genre, it's the stuff of movie soundtracks and hit radio songs. The lyrics, however, are instructive: "I got no job to worry me, No big, fat boss to hurry me ... don't know where I'm goin', I don't care where I'm goin'." The song celebrates the virtues of empty-headedness and the welfare state. The notion explicated is that the poor are poor because they want to be. Between the loftiness of his status as Chad Gates in *Blue Hawaii* and his lowliness as Toby Kwimper, Presley is the musical glue holding the American economy together.

Together with Pa Kwimper (Arthur O'Connell), adopted sister Holly (Anne Helm) and the twin boys who mug shamelessly, Toby sets up a squatter's encampment on a vacant stretch of Florida beachfront property. Toby busies himself by keeping his mind off sex, mentally rehearsing multiplication tables from one times one through one times nine. Meanwhile, Pa Kwimper's American Dream is to have an indoor toilet. Holly's endeavors rounds out the family motives in her efforts to get Toby's romantic attention. Absent from this assembly of synthetic archetypes is any reference to a Ma Kwimper character. As with the Beverly Hillbillies, the Kwimpers are people of the soil, without beginning or end. America itself is their mother. Simple, humble and honest, with a guilelessness that pierces the pretenses of sophisticated, urban folk, the Kwimpers are a star-spangled version of Socratic irony. It's an irony funneled through romanticism, as per the likes of poet and artist William Blake's *Songs of Innocence and Experience* (1789). Those identified with nature, the Kwimpers, have a moral superiority that triumphs over the wiles of urbanity without even trying, or realizing there's any need to try.

The Kwimpers have subsisted off a disability pension that Toby receives for a back injury sustained doing army judo. As in earlier films, another nod is given to Presley's familiarity with martial arts, and his militarized patriotism is referred to yet again. When Toby helps a passing motorist reel in a big fish and is generously remunerated for it, Holly gets the idea for the Kwimpers to set up a rod and reel rental shop. Presley's character is again affiliated with the leisure activity and entrepreneurship. Toby and Holly go the local bank for a start-up loan for their business. Through a mildly comical misunderstanding, Toby is mistaken for a bank robber. Disaster is averted when the benevolent bank president arrives. As it turns out, the banker is the same man whom Toby helped reel in the big fish. Contrary to the resistance offered by an antsy bank manager (Howard McNear, who played the antsy tour guide boss in *Blue Hawaii*, also familiar to mass audiences of the time from *The Andy Griffith Show* as the antsy Floyd the Barber), the bank president knows you can trust simple folk and authorizes a "character loan."

The more menacing side of the entrepreneurial spirit surfaces when a roving band of gangsters and their traveling casino learn of the tax-free, legislation-free status of the property on which the Kwimpers have set up shop. The legacy of the homesteader which, by 1962, had deteriorated into the stuff of folklore, proves impervious to all violent attempts on the lives and business of the Kwimpers. Their ignorance of evil is their saving grace. As per a Garden of Eden in this Promised Land, their not knowing is their unassailable protection. It's by virtue of the Kwimpers' intellectual limitations that they are destined to arrive in a new variation on the Promised Land. With the ingenuity of a bad Bugs Bunny cartoon, the ruthlessness of the gangsters is thwarted by the Kwimpers' guilelessness. The Kwimper family's victory over the gangsters is a victory of myth over history, disregarding the fact that the first White

American settlers were predominantly deported criminals. The caricatured Mafiosi are expelled from the new Eden, not so much because they are thieves and killers, but because their monopolistic intentions cannot coexist with free enterprise. Ironically, the expulsion of the gangsters means that it's the Kwimpers who'll have a monopoly over the contested property.

The token bureaucratic bad apple, Mr. King, sends the beautiful but devious social worker Alisha Claypoole (Joanna Moore) to investigate the Kwimpers. Miss Claypoole demonstrates an almost burlesque sexual aggression in response to Toby's raw, animal bumpkinism. Toby proves to be totally immune to her attempts at seduction and psychoanalysis. The simultaneity of the two strategies suggests an equality between them. It's implied that psychoanalysis is a kind of illicit sexual enterprise. A jealous Holly shoves Miss Claypoole into a lake and, with puritanical disgust, denounces her as "a dirty, dirty thing."

As if the gangsters were conspiratorially in league with un-American forces of bureaucracy, Miss Claypoole testifies against the Kwimpers in a climactic courtroom scene. At stake are both custody of the Kwimper twins and the Kwimper right to squat. Toby steps in as Kwimper family attorney. His courtroom oration focuses on extolling the infallibility of Pa Kwimper's understanding. The conformism to parental authority by the previously rebellious king of rock & roll reinforces the idea of a Presley rehabilitated from his rock & roll past. The jilted Miss Claypoole, "a qualified psychologist," explains to the court how Toby "may mean well consciously, but his subconscious motivations are all that really matters." She administers a written word-association test, presumably to Pa Kwimper. She then analyzes the results. She concludes that Pa Kwimper is a criminal, a child labor profiteer and an alcoholic. As it turns out, it was the results of the judge's handwritten responses to the test that Miss Claypoole was analyzing. With psychology completely discredited, bureaucracy defeated, the custody of the twins secure and the Kwimper's homestead and business intact, the judge proclaims how "thrilling it is to know that the spirit of the pioneer is still functioning today."

This massacre of the aforementioned Golden Age of Psychiatry in the cinema, while still in its infancy, communicates the notion that the life of the mind must be overcome for the utopian happy ending to be realized. With Miss Claypool's credibility and all it stands for completely undermined, another facet of the sexism of Presley movies is thus revealed: the real adversary to happiness is shown to be the educated career woman.

The courtroom has often been a favored Hollywood cinema setting where narrative conflicts are resolved and stories arrive at their most essential conclusions. A theological undercurrent is thereby cast in secular terms. Allowing the audience to scrutinize what's presumably most significant about their lives for nearly ninety minutes, the audience then has the opportunity to witness their final judgment. Comedically, this tradition goes at least as far back as Frank Capra's screwball production of *Mr. Deeds Goes to Town* (1936). A guileless hick played by Gary Cooper triumphs over all the wiles of the American judiciary and over psychiatry, retaining a massive inheritance that an assortment of unscrupulous types, led by a larcenous lawyer, attempt to misappropriate. The courtroom in American mass culture has become a ritual setting for resolving and concluding the narrative.

The popularity of the courtroom ritual as plot device gratifies Americans' belief in their country as a nation of laws, as well as a perception of themselves as a fundamentally law-abiding people. Perhaps, for the better part, the singularly most outstanding feature of this device as a form of myth is that, for the most part, Hollywood presents the courtroom as a place facilitating happy and just endings. Despite the often seeming insurmountable twists in the opposite direction, American movies and television frequently present their courtrooms as places wherein truth is revealed and justice is meted out. Even in otherwise cynical scenarios, a near-religious belief in the American legal system is promoted. Contrarily, and as philosopher Gary Brooks has observed, courtrooms are often inherently violent places, places where relationships can be severed or destroyed, reputations ruined, financial holdings and other valuables seized, personal freedoms or even life itself taken away. As America continues distinguishing itself as a violent society, and the most violent in terms of gun crime, the untenable quality of this fiction becomes ever more threadbare. Among the great contradictions manifested, as well as the great irony in the American social order, is the chasm between the extent of its gun violence and the litigiousness of its citizenry, a great many of whom demonstrate an ongoing eagerness to sue each other.

American popular culture's tired device of the courtroom as the theater wherein conflicts are resolved is, in *Follow that Dream*, the setting where Elvis Presley, as a hayseed rube, emerges victorious as self-made attorney. As an attenuation of the American Dream, it's indicated, victory in the legal system is relatively straightforward for those who are good-natured. Presley's Toby Kwimper is a screen expositor for American humanism. Renaissance-based humanism stressed the importance of critical thinking and empiricism, as well as the value of man in his capacity to function as rhetorician, in his capacity to verbally persuade. As if suggesting a more civil diminishing of assassinated Louisiana governor Huey Long's motto of "Every Man a King," Toby Kwimper implies "Every Man a Lawyer."

Having won in court, Toby is free to pair off with his adopted sister Holly. Her status as an adopted family member means that she and Toby can marry without the taint of blood-relation incest or the hazards associated with inbreeding. Their snuggling on the porch, accompanied by the strains of Toby singing "Angel," is punctuated by the movie's running gag: the explosion of Pa's dream toilet. This coda manifests the mass cultural appropriation of what critic Wayne Burns has called the Panzaic Principle, after Sancho Panza of *Don Quixote*. It's an undercutting of a moment of romanticized idealism by the incursion of the visceral or the scatological. Rather than deflating some exalted principle or vision, however, concluding the movie with exploding sewage expresses an infantile delight in the fecal.

The tangled and untenable reasoning of *Follow that Dream* resides in the extent to which it shows that the triumph of true love depends on xenophobia, animosity and the suspension of reason. Turnabout toward a discrediting representation of psychology suggests limitations to the compassion of the American welfare state. Helping profession or no, Uncle Sam's pockets are only so deep. In its anti-intellectualism, the movie doesn't simply oppose critical reasoning and any serious attempt to dignify the life of the mind. A fundamental question emerges, this despite popular culture's tendency to deter questioning or anything else that might otherwise cause audiences to think. Although not a math comedy, the difficulties this movie presents respective to what's necessary for true love to run its course are comparably twisted and arduous.

AND IN THIS CORNER . . .
ELVIS PRESLEY!

Kid Galahad (1962) commences with the familiar opening of Presley's character having just been discharged from the army. The movie is a musical retooling of a 1937 gangster yarn of the same name, which starred Edward G. Robinson and Humphrey Bogart, mainly set in the world of prizefighting. Respective to the substantial liberties taken in the plotting of the updated Presley version, even retaining the title of the original looks to have been wholly unnecessary. Possibly chief among differences in the two productions is that the original was a Depression-era tale. Alternatively, in addition to starring Elvis Presley, the later movie was made during a time of great prosperity.

In the 1937 original, bellboy Ward Guiseberry (Wayne Morris) comes to the aid of a woman in a hotel room party by landing an overpowering punch in the face of gangster Turkey Morgan's (Bogart) masher of a champion fighter. The blow catapults Ward into an auspicious rise amid the world of professional boxing under the management of gangster Nick Donati (Robinson). Turkey Morgan is the bad gangster; Nick Donati is the good gangster. This is standard Hollywood Americana. One minute you're a bellboy, the next you're well on your way to being crowned heavyweight champion of the world. The circuitous story is well-padded by a covertly budding romance between Ward and Fluff (Bette Davis), Nick's moll. After Ward wins the title, Nick makes way for Ward and Fluff to officially pair off when he and Turkey conveniently shoot each other to death. The nihilistic ending makes way for an otherwise impossible romance to come to fruition. Their mutual annihilation seems an illustration of philosopher Alfred North Whitehead's idealistic claim that evil eventually collapses due to the stress of its own internal contradictions. Though perhaps possible at times, reliance on such a principle might also result in complicity through passivity. Historical examples indicate that it can sometimes be judicious to give evil a push to help it collapse. Typical of American gangster movies, a moral relativism is presented wherein a comparatively good gangster is pitted against a more evil gangster. Persuading audiences to root for the lesser of two evils is encouraging them to root for evil nevertheless.

Another major distinction in the 1962 *Kid Galahad* is that the boxer is the hero of the piece. Though heroic in the 1937 version, Ward the boxer is clearly second banana to Nick the gangster. While criminal goings-on only frame the narrative in the Presley version, they're central to its predecessor. Between them, they present a shared optimism. Both identify prizefighting as something that a young man can excel in and remain morally unsullied despite being surrounded by corruption.

The Presley version opens with naturalized surrealism. Presley sings the theme song while dangling his legs from the back of a speeding freight truck. The song itself is the gospel-ish-without-being-gospel "Sing, Brother Sing." As per "What a Wonderful Life" at the opening of *Follow That Dream,* it's a tune extolling the carefree virtues of being broke. In *Kid Galahad,* worldwide aristocratic status is attributed to that condition: "A poor man wants to be a rich man, a rich man wants to be a king, but a man who can sing that he hasn't got a thing, he's a king of the whole, wide world." Musically carrying on in his army uniform, he's oblivious to how easily he could fall or be knocked from his rapidly moving perch. Presley is as comfortable as a reckless adolescent, even when in danger of extreme physical injury. The same indifference to danger will be brutally restated through his unique quality as a boxer: a head of solid concrete.

As humble everyman Walter Gulick or "Kid Galahad," Presley the newly discharged soldier is a triple threat as singer, mechanic and boxer. His character is again an orphan, someone to be sympathized with, someone to become completely "self-made", someone who, like rock & roll itself, has no parents. Walter wanders into an afterthought of a small town called Cream County in a mountainous, pastoral region of what's supposed to be the Catskill Mountains of New York State (though the film was shot in California). The gangster story central to the 1937 production is relegated to little more than window dressing. Resort owner and boxing team trainer Willy Grogan (Gig Young), who's indebted to organized crime, is given an early introduction. So too is Walter's first on-screen foray into the ring. "It's not that I want to be a fighter," Walter tells Grogan, "I've got experience. I need the money." For five dollars pay to be a sparring partner, Walter enters the squared circle. After a rapid succession of punches to the head and making no attempt to cover up, Walter K.O.'s his presumed pugilistic better. His itinerant, youthful disdain for riches is again melodically expounded when he then entertains the training camp with "This is Living." The tune features lyrics such as, "I wouldn't care to be a millionaire, don't wanna' settle down, I gotta' move around." Again, in America, the only reason for not being rich is not wanting to be rich.

Speaking to trainer Lew Nyack (Charles Bronson, walking with a limp as if henchman to Dr. Frankenstein), Grogan pinpoints the special attributes that make for Walter's winning combination as a boxer: "He's got an ax in his right hand and a bowling ball in his head." As if validating the movie's opening and Presley's indifference to injury, Presley's Walter Gulick is someone for whom injury and mortality have no relevance.

As per the theme of many Presley movies, America and other liberal democracies are superior to the then-communist world because they afford people more opportunities for pleasure. In the most punishing of all athletic contests, Presley the star athlete is incapable of experiencing punishment. *On Boxing* (1987) author Joyce Carol Oates, who doesn't consider boxing a sport because, among other things, "There is nothing fundamentally playful about it," likens the role of the boxer to that of a prostitute. Both sell their bodies to give others pleasure. Both tend to have very short careers. As an entertainment, Oates sees boxing as "akin to pornography." As if asking yet again, "What is Elvis Presley?," while several of his previous roles and rock & roll identity at large had suggested as much in different ways, he is here the utopian body. Completely unhindered by pain, he's given free rein to inflict pain on others and is widely adored for doing so.

Walter demonstrates his mechanical know-how and accepts a job as a singing grease monkey. The designation rounds out Presley's character as the total American renaissance man: soldier, singer, boxer and working stiff. He rescues Willy's girlfriend Dolly Fletcher (Lola Albright) by beating up someone, which garners him the nickname "Galahad." Willy seizes upon his new find and Walter "Kid Galahad" Gulick's predictably ascends toward having a title shot.

While he's still working as a mechanic, there appears an anti-Semitic representation of the local Jew, Mr. Zimmerman (Judson Pratt) the only instance of an overtly Jewish character in any Presley movie. "There goes a real fast man with a buck, that Zimmerman," comments Walter's co-worker, after

Walter declines payment for a slight automobile repair and Zimmerman quickly departs. When Willy's beautiful younger sister Rose shows up (a recycled Joan Blackman, reconfigured as a Caucasian after her turn as Maile in *Blue Hawaii*) she and Walter strike up a romance. We are treated to a musical number that can only be described as the de-vulgarization of Elvis. He sings the bland "I Got Lucky." In the familiar movie environs of a county fair, Presley does a version of the twist that looks like it was choreographed for rest home residents.

The few other songs presented, the upbeat "Riding the Rainbow," with lyrics such as "I'm free to have fun, it's fun to be free," as well as the more balladic "Home is Where the Heart Is" and "A Whistling Tune", are even more remote from rock & roll. Inexplicably, Presley sings the latter of them to Rose. Lyrics include, "It's a whistling tune for walking in the night . . . It's wonderful to walk beneath the Moon," as they stroll together in broad daylight. Musically, *Kid Galahad* presents an Elvis Presley who's musically disowned his rock & roll past. Meanwhile, his Walter Gulick character has retained the essence of rock & roll: violence. In short, as per the nihilistic qualities of rock & roll itself, these are the politics of nihilism, situating Elvis Presley so central to a movie that, by implication, treats its rock & roll subject with such contempt.

That songs rejected for one movie would be used for later ones also reflects how interchangeable some of the Presley movie plots were becoming. Production choices were increasingly driven by what made for the most profitable packaging of the accompanying soundtrack albums. Inclusive of Presley's singing in his movies, this became an early form of what's now known as product placement. As a result, Presley's songs lack specific relevance to the movies in which they're performed. Within their cinematic context, the songs, and subsequently the singer, are rendered meaningless. Alternatively, the entirety of the film narratives that surround each song's performance are rendered meaningless. At the very least, music ceases to either build on or expand the narrative. Between the flow of the narrative and the stasis of the production numbers, there arises an irrational tension stressing who's asserted as the focal point and chief object of worship: Presley himself. Presley the actor is at once idol and advertisement for Presley the singer. Decades later, music videos would condense matters into much briefer, more intense expressions of pure promotion. In the 1960s, the mass audience still needed to be wooed, flirted with and fought over, alongside having their longer attention spans catered to. Presley still resonated with the presence of being the purveyor of thraldom. By contrast, the music video is a quickie.

As with the ecstatic endings of *Blue Hawaii* and *Follow that Dream*, *Kid Galahad* concludes with an orgy of resolved conflicts. The mob's attempts to fix Walter's championship bout come to nothing. Yes, they broke trainer and fight doctor Lew's hands, but he'll live to play the oboe again. Despite his shady affiliations, Willy is exonerated for having earnestly looked out for Walter's best interests all along. Walter retires from the ring undefeated, presumably to marry Rose and open his own garage. It's telling, however, that in order to achieve this aim, he must establish himself in an entertainment medium, albeit a brutal one, toiling in the savage trenches of the leisure industry. The Jewish Zimmerman and the Irish Roman Catholic priest, Father O'Cliche (Liam Redmond), strike up a friendship in the aftermath of the climactic last fight. If there's one thing Catholics and Jews can agree on, it's their love of Elvis Presley.

While *Kid Galahad* is another mediocre Presley musical melodrama, familiar tropes, the involvement of organized crime in the professional boxing world, the anti-Semitic stereotype of a financially opportunistic Jew, along with a young fighter getting involved with a promoter of ethically sketchy tendencies. All resound with the theme of the exploitation of the Presley character. In these respects, it's the most realistic of

Presley's entire movie career. It stands as an expression of bad conscience on behalf of those responsible for the crafting of the Presley movies, including manager and ever-present "technical advisor" Colonel Tom Parker. Yet as an exposition of the idea that youthful talent will inevitably transcend exploitation, *Kid Galahad* is pure fantasy. The exploitation of Presley is exhibited as a kind of athletic pageantry. In an interview with Barbara Walters years after Presley's death, Priscilla Presley said of the mediocrity of so many of the Presley movies that Elvis knew they were cash grabs for the Colonel, something Elvis could have confronted the Colonel about and, presumably, put a stop to. Why the star never did try to halt his degrading exploitation is quite possibly the greatest mystery of his phenomenal career.

GIRL$ GIRL$ GIRL$

*G*irls! *Girls!* *Girls!* (1962) looks like a cheap attempt to duplicate the commercial success of *Blue Hawaii*. Freewheelin' powerboat and sailboat tour guide Ross Carpenter (Presley, in yet another branch of the leisure industry) cruises the waters around Hawaii. This time Presley's character is introduced with five bikini-clad water skiers in tow. Simultaneously, he divides his attention between feeding his girl-watching impulses and singing the title song from atop a powerboat. For the moment, the movie appears to deliver what its title promises. Another pair of bathing beauties wave to him from a passing sailboat. Even when playing a financially struggling individual, it's through the reification of women, their being made thing-like, that the Presley character is identified with wealth. If one woman appears desirable, the appearance of five or seven women at once is five or seven times as desirable. As the Presley movies gravitated in the direction of being expressions of American imperialism, as is the case here, the Presley protagonist is increasingly associated with multitudes of comely young women as a cypher for wealth.

After reeling in a jumbo swordfish for a pair of married tourists, Ross rebuffs the woman's advances and promise of easy money. "Mrs. Morgan," he says angrily, "I don't accept charity from anybody. I earn what I get." Presley's character is as stridently independent as ever. Upon his return to the marina, we learn that Ross doesn't own his own boat, but works for benevolent, elderly couple Papa and Mama Stavros. Papa and Mama are selling both the powerboat and sailboat named The West Wind, a boat that Ross built with his late father. Health concerns for Mama Stavros have prompted the couple's bid to move to a drier climate. Because Ross also lives on the Stavros' sailboat, he's threatened with not only unemployment, but homelessness too, though that implication isn't addressed.

Ross' mother died giving him birth. Though his character had parents at one point, Presley's Ross Carpenter is still without parents at a fairly youthful age. The ongoing repetition of this Little Orphan Elvis protagonist harks back to the enlightenment era's stressing the importance of personal independence. Contrary to this idealization of individual self-sufficiency, however, personal independence can be more disempowering than empowering. That most people fare better in life by living in families, in communities or both is repudiated by the independence of Presley character.

The boats are purchased by unscrupulous businessman Wesley Johnson (Jeremy Slate). Johnson agrees to let Ross use his seamanship on Johnson's tuna boat to buy back The West Wind. Ross vents his musical impulses at the local nightclub, The Pirate's Den. There his ex-girlfriend Robin Ganter (Stella Stevens) headlines and the former couple still bicker with each other. His first song in the Pirate's Den, "I Don't Wanna Be Tied," is of a more rock & roll vein than has been heard in a Presley movie for some time. It's enjoyable to see that Presley can still perform something of a high-octane quality and do it well. Yet his corresponding movements are a processed version of familiar elements of past stage presentations. Summarily, the song performance rings of being a contrivance as much as, or more than, a musical expression. It still works though, and Presley looks confident that it does. He's not offering anything new, however: only a streamlined packaging of something formerly of a more spontaneous quality and livelier in appearance.

Following the performance at the Pirate's Den, Ross hooks up with the secretly wealthy Laurel Dodge (Laurel Goodwin). Together they attend the Stavros' anniversary party, where he charms Mama Stavros with a love song. During a moment of private dialogue between them, a nod is given to Presley's character having been orphaned by his mother at birth and, later, by his father, for unspecified reasons. There's a meandering digression when Ross and Laurel visit a Chinese family who are friends of his. Two cute girls, Mai Ling and Tai Ling (Ginny and Elizabeth Tiu) glaringly aware of their own cuteness, accompany Ross to perform a childish, mock-Chinese ditty. It's all made palatable by being coated with cascades of sugar. Lengthy and meandering, too, are verbal exchanges between Ross and marina businessman Wesley Johnson (Jeremy Slate). Courtship and business are both shown to be forms of conflicting negotiations.

Concurrent with Presley the lover who doesn't need sweet talk, who only sings to win over his intended, Presley the businessman emerges. He haggles for his wages, haggles his way out of one romance and into another. Determined to buy back The West Wind from Johnson, Presley's Ross Carpenter captains Wesley's tuna boat and turns professional singer at the Pirate's Den, reluctantly, of course. In that setting Presley, sings his hit song "Return to Sender." It's a good number and Presley puts it across well, but the staging and the set on which he performs look noticeably cheap. The cheapness isn't due to the song being performed in cheap nightclub, but because of ramshackle film production values. The blocking, the physical positioning of Presley and the band, is cramped, their backdrop blandly tacky, the camera angle static.

Aside from being a lead-in for Presley, Stella Stevens' Robin Ganter character never gets past acting as the redundant, cyclically recurring, carping shrew in his life. Accounts of the production record that the two had a strong personal dislike for each other and, adding a touch of realism to the movie, it shows. A flaw in the script is that, aside from the night he spends at his Chinese friends, there's no indication of where Ross sleeps after Johnson buys The West Wind. Ross transforms labor into fun as he leads the tuna boat crew in a Kingston Trio-like piece of pop music pantheism, "Thanks to the Rolling Sea." Co-laboring to help haul in the nets, the idea of Presley/Ross Carpenter as blue collar worker is reasserted, though he's decked out completely in black throughout most of *Girls! Girls! Girls!*. Is the black apparel to convey his toughness? His sexiness? His grieving over a once-promising movie career? The project ought to have quit before assigning Presley to sing "Song of the Shrimp." Nor does the musical reprise, "We're Comin' in Loaded" salvage any determination there might have been to the contrary. Such inclusions might have been appreciable if, instead of *Girls! Girls! Girls!*, the movie was called *Fish! Fish! Fish!*.

Plot development hovers between showing finer points of the courtship between Ross and Laurel, buttressed by business conflicts between Ross and Johnson. Once sufficiently explicated, and a few more banal musical numbers interspersed, an odd closure is imposed on the proceedings. Wanting to help Ross out of his financial predicament, Laurel gets enough money from her wealthy father to buy The West Wind for Ross. The central conflict of the movie then centers on how Ross can continue his relationship with Laurel, get back The West Wind and remain as proudly opposed to receiving charity as ever. Upon learning that Laurel has bought The West Wind for him, an incensed Ross fumes, "I don't take handouts from anybody. I don't wanna be kept!" It's a reiteration of how he's first introduced as after his singing, as someone who accepts no charity. Simultaneously, the statement is an angry rejection of socialism.

As art historian Arnold Hauser observed, the much imitated, so-called math comedies of Ancient Greece were concerned with showing the adversities of romantic love to turn their audience's attention toward the presumably more practical pursuit of material interests. *Girls! Girls! Girls!* presents the adversities of heterosexual love relations harmonized with a depiction of the adversities of business. Romantic love is relegated to the level of being just another form of business. The snake Johnson, the boozing serpent in the Hawaiian paradise who cheated the Stavros on the sale of their boat, and who shortchanged Ross on his wages for tuna fishing, tries putting the moves on Laurel. She finds Johnson repulsive, but agrees to go on a demonstration cruise aboard The West Wind with him. Just as Johnson is at his most physically forward with a resistant Laurel, Ross is told about the situation by an inscrutable friend. He speeds to her rescue. Ross gives Johnson a good beating, earlier they'd fought to an unheard-of unsatisfying draw, and demands that Johnson buys back The West Wind from Laurel. The hypocrisy of the movie is thereby made plain. For all that is valuable about learning how to be a good businessman, as is Ross, recourse to physical violence is shown as the most necessary and moral element for determining a favorable outcome. With Johnson forced bodily into an agreement, Ross has established himself as victorious in pugilism, business and love. The altercation is as much about establishing Ross' manly independence as it is about saving Laurel. No attention is paid to the detail that, for the time being, Ross will be homeless.

Jumping from sea to land and day to night, Ross then proposes both marriage and a business venture to Laurel. He pops the question that they build a new boat together. She consents. A co-mingling of love, sex and romance with business, this is what the movie has been intertwining all along. The goal of this distortion of the romantic musical comedy hasn't so much been the resolution of conflict through marriage, but the glorification of the deal. As Ross reprises the title song, he's suddenly flanked by hordes of hula dancers. Beauties in flamenco dresses, geisha girls, young women in other elaborately ornate forms of Asian costumes, along with a pack of young White women in contemporary dress dancing the Twist, some of them uncharacteristically homely by Hollywood standards, all show up out of nowhere.

Laurel waves Ross on approvingly, happily accepting that, as the epicenter of global adoration, her man belongs to all women. He is, as the self-promoting theme song puts it "just a red-blooded boy and [he] can't stop thinking about Girls! Girls! Girls!" Established as absolute victor in matters of love, commerce and, not insignificantly, the use of force, Presley's character is celebrated as *global* champion of all cultural, sexual and commercial enterprise.

Mutual acrimony between Presley and Stella Stevens notwithstanding, the movie's finale is its most honest moment in terms of what it reveals about its significance as propaganda. The twist was arguably the most popular dance in rock & roll history. Just as Presley brought the sound of Black music to White audiences, the twist called for White people to make use of their hips while dancing, a veritable first for most. Subsequently, the concluding production number is a choreographed metaphor of how the idolatrous revolution of rock & roll exported an Americanized hedonism to the world, particularly by way of programming young women and girls into pre-marital and non-marital sex. As a political agenda, this had little, if anything, to do with the genuine advancement of personal freedoms. Rather, it had everything to do with securing, strengthening and exporting a cultural basis for a form of political economy.

AN IDOL WITHIN AN IDOL

The 1960s cycle of Presley movies seems to recognize that there's something implicitly preposterous about Presley playing anyone other than himself. In *It Happened at the World's Fair* (1962), Presley expands his repertoire of playing average singing Joes: singing convicts, singing tour guides, singing boxers, and so on. This time as singing crop duster pilot Mike Edwards, as often occurs in Presley's movies, his typical screen persona is downplayed until he breaks out into song, thereby compelling every young woman within earshot to become his doe-eyed love zombie. Musically, in his movies of the 1960s, Presley functions predominantly as a crooner, someone who owes his career to the electronic amplification of his singing voice. The later Presely movies employ him as a throwback to an arrested phase in the development of popular music, an era that persists as if rock & roll had never happened. From expediter of the American Dream to irresistible wandering troubadour, on the big screen Presley continued as the self-made man and repository for the residual feelings of mass thraldom he'd evoked years earlier. In *It Happened at the World's Fair,* Presley the ceremonial celebrity is presented as if he were married to the real-life spectacle of a ceremonial world event.

The soundtrack of *It Happened at the World's Fair,* as with many other Presley movies, is an amnesia-promoting auditory cocktail, with the seeming purpose of giving rock & roll a genteel burial. As Mike Edwards, Presley burbles through nearly a dozen forgettable tunes. None of them rises above the level of overproduced ditty. The film opens as Mike and co-pilot Danny Burke (Gary Lockwood, back from the dead after being punched into an Elvis-induced cardiac arrest in *Wild in the Country*) get their biplane impounded due to Danny's compulsive gambling debts.

They hitch a ride from Chinese truck driver Walter Lin (Kam Tong) and his eight-year-old niece Sue Lin (Vicky Tiu) to the Seattle World's Fair. Through the inclusion of Asian characters, it's reiterated that the love of Elvis is universal and not subject to demographic boundaries such as age or ethnicity. Mike and Danny part ways briefly. That development makes way for movie's focal point, an Elvis-hosted tour of the World's Fair. Presley approaches his role with professionalism, seemingly comfortable with putting across infantile songs, seemingly comfortable wandering through a half-baked movie plot, seemingly comfortable reciting hackneyed dialog, "seemingly" because his growing disenchantment with his movie roles of this period has been well-chronicled elsewhere.

Once on the ground, suit-and-tie-clad Mike consults his little black book to see what female companionship is available to him in the vicinity. Presley enacts this consultation with all the detached casualness of someone consulting a luncheon menu. Presley's Mike Edwards is someone for whom promiscuous womanizing is as natural as breathing.

As Dorothy Johnson, the exceptionally shapely Yvonne Craig is displayed tightly packed into a low-cut, buff-colored cocktail dress. Less than a year later, in *Kissin' Cousins*, Craig will be more far more cooperative with Presley's advances. Here she struggles to restrain herself and him, simultaneously indicating she'd really rather capitulate to instant intimacy with her transient suitor. The scene unfolds to the strains of Presley's easy-listening anthem of seduction entitled "Relax."

Dorothy begins succumbing to Mike just in time for her parents' return home, and for her father to chase Mike away with a shotgun. The entire episode of visiting Dorothy Johnson's house contributes nothing to the movie's plot, it only comments and promotes an ethos that harmonizes with the slipshod production values of most of Presley's movies: throwaway relationships, throwaway sexual intimacy, throwaway quality of movie-making, cumulatively adding up to throwaway movies, Returning to his more specifically Mike-ly role, Presley finds Danny losing badly in a back alley poker game. The two pilots resolve the situation handily by beating up the five other men to whom Danny owes money. Whereas depersonalized erotic expression is shown to be legitimate, the same won't be implied about gambling in a Presley movie until the release of *Viva Las Vegas* fourteen months later. While welshing on a bet isn't The American Way, all can quickly be forgotten, as is shown by the effective use of violence by those to whom the audience's sympathies belong. The friendship between Mike and Danny makes clear how even healthy young men can love Elvis, in a manly, heterosexual, compulsive gambler sort of way.

Little Sue Lin further sweetens matters when she joins Mike's tour of the Fair. She adds a touch of drama when they're briefly separated from each other. He locates her at night in the backseat of a futuristic "Dream Car," less an automobile than the musings of an engineering team inspired by Buck Rogers. Rare are those instances that don't later prove to be an embarrassment for those who attempt to convey what future goods and future culture will look like. Presley's winning ways with little Asian children, previously seen in *Blue Hawaii* and *Girls! Girls! Girls!,* allow those wanting a gentler idol to see in him someone meekly avuncular. Adult Asians are presented as fundamentally decent in these movies, yet are still a types of children.

In the movie's inevitable romance, Nurse Diane (Joan O'Brien, looking lovely in a nuclear beehive hairdo) is an employee of the World Fair's medical clinic. Mike first encounters her when Sue Lin is seized by Fair-food indigestion. Unlike almost every other woman and Chinese truck driver in sight, Diane is impervious to Mike's charm. Naturally, he manages to melt her, only to lose her, then get her back again. Along the he-gets-her, then-loses-her, then-gets-her-back-again way, Danny's gambling sparks a couple of improbable fight scenes, possibly to keep the audience awake. After Mike's failed attempt to cozy up to Nurse Diane, he pays a young Fair-goer (Kurt Russell) to kick him in the shin, giving him a plausible excuse to see Nurse Diane again.

As Mike, Presley likes to get down to business immediately. The well-starched Nurse Diane tersely fends him off. Whether it's due to his residual rock & roll identity or Hollywood's glorification of the power and authority of good looks, in many if not most of his movies, Presley regularly conducts himself towards beautiful women in a manner for which any lesser man, or less physically attractive man, would be called a pig. It should be added that attributing any swine-like qualities to Presley is much at odds with what had been his gentlemanly offscreen demeanor.

Nurse Diane's choice of reading matter reveals that she plans to go into space, possibly to introduce intergalactic sexual austerity measures. Mike feigns starvation to persuade Diane to join him for a meal in the Seattle Space Needle's revolving restaurant. Their meal spans from daytime to dark of night, and Mike concludes their rotations together by singing "A World of Our Own." They kiss, then exit to the applause of the other restaurant patrons. It's unclear whether they're applauding his singing or his romantic conquest.

Danny arrives at his and Mike's motel room with money and a promise of another flying job for them. Unknown to Mike, the job Danny has arranged is for them to smuggle contraband into Canada. It's the lone instance of a mention of Canada in any Elvis Presley movie. He explores the antidepressant properties of his singing by performing the bland "How Would You Like to Be" to a glum Sue Lin. She quickly livens up to dance a child's version of the twist. This is the movie's lone reference to rock & roll: a little girl shaking her body to a song with no musical connection to rock & roll, aside from the man singing it. A child welfare agent shows up to take Sue Lin into custody for her having been abandoned by her parents. Is this dramatic tension, or necessary punishment for exhibiting rock & roll tendencies?

Sue Lin escapes custody to stir up more intrigue. She leaves a note for Mike to meet her at night at the Dream Car. The automobile is the utopian setting wherein things move toward being set aright. Then, in a warehouse, Mike, Sue Lin, Danny and, somehow, Nurse Diane meet up with Vince the smuggler. "The deal's off!" Mike tells Vince, upon detecting illegality. A brawl ensues with Mike and Vince landing many blows into each other's faces, neither of them any the worse for wear. Eventually, Vince collapses, possibly due to disinterest.

At the police station, Danny fesses up that it was he, not Nurse Diane, who had child welfare services impound Sue Lin. His punishment, such as it is, is to be rejected by the female welfare worker he asks out. Mike and Nurse Diane promenade hand in hand down the fairground fairway, a huge brass marching band following in their wake. "[Give Me a Story with a] Happy Ending," Presley sings. The lyrics seem dishonest. What's preceded them has been less story than a showcasing of a spectacle and Elvis Presley for propaganda and promotion purposes. The American can-do determination of the world's sexiest male entertainer has just won another seemingly impossible romantic conquest, as if there might possibly have been a moment's doubt that he would. The wager instrumental to Presley winning over Juliet Prowse's Lili "The Iceberg" in *G.I. Blues* is harked to, although the story line of that feature had more substance. In *It Happened at the World's Fair,* the conclusion occurs as an extravagant promotion for a future that, like its Dream Car, never arrived. World fairs, Expos and such are places for mellontolatry—the worship of the future, as much science fiction is implicitly. The vehement escapism inherent to mellontolatry relates an idealism greatly superseding that which is associated with nostalgia, not merely because it postures at eagerly looking forward instead of fondly looking back. Chief to what mellontolatry and nostalgia have in common is an appeal that is at least partially rooted in the perception of a barely tolerable now. Mellontolatry's escapism rejects the present for a paradoxically non-transcendent secularist religion, one that fatuously posits a greatly superior, man-made religion. At the center of that synthetic faith is still a non-transcendent, unregenerate humanity. The World's Fair is another setting for forgetting who Elvis Presley once was. As author and pastor Tim Keller keenly observes: "Technology hates the past and secularism hates transcendence." Absent from such mellonolatry-based faith is any reckoning with what makes the present so intolerable, what hastens the speculative: the ongoing problem of human nature itself.

EL ELVIS

Shot in Hollywood and starring Presley as singing trapeze artist and lifeguard Mike Windgren, 1963's *Fun in Acapulco* is neither fun nor was shot in Acapulco. The movie opens with Presley in captain's attire aboard a cabin cruiser, fighting off the advances of a hot-to-trot teenybopper (Terri Hope). The scene is a reminder that, despite the flimsy artifice of his screen persona, this is still the same man who, not many years earlier, caused adolescent girl populations of nations to shriek and swoon. He goes into a cantina where he sips a beer and sings, backed by a group of Mexicans who sound suspiciously similar to his trusty Jordanaires. Having distinguished himself with his musical ability, here serving as audio wallpaper, he's introduced to beautiful bullfighter Delores Gomez (Elsa Cardenas). She's surrounded by male suitors. Seeing the amorous teen he'd fought off on the cabin cruiser now awaiting service in the cantina, Presley as Mike reprimands her just in time to be joined by her father. When the scorned girl blames Mike for ordering her liquor, her angry father fires him. The girl is never addressed by name. In her desire for Presley, she's every teenage girl.

Within the short span of the cantina scene, Presley performs two tunes: "Vino, Dinero y Amor" and "I Think I'm Gonna Like it Here." For the latter, he's aided by the audio aberration of a do-wop mariachi sound. As is typical of many other Presley production numbers in his movies of the 1960s, these aren't songs so much as songlets, brief and, for the most part, musically unremarkable. The chief function of their inclusion seems to be to serve as reminders that Presley was a singer.

Without skipping a beat, Mike takes on a ten-year-old Mexican huckster named Raoul (Larry Domasin) as his business manager. This preposterous development is an amplification of another aspect of the Presley film formula. Presley is shown to be instantly appealing to people of all ages, genders and ethnicities. As with Sue Lin in *It Happened at the World's Fair,* the twin orphans in *Follow that Dream* and, to a lesser extent, by way of his rapport with children in *Blue Hawaii,* Mike Windgren is likable in a manner comparable to Ronald McDonald: each amiably introduces children to his product. As a benign variation on the Pied Piper, Presley's characters have an enchanting quality to which children are inexorably drawn. Raoul demonstrates that business savvy requires no more understanding than something a ten-year-old can grasp. Simultaneously, Presley is subordinate to a ten-year-old boy.

Mike and Raoul (or "Rowl," as Presley pronounces it) make a deal for Mike to have a part-time gig at the Acapulco Hilton on the headliner's nights off. The idea that being an entertainer isn't real work, a theme articulated most resoundingly in *King Creole*, indicates that Presley's main identity is rooted in his having a good time. As if to assure the manager that he's not accepting the charity of a free room in exchange for singing, Mike volunteers to pull double duty as a lifeguard at the hotel pool. Having secured the deal, Mike and Raoul bicycle together to sing the promotional ditty "[Life Begins When You're in] Mexico." Again, a dialectical relationship between Presley and a glamorous setting is intimated, albeit less convincingly, since he never set foot in Mexico.

This development picks up steam when he meets the hotel's full-time lifeguard and reigning cliff-diving champion, Moreno

(Alejandro Rey) and his voluptuous girlfriend Marguerita Dauphin (Ursula Andress). Contrary to her last name, she bears no resemblance to the eldest son of a king of France, but is an exile from an Iron Curtain country. Her father, Arch Duke Maximilian Dauphin (Paul Lukas) is working as a chef at the hotel. The Cold War makes an incursion into the most unlikely of circumstances here. Whereas American democracy would have every man be a king, communism forces every aristocrat into becoming kitchen help. As cliff-diving champion and boyfriend to a duchess, Moreno too is an aristocrat of sorts.

On the opening night of his run in the hotel ballroom, Presley performs a Mexican-esque ballad about a dying matador, "El Toro." Other songs featured in the movie, "Marguerita," "The Bullfighter Was a Lady," "[There's] No Room to Rumble in a Sports Car," "You Can't Say No in Acapulco" and the finale, "Guadalajara", all have the chintzy taint of mariachiness superimposed on a banal pop score. Insofar as that does anything to establish or maintain a sense of setting, it's more overt function seems akin to advertising. Over and over again, the audience is melodically told they're having fun in Acapulco with Elvis Presley. Was there something dangerous about allowing Presley to sing rock & roll in his movies? Perhaps giving Presley musical pap to perform was, in part, a strategy to be more inclusive of a mass audience that was still divided in its estimation of rock & roll.

Once in a rare while, rock & roll–hungry movie fans might be tossed a bone, as in *Fun in Acapulco* when Presley performs "Bossa Nova Baby." It's a telling oddity as Presley races to the hotel stage to sing it, then leaps off immediately afterward. The tune isn't just fast as an up-tempo, rock & roll number: everything about its presentation has a hurried, let's-get-this-over-with quality to it. The accompanying choreography of his moves too, though distinctly Presleyan, is greatly condensed. It's as if he's flashing the audience with a hit-and-run reminder of who he used to be and, perhaps, still could be if he had to.

A flashback reveals that, as a trapeze acrobat with the Flying Windgrens, Mike failed to catch his brother one night, causing him fall to his death. Subsequently, Mike is afflicted by P.T.S.D. (Post-Trapeze Stress Disorder). He's uneasy around high diving boards and the tall, rocky crags that Moreno dives from so expertly. The boy-loses-girl juncture occurs for Mike when he mistakenly concludes that Marguerita is only interested in him as her meal ticket to America. They have a brief falling out until His Excellency, Marguerita's dad, informs Mike that it's he, not his daughter, who wants to go to the States. Rather than approach the duchess to offer a simple apology, Mike, or rather, Presley's stunt double, scales a towering rock face to dive into a narrow, ocean inlet. A host of spectators looks on from a large patio nearby. The group includes some American astronauts. The cliff that Mike has climbed, nature in all its intimidating grandeur, is the medium by which he affects a reconciliation with Marguerita, as well as winning the admiration of the crowd and the U.S. space program.

Even the great Moreno, whose thunder was stolen when Mike performed in his place, now with one arm in a sling thanks to a bout with Mike, has been won over. He compliments Mike on his diving prowess and the hardness of his jaw. With no objection from Moreno, Mike and Marguerita embrace and kiss. Presley gets the girl back again and is implicitly established as heir apparent to Arch Duke Maximilian's soup ladle.

The successful execution of what is essentially a stunt suggests a multi-layered conclusion. Mike overcomes his phobia, redeeming himself respective to his past tragic acrobatic blunder. He's found favor as a Roman Catholic, crossing himself prior to plunging. He's conquered a foreign nation on their own cultural terms by outdoing their champion cliff diver, winning over the hearts of locals and tourists alike. Upon his surfacing from the dive, Raoul crows over him: "Mike, you're not crazy after all!" Whatever Elvis Presley might be, he's proven he isn't insane.

In a dizzying reversal of moral values, Mike hasn't just moved in uninvited on Moreno's hotel occupation and his woman. After some verbal provocation, he's subjected Moreno to a shoulder-breaking beating, opening the door to trumping Moreno's known cliff-diving accomplishments. Successfully courting both the lady bullfighter Delores and Marguerita, he's established himself as U.S. surrogate royalty as confirmed by the presence of NASA. All this transpires to establish Presley as a universally loved hero.

In his time of triumph, Mike is asked by Marguerita, "Can anyone get in on this act?" He replies, "Only the usual customers." The verbal irony acknowledges that the stunt was just that, a stunt, and one performed by a body double to boot. The Presley character is once again a prostitute of sorts, as was suggested in both *King Creole* and *Kid Galahad,* though with *Fun in Acapulco,* he retains his right to sexual non-exclusivity.

THE MILITARY
INDUSTRIAL ELVIS

Film historian Leslie Halliwell spared no venom in his
appraisal of 1964's *Kissin' Cousins,* dismissing it as "a feeble
production in every sense, even below its star's usual standard."[6]
However, to view the movie and Presley's function in it as
exemplary of ideology wedded to commerce, militarism and
imperialism, *Kissin' Cousins* warrants a closer look. On the
surface, it's difficult to see how Presley, by 1964 largely spent as
the revolutionary cultural force he was when first exploding on
the scene, might have regained his earlier relevance. Yet for all
the ballyhoo about the so-called British Invasion of rock music
in North America, also commencing in 1964, *Kissin' Cousins*
was more politically relevant than anything the Beatles, the
Rolling Stones and all other cultural pond jumpers combined
brought with them.

As Lieutenant Josh Morgan, Presley is more military
ambassador than any role he'd played since *G.I. Blues.* The
army wants to exploit Josh's hillbilly family connections, the
Tatums, to establish an intercontinental ballistic missile base
on their Smoky Mountain backwoods property. As fortune

---

6   Leslie Halliwell, *Halliwell's Film Guide,* 1995, p. 600.

would have it, in the adjacent Kittyhawk Valley, "there ain't been nuthin' but girls born for 20 years." A large roving band of sparsely clad, sexually eager young women roam the Tatum's property. American militarism is coupled with male fantasizing about polygamy, suggesting an unbroken continuum between warfare and human sexuality. Anticipating the Tatums' hostility to government, Josh gets permission to don his civvies when visiting the Tatums, thereby allowing the audience to see the star in fashionable form. The soldiers accompanying him are fully armed and in full uniform. Even when approximating a regular guy, Presley travels backed by a military entourage. After Presley as Josh arrives at Smoky Mountain to a gunfire reception from his cousins Selena Tatum (Pam Austin), Azalea Tatum (Yvonne Craig), and Josh's identical twin cousin Jodie Tatum (Presley in a blond wig with the help of trick photography), Josh out-wrestles Jodie, and overcomes all hostility by explaining that he's kin folk. Despite their obvious physical maturity, Salena and Azalea consistently speak and otherwise behave like eight-year-olds.

This time, the exoticism of Presley's surroundings is established by way of the marauding, sexually aggressive kittyhawks. The kittyhawks are young women so starved for male company that they subdue soldiers with hugs and kisses. Josh commences singing the egregious "One Boy and Two Little Girls" and "Show Me How to Kiss" to Jodie and the buxom Salena. Shades of the sexual revolution seem immanent by way of the instant intimacy between Josh and Azalea, as well as between the uniformed soldiers and the kittyhawks. Josh's singing makes clear from the outset that he's using his vocal talent to seduce both Selena and Azalea. He's winning them over to support the planned missile base. All of Presley's seductive power is in the tactical servitude of advancing U.S. nuclear ambitions and, simultaneously, his character's personal gratification. Presley's pleasure has become synonymous with U.S. military aims. The musical interlude shows how two women can peacefully co-exist while sharing the same man. The main thing, apparently, is that he enjoys himself. If lyrics such as "But right now I'm having such fun I just can't give up either one" are any indication, in the role of Josh, he clearly is succeeding in that main thing.

Soon thereafter, Josh focuses his attention on Azalia to sing "(I'm) Catchin' On Fast." He asks the musical question countless women would presumably want him to ask of them: "Won't You Show Me How to Kiss?" The tune is a watered-down simulacrum of rock & roll. As has often been the case when American movies and television allude to a rock & roll sound, there's a discrepancy between it and the real thing if, as the primary medium for the spreading of rock & roll, one cites radio. Exceedingly rare are those rock & roll-ish instances of Presley's 1960s-era movies that don't manifest similar discrepancies. Again, it's as if there is something dangerous about giving Presley a chance to show what he does best, that rock & roll music was something best kept either under wraps, abbreviated or greatly diluted.

Josh philanthropically persuades his captain to have the army spring for a shopping spree for Salena, Azalia and the kittyhawks. Josh drives up to the Tatum homestead in a Jeep full of women in bikinis, the official uniform for young women in Presley movies of the 1960s. Unlike other bikini-laden Presley flicks, however, there's no evidence of any nearby body of water or pool to justify the display of bodies. As one anonymous woman in John Berger's documentary *Ways of Seeing* (1972) stated, when commenting on the depiction of the female nude in classic European oil painting, it's a uniform that says, "Okay, I'm ready for sex now." Even while engaged in military duty, the Presley protagonist is established in his truest cinematic element when surrounded and draped by tantalizing young women. The image of Presley driving an automobile full of provocatively attired females would recur in *Spinout* (1966) and

Stay Away, Joe (1968): Presley, the ideal American man, driving the ideal motor vehicle.

In his role as Josh, Presley even brings pretty Private Midge Riley (Cynthia Pepper) to occupy cousin Jodie, thereby identifying the military with the role of matchmaker or perhaps even pimp. Cousin Jodie serenades Midge with a voice identical to that of Josh, not surprisingly, since they're both played by Presley. Ma Tatum (Glenda Farrell) opts against the building of the missile base because preventing World War III would interfere with Selena and Azalea doing their chores. An impromptu rescue team led by Josh saves Pappy Tatum (Arthur O'Connell) from falling down a cliff after he somehow affixes himself to a tree branch. The successful rescue leads to a hoedown at the Tatum homestead, complete with moonshine. Initially, Pappy is immune to all incentives from Josh to have a missile base. He surrenders to the idea when told that, in addition to the promise of money and a new road, all government agents would be prohibited from visiting the Tatums' shack, which establishes the Tatum household as off limits to "revenuers."

Accompanied mostly by male dancers in servicemen uniforms, Josh launches into the saxophone-heavy "Once Is Enough." With such decadent lines as, "If you live every sec, what the heck, once is enough," lyrically, the song communicates a rock & roll ethos: eat, drink and be merry, for tomorrow we'll dance the twist no more. Therein is invoked what poet and young casualty of war Wilfred Owen called "the old Lie: *Dulce et decorum est Pro patria mori*" ("it is sweet and becoming to die for one's country"). The musical aesthetic, the beat, was what the military couldn't yet show any sign of capitulating to. In the deal made with Pappy, however, an allotment for a certain measure of contained chaos is sanctioned. It's a fictive arrangement that parallels the real-life allotments made by America, still quite conservative even in its liberalism of the time, to accommodate the rock & roll revolution.

As both Josh and Jody, Presley sings the title song in a duet with himself. Surrounding the two Elvises (Elvi?) are couples fondling each other on a mound of grass in a now tax-free Titian-esque bacchanalia by way of cartoonist Al Capp. Free from the inevitability of taxes, are they now correspondingly free from the inevitability of death as well?

Kissin' Cousins exemplifies a variation on Cold War culture that sought to assuage the anxieties of living in a politically polarized atomic age. The only instance of a nuclear weapon being shown in the movie is when Josh momentarily flashes a small, aged newspaper picture of a missile in order to explain to Pappy Tatum what a missile is. The danger of a nuclear holocaust is thereby diminished, made as minimal as possible while still being acknowledged. What the movie presents as being most pressingly at stake is not the direct threat stemming from a hindrance to U.S. nuclear capability. Rather, Josh's commanding officer Captain Salbo (Jack Albertson) is threatened with a transfer to Greenland should the mission to establish a missile base fail. In turn, Salbo threatens Josh with a transfer to the Arctic Circle should they be unsuccessful.

Aside from implicating the military as a pimping service, two different Elvis Presley characters in the same movie, one of them blond, might have led to interesting narrative developments. However, that potential was left largely unexplored. The publicity appeal of twice the Presley might suggest two times the thraldom. Alternatively, might a blond Presley as lemon-scented Presley, or Presley Lite, have been on the minds of the architects of this fiasco? In the modern era, Fyodor Dostoyevsky's novella *The Double* (1846) explores the humorous facets of a double in a bureaucratized society. Correspondingly, twice the Presley isn't just twice the fun. In spite of the movie's glorification of Presley, it might also suggest his growing redundancy to the ideological purposes he'd been in the servitude of for years.

The use of a double also has significant ramifications for both Presley and *Kissin' Cousins* as propaganda tools. In his 1919 essay "The Uncanny," Freud identifies as uncanny that which "arouses dread and creeping horror ... it tends to coincide with whatever excites dread."[7] He goes on to relate the centrality of the double to the uncanny: "This invention of doubling as a preservation against extinction has its counterpart in the language of dreams ... Such ideas, however, have sprung from the soil of unbounded self-love, from the primary narcissism which holds sway in the mind of the child as in that of primitive man; and when this stage has been left behind the double takes on a different aspect. From having been an assurance of immortality, he becomes the ghastly harbinger of death."

The essential childishness of *Kissin' Cousins* aligns its psychology with what Freud identifies as the earlier, more primitive role of the double. Jody is not the "ghastly harbinger of death." Rather, he's the assurance of the indestructibility of the American ego, the preservation of Presley as potential soldier and entertainer and, by extension, the preservation of his audience. Yet for the mass audience to enjoy the idealism of surviving a nuclear war requires that, at some level, they re-orientate their own egos within an intensely regressive, childish value system. As such, *Kissin' Cousins* stands as a document of the incalculable chasm between the scientific sophistication required to engineer doomsday technology and the primitiveness of the martial mentalities behind the arms race.

---

[7]   Sigmund Freud, "The Uncanny", p. 122

WHAT DIDN'T
STAY IN VEGAS

Las Vegas was among the most mobbed-up of American cities in the 1960s. Hence it's unlikely that *Viva Las Vegas* (1964) was made without both the approval and involvement of organized crime. Of noticeably higher production quality than Presley's other movies of the 1960s, although still lightweight, it proceeds as if designed to do for the gambling hub what *Blue Hawaii* did for the fiftieth state. As a site for perpetual pleasure, Las Vegas was well-suited for Presley as someone perennially associated with leisure, amusement and recreation. The movie is a commercial travelogue for Las Vegas. There was more at stake monetarily than the usual advocacy of the American Way. Hence the direction is sharper, the musical numbers more polished, the overall production superior to anything Presley had appeared in since *Blue Hawaii*. In 1964, those managing Las Vegas probably wouldn't have stood for anything less.

As singing racing car driver Lucky Jackson in *Viva Las Vegas* (1964), Presley makes his entrance looking slick in his familiar black attire. This time the setting is a casino where he takes a turn at shooting craps, but we don't see the outcome. Whether he wins or loses isn't the point. The point is to simply establish that *he plays*. It's a fleeting introductory scene, abruptly followed by the introduction Lucky's second-in-command, his mechanic Shorty (Nicky Blair). Shorty's at an auto dealership trying, unsuccessfully due to limited finances, to get a new motor for their racing car. This prelude introduces us to the movie's brass tax: Lucky working on his race car in a garage. The man who'll soon be established as his rival is racing car driver Count Elmo Mancini (Cesare Danova). The object of their rivalry is the beautiful Rusty Martin (Ann Margaret, introduced as only visible from the waist down in her short-shorts). Although it isn't granted, Margaret's derriere receives sufficient screen time to merit its own credit. The damsel in distress needs car repairs. Lucky and Count Elmo resort to a friendly ruse to keep her car and, quite probably, her attention, overnight.

Most Presleyphiles know of the real-life romance between Presley and Ann Margaret, a romance that intrudes noticeably in their first exchange of dialogue with each other. It's a fairly commonplace occurrence among co-stars. Margaret is said to have nearly edged out Priscilla to be Mrs. Presley. Screen couples such as Tracy and Hepburn, as well as Bogart and Bacall, managed to integrate their sexual chemistry to serve as naturalistic components of their characters and on screen relationship. At first in *Viva Las Vegas,* the two stars appear to be showing up for work to deliver line readings comingled with their flirting with each other.

That night, circumstances prompt Lucky and Count Elmo to tour the town's casinos in search of Rusty. It's a pretense to promote the better-known casinos and their floor shows to moviegoers. Emphasis is on displays of sexy showgirls, some in ethnic costumes. The internationalism of this pageantry is reminiscent of the multi-ethnic frenzy of female adoration that Presley receives at the end of *Girls! Girls! Girls!* However, this time, the adoration appears available to any man who makes the pilgrimage to mankind's most famous playground.

Lucky and Count Elmo crash a Texas-themed bar night where a free-for-all has broken out. Lucky takes it upon himself to restore order by donning a cowboy hat and singing the state song "The Yellow Rose of Texas." The inclusion is filler, but it's filler with an ideological purpose. The filmmakers could have resorted to innumerable other ways to pad the movie so it would reach its spare eighty-six-minute running time. The incorporation of Texas, cowboy hats and six-shooters remind us that Las Vegas is part of America.

It's not until the next day that Lucky sees Rusty again, this time in the first of several appearances she'll make while effectively filling out a red, one-piece bathing suit. It's certainly an occasion for song, and Presley obliges in a duet with her, "The Lady Loves Me." To his every good-natured proclamation to the effect that she just hasn't yet realized her true affection for him, Rusty counters with such lyrics of protest as "The gentleman needs a psychiatrist." Capping off the song, Rusty pushes Lucky off the high diving board, suit, tie, acoustic guitar and all. Presley's wardrobe alternates between tasteful windbreakers with slacks and several well-tailored suits, attire quite remote from his earlier rock & roll identity.

In order to pay for a new engine, Lucky and Shorty take jobs as waiters at the hotel where Rusty works as a diving instructor. The disparity in dignity between the two men, Shorty clearly functioning as Lucky's lackey, illuminates another constant in Presley's movies: Presley never appears to have a friendship with any man on equal ground. His male friends are either his subordinates or, in a few movies, father figures to him. All other men who might somehow be perceived as potential equals, such as the suave Count Elmo Mancini, are rivals who'll inevitably be defeated by Presley. The constancy of this formula not only further exalts Presley. It's a device that implicitly instructs both male and female viewers to disdain, to see as less than ideal, those men who do relate to each other as equals.

Rusty rebuffs Lucky's advances once more, but warms up to him enough to invite him to visit her dance studio the next day. At the dance studio, a dance number led by Rusty provides some indication of why Margaret was promoted as "The Female Elvis." Wearing the perennial fashion favourite of a heavy sweater and black tights, it's a calculated combination of over-determined modesty and over-determined exhibitionism. As fashion statement, her attire parallels Andy Warhol's claim in *The Philosophy of Andy Warhol: From A to B and Back Again* (1975), that beauty isn't sex and sex isn't beauty.

Still prickly toward him after her dance number, Rusty dares Lucky to dance. He declines, verbally, but takes her up on her asking him to sing, soon dancing too anyway. For the male as for the female then, no is meant to really mean yes, or can be easily be cajoled into a yes. Wearing another suit, Lucky performs the rock & roll–flavored "C'mon Everybody"—not to be confused with Eddie Cochrane's more authentic rock & roll classic "Come On Everybody," although Cochrane also performed in suits during his short life. Lucky effortlessly integrates his dancing with Rusty into his singing and, by the time it's done, he's won her over. As often happens when Presley sings in his movies, his talent is shown to be an irresistible sexual force to women. Possibly, Presley's singing mystifies the constituents of what goes into bringing a man and a woman together, simultaneously censoring genuine intimacy.

In lieu of directly representing how such intimacy occurs, a substantial digression, without any dialogue, shows Lucky and Rusty at a shooting range together, riding motorbikes together, at play with each other in a mock shoot-out, enjoying a helicopter tour together, water-skiing together and dancing with each other to an ersatz Afro-American rhythm & blues band at a nightclub. They seem to participate in everything Las Vegas has to offer *except* for sex and gambling. In this life-imitates-Elvis series of vignettes, what was first cynically depicted by Presley's Vince Everett in *Jailhouse Rock* as something that Everett did as movie publicity junket is here expressed as a romantic celebrity endorsement for Las Vegas. Intimacy is shown as something that happens when two consumers partake together of services provided by the leisure industry. The rhythm & blues band, artificial aside from being comprised of actual African Americans, sounds anemic. The musical contrast is heightened when Lucky performs a rousing cover version of Ray Charles' "Tell Me What'd I Say?"

Musically, Lucky out-Negroes the Negroes. Melodically, it's the most lively that Presley has appeared on screen for several films. Yet as if again disavowing Presley's rock & roll star past as in various other Presley movies of the 1960s, his musical performance sets off variations on the more dated Jitterbug and Lindy Hop dance moves among the nightclub crowd. That's followed by one of the shortest boy-loses-girl intervals in movie musical history. Rusty walks out on Lucky when he refuses to forsake the dangers of auto racing for her and for the little house with the tree in front that she confesses to craving. She's reconciled to him in the next scene when she discovers he's left a potted tree for her at her doorstep. Why this component of the narrative is deemed imperative, as if somehow the story line would otherwise be unrecognizable, suggests something at once mellifluous and menacing. Romantic love, it's suggested, is unavoidable and inescapable, regardless of free will.

When the two lovebirds enjoy a flight together in a helicopter manned by Lucky, Rusty again replicates Juliet Prowse's Lili from *G.I. Blues* by providing a travelogue narrative, including many fun facts about Lake Mead. Far more than Prowse's tacked-on information service, Ann Margaret's Rusty sounds like she's encouraging audience members to perceive themselves as real-life tourists, to dream of one day walking in Elvis's footsteps, possibly flying along one of his flight routes.

The momentary acrimony between Lucky and Rusty turns into a friendly competition between them at a talent contest. Decked out in a virginal white fur coat, Rusty sings about an old sugar daddy who spent lavishly on her "to show his *appreciation*." She then strips off the fur and with it her exclusivity. Wearing only a sheer lavender body stocking, a half-dozen dancing men rush to her side. She becomes more democratically available thereby, someone whom all men are free to imagine themselves groping.

Lucky trumps her, however, by reprising the movie's title song. He undulates in between a series of excessively ornate showgirls with such lyrics as "I'm just a devil with love to spare." As is the case with the female Elvis, this boast of profane virility is his self-advertisement of sexual availability. Audience response results in a tie between Rusty and Lucky. The contest winner is decided by a coin toss. It's a fitting victory by both Las Vegas and pop culture standards. Neither individual effort, talent nor even the subjectivity of audience response is the decisive factor in winning, only chance, the metaphysical dynamic of the marketplace. And chance in this instance favors the performance that most overtly pays homage to Caesar or, in this case, to Las Vegas. Rusty's second place winning is a pool table, a somewhat masculine item. Lucky wins a trophy and a two-week honeymoon, worthless items to a single man in need of money.

Lucky wanders alone amid various young couples kissing and fawning over each other. "I Need Somebody to Lean On," he sings mournfully. The song is a musical extrapolation on the notion that, in a society that promotes coupling as a supreme value, singleness is among the worst of conditions. As is frequently the case with second bananas to the leading man, Shorty miraculously obtains a new engine for Lucky's car, making it possible for Lucky to race in the Las Vegas Grand

Prix. Another reconciliation commences when Rusty and Lucky commiserate over the futility of the talent competition.

Alone in Lucky's garage, Rusty reflects on the presence of Lucky's race car, singing the musical question "Does He Love Me or Does He Love My Rival?" In so doing, she embraces her identity as an object, melodically pondering whether she is of more value to her man than a car. During one of the bumps in the road to true romance, Rusty has dinner with the suave Count Elmo. Intervening to act as their waiter, Lucky sabotages Count Elmo's seduction efforts by making a mess of both their meal and the Count. American guerilla tactics win handily over legendary Latin charm, as Lucky leaves the pair with the Count drenched in champagne and Rusty laughing about it. The victory is sufficient for Lucky's purposes. However, he must also must also prove U.S. race car driving superiority over the Italians by beating Count Elmo on the race track as well. Shades of Presley's Mike Windgren out-cliff- diving a Mexican community for whom cliff-diving is their culture is Lucky's remaining challenge.

The first running of the Las Vegas Grand Prix extends from dark of night into broad daylight. Race cars even speed through the pedestrian-filled streets of the Vegas strip. Could the risk to onlookers be part of the fun, or is it just stupid? Cheering on Lucky from an overhead helicopter are Rusty, Shorty, and Rusty's father (William Demerest). Editorializing reaction shots might have made the road race more engaging to audiences of the day, but it's still fairly tame. Shots of Presley behind the wheel are the dramatic focal point, but he must win or his character's name, Lucky, would be a sad irony. It's a rarity to see a Presley movie where he doesn't get into at least one brawl. Possibly that was deemed at odds with this feature being designed to lure tourists to Las Vegas. Additionally, taking recourse to fisticuffs would have undermined his out-doing Count Elmo in the civility department.

The suave Count Elmo is vanquished in a dramatic wipe-out with, perhaps, a chance of surviving to pose in cigarette ads. The American can-do spirit triumphs over European charm and cultural refinement. When Lucky wins the race, Shorty blurts out ecstatically that it was Rusty's father taking out a loan that financed the new engine for Lucky. This is the closest the Presley protagonist ever gets to accepting charity. The loan acquisition turns out to be less an act of charity than a wager on Lucky's superior skill and predictable victory. Having undergone great risk to his personal safety, demonstrated great skill and daring, the protagonist earns the good luck to participate in the societal norm of married life. Yet it's to the dad in the machinery that he owes his victory. The movie concludes with two musical reprisals on a split screen, a very 1960s cinematic device. Presley again sings the title track on the right, and the lavender body stocking-clad Margaret convulses on the right. Cumulatively, it's a pure summation: Long Live Las Vegas, Long Live Elvis and Long Live the Objectification of Women. To the modest extent that it makes incursions into matters, placing rock & roll, as well as Presley, in the servitude of an eighty-six minute commercial for Las Vegas, again proves the complete malleability of Elvis Presley and rock & roll to be shaped to suit any agenda.

THE PRESLEY GROTESQUE

I f, as Russian literary philosopher Mikhail Bakhtin claimed, "the popular festive carnival principle is indestructible,"[8] and if, as was stated by Malcolm McLaren, the late manager of The Sex Pistols, popular culture is about plagiarism, then it was inevitable that the popular festive carnival principle would eventually infiltrate an Elvis Presley movie. As hot-tempered, singing tough guy Charlie Rogers in *Roustabout* (1964), Presley takes on a position as a carnival hand or "roustabout." The relatively exotic title is the lone instance of a Presley movie that takes as its name the hero's role as a laborer. One wonders if the title of *Gopher* wasn't considered. *Roustabout* is, again, less than stellar cinema.

Simultaneously, however, the movie is possibly the cleverest merger of Presley's most typical 1960s movie persona, someone synonymous with recreation who's also wedded to a working class identity. Eventually, both categories are transcended by way of his talent as a performer and his coupling with the right girl.

A brief stay in jail results from Charlie using his karate skills on a few college types who rudely didn't cotton to his stage act. Having opened by propositioning one of their girlfriends, and

---

[8]   Mikhail Bakhtin, *Rabelais and His World,* p. 33.

in response to their sophomoric heckling, he further invokes their wrath by singing the anti-academic anti-paean "Poison Ivy League." The catalytic instance propelling Charlie into motion is envy over his superior sexual attractiveness and a song expressing class-based resentment toward higher learning. The song is peppy, as if at least having rock & roll aspirations, and it features lyrics that mock academia: "They'll even pay someone to take that test … They're so full of bunk," and other lines that might have inspired Pink Floyd's *The Wall*. That which is most particular to the rock & roll-ism of the song is its hostility toward authority, education and formalized intellectual life, all of it framed within a sexually-related context that's a prelude to violence.

After an enamored waitress bails Charlie out of jail the next day, he abandons her to take to the road on his motorcycle. This is the occasion for the song "Wheels on My Heels," which includes such stirring lyrics as "I gotta keep rollin', rollin' along." This musical expression of intention grinds to a halt when irate carnival owner Joe Lean (Leif Erickson) runs Charlie off the road. Joe is angered by the highway high-jinx of Charlie flirting with his pretty daughter Cathy (Joan Freeman). Insofar as a father-figure to Presley's character can be identified in this movie, it's Joe. His disposition: he's enraged, hard-drinking and homicidal, first directly addressing Charlie with the words, "Ya fresh punk!" Even at his introductory worst, there's an effeminacy to Joe, in the vernacular, "fresh" was a verbal designation reserved for use by women when referring to the sexual aggression of male youths and men.

In what looks like an effort to compensate for Joe's malfeasance, carny matriarch Maggie Morgan (Barbara Stanwyck) hires Charlie to work as a roustabout. "It's hard work," Maggie tells Charlie. When asked by her where he's from, he casually replies, "A little swamp outside Shreveport." Although only fleeting mention occurs thereby, a reference is again made to the question of *"What* is Elvis Presley? A swamp thing?"* His motorcycle damaged, his guitar ruined and, with a band-aid on his head as the segue evidencing transition from his freewheelin' life on the road to roustabout, Cathy gives him a tour of the carnival. He forces a kiss on her. She slaps him and storms off. To Maggie's arriving to say of the rejection from Cathy, "Strike three," he arrogantly states, "She'll be back."

Presley's character is again entrenched in the business of amusement, amusement through which he'll eventually be either reformed or rehabilitated. Familiarly, Charlie is yet another orphaned Presley protagonist, thus explaining his antisocial disposition. That cool, with-it Elvis Presley so frequently plays characters who've dispensed with civility or never learned it suggests that civility is unnecessary. The socially regressive is upheld as the fashionable norm. Again reiterated is the resonance of Presley's rock & roll identity, forcefully asserted in *Roustabout* by way of his attire: a black leather jacket, matching pants and riding boots. Both he and rock & roll seem the result of some real, imagined or emerging societal failure to sustain the conventional family, or were possibly even marketed in an economic and political effort to encourage such a failure.

Charlie commences pursuing Cathy romantically, although not exclusively. He also steals the bath towels of two carnival showgirls as they shower, diddling around with sexually aggressive, carny fortune-teller Estelle (Sue Ane Langdon) who goes by the professional moniker of Madame Mijanou. A bit of innuendo-laden banter between the two in which he likens women to wine concludes with Charlie metaphorically stating, "I'm an alcoholic."

Roustabout is exemplary of a pop culture counterfeit of the carnival principle, a latter-day manifestation of Bakhtin's identification of what he called "the indestructible festive character," once synonymous with medieval spectacles, which "had to be tolerated and even legalized outside the official sphere and had to be turned over to the popular sphere of the marketplace."[9] As such, it's not emancipating in the same sense that Bakhtin meant. The pop culture counterfeit presented in *Roustabout* might have been an early precursor to the counterculture.

Roustabout also falls short of genuine carnival in its humorlessness. Bakhtin stresses the unbreakable link between authentic carnival and laughter as an indicator of social freedom. *Roustabout* has but one perfunctory scene acknowledging the connection between carnival and humor. In a scene with the resident sword-swallower and fire-eater, Presley delivers his lines with the levity of a distracted priest administering the last rites. The inclusion at the scene's end of little person Billy Barty as Billy might have been meant to have some comedic quality. Even if the inclusion of Barty falls flat as attempted comedy, the exoticism of a very short man reminds the audience they're seeing Elvis in an exotic locale (in the company of a very short man, not as a short man). There's an exchange of a few one-liners between Elvis as Charlie and the sword-swallowing fire-swallower. Glimpses of Presley's sense of humor in later concert documentaries aside, comedy wasn't his on-screen strong suit.

The ad hoc negligence with which Presley's musical numbers were thrown into the mix is apparent when he goes on a Ferris wheel ride with Cathy. In a sequence incomprehensible to his up-to-that point surly, macho character, he blurts out singing "It's a Wonderful, Wonderful, Wonderful, Wonderful World." Next, he assumes the role of singing shill for Cathy with "It's Carnival Time." In so doing, he reveals his ability to draw a crowd. This scene is the first of three instances of Presley singing backed by what, by 1964 standards, must have been the steamy sight of flashily under-dressed young women dancers promoting a carny "girlie show." Angered by Charlie's

---

[9]   Mikhail Bakhtin, *Rabelais and His World,* p. 9.

unasked-for intervention, Cathy demands to know of him, "What are you, some kind of sex maniac?" Yet again and here most directly, the question is raised: *What* is Elvis Presley?

Maggie recognizes that Charlie's talent for singing can save her cash-strapped carnival, a business heavily in debt, sued because drunken Joe Lean failed to rig a ride properly. Whether performing privately to woo Cathy, or more publicly for fair-goers as he will soon thereafter, there's a schism between Charlie's tough rebelliousness and the saccharine songs he sings. Imprisoned by the false happiness of those songs, songs much at odds with everything else observable about Charlie, as a musical, *Roustabout* presents Presley as a living, breathing, talking, singing contradiction.

The boy-loses-girl facet enters when Cathy sees Charlie kissing Madame Mijanou. Afterward, he rescues Cathy from a golden-armed carnival patron who subjects her to a punishing series of soakings when she works the dunk tank. The scene shows what Bakhtin describes as "turnabout", that aspect of carnival in which there is "a continual shifting from top to bottom, from front to rear, of numerous parodies and travesties, humiliations, profanations, comic crownings and uncrownings, a second life, a second world of folk culture is thus constructed."[10] Parodying the religious rites of baptism by total immersion, the dunk tank also facilitates the humiliation of a beautiful young woman. Charlie intercedes violently. He functions as the agent of prohibition against carnival laughter, the universal laughter of the people.

During Charlie's brawl with him, the golden-armed patron loses his wallet. A drunken Joe is held responsible and jailed. Later that night, Charlie finds the wallet, but like a dog returning to his vomit, he gets distracted by Madame Mijanou and advances on her. Amorously inclined toward him though

---

[10]   Mikhail Bakhtin, *Rabelais and His World*, p. 11.

she is, the good Madame rebuffs Charlie's offer to make love due to his brutish insistence that they do so outdoors. Charlie apologizes to Cathy for calling her father Joe a pig and for stationing Cathy at the dunk tank.

He declines signing a contract for Maggie, stating a once famous mantra of the later 1960s: "I don't wanna get involved." The morning after making up with Cathy, Charlie gets distracted while en route to return the wallet to the police, as a fellow carny dares him to attempt the carny's dangerous "Wall of Death" motorcycle ride. Being told that all he needs is "guts," he still declines the challenge on the grounds of cowardice. The fellow carny then derisively calls him "dear." It's the only instance of anyone ever casting an aspersion on the heterosexuality of a Presley movie character. He immediately responds by risking his life, speeding his motorcycle along the steep, circular carnival ride and thereby irrefutably proving his straight sexual orientation.

He masters riding the "Wall of Death," but not stopping the bike he crashes. It's then discovered by Cathy and his fellow carnies that he has the golden armed patron's missing wallet, the reason for Joe's incarceration. Soon after getting sprung, Joe subjects Charlie to a beating that Charlie submits to without fighting back. The scene is evocative of writer and teacher Jerry Zaslove's comment that, when the authoritarian state is perfected, the criminal will punish himself or, as is suggested here, will volunteer for his own punishment.

Of course, in a Presley movie, such an attack won't go unanswered indefinitely. Later, Charlie lays a good old-fashioned American pounding on Joe, and without resorting to karate. Charlie defects to the bigger, more successful carnival of the opportunistic Harry Carver (Pat Buttram). Carver's carnival represents what Bakhtin might have called the official cultural version of carnival, in this case a counterfeit of a counterfeit. To watch Charlie's performance at Carver's carnival suggests a mind-blowing analogy. He sings the burlesque ballad "Little Egypt" to one nearly nude Cleopatra-esque dancer accompanied by other similarly dressed female dancers. The number features an ancient Egyptian-styled backdrop, as well as mock Egyptian clarinet and drum musical backup that Hollywood has codified as synonymous with Ancient Egypt. In *Roustabout,* this appeal aligns the carnival of official culture with a regression to the most static, slave-based civilization the world has ever seen. It's by means of this salaciously backward-looking contrast that the carnival of Cathy, Joe and Maggie is shown to be the genuine carnival article, even though it too has peep shows. It's difficult to imagine a cultural reference point more at odds with the spirit of carnival than that of Ancient Egypt. For as Bakhtin states, "during carnival there is a temporary suspension of all hierarchic distinctions among men and of certain norms and prohibitions of usual life."[11] The Ancient Egyptian civilization was the most long-lived, rigidly hierarchical form of societal organization in history. Mass cultural references to Ancient Egypt such as this express or promote a longing for an intensely regressive mode of society and existence.

Madame Mijanou persuades Cathy to lure Charlie to return to their carnival. In the same breath she observes, "He's a louse. He uses people." This needs pointing out because we're not really seeing a radically different Presley here. He's no worse a character than, say, handsome-but-ugly-American Mike Windgren of *Fun in Acapulco,* or the selfishly sulky Deke Rivers in *Loving You.* Cathy sees Charlie performing at Carver's carnival, and then compliments him on having "found his voice." She fesses up that she came to do whatever it would take to draw him back, but doesn't have the "guts" to go through with it. The virtuous young woman is revealed as merely missing the nerve to barter her sexuality. Guts for a woman,

11   Mikhail Bakhtin, *Rabelais and His World,* p. 15.

prostituting herself, is the female equivalent of a man risking his life on a motorcycle.

Charlie breaks his contract with Carver's carnival and returns to Maggie and Joe's carnival. Charlie brings back sufficient earnings to keep the creditors at bay: his earning power has completely rescued the humbler amusement park. Maggie and Joe demand to know why Charlie is so charitable. He confesses that, shucks, he's in love with Cathy. Charlie's admission is greeted with much laughter by those carnies present. It's what Bakhtin calls the universal laughter of carnival, a laughter of all the people that's directed at all the people, including carnival's participants. Additionally, it's the simulacrum of the carnival moment of unmasking, in this instance not a literal unmasking, but the redemptive revelation that Charlie's love for Cathy means he isn't such a louse after all.

To the enchantment of the entire carnival staff, Charlie, who's just revealed that he's really been the lovable Elvis all along, launches into the movie's closing song, "There's a Brand New Day on the Horizon (and the Whole World's Gonna be Mine)." As Presley sings the climactic closing number, the grotesques, the truest inhabitants of the carnival, are shown. The fire-eater, the world's tallest man, the bearded lady, the fat lady and a female dwarf all show up. As Bakhtin observes regarding the grotesque, "images of the body are offered ... in an extremely exaggerated form."[12] By inverse contrast, this irregular assortment reasserts the perfection of Presley as the utopian body. Memorably displayed in a black leather jacket, matching pants and riding boots, he dons the garb of not just a king, but also high priest of rock & roll, a Melchizedek of popular culture.

Depending on whose account of production details you side with, even Presley himself takes on grotesque overtones

---

[12]   Mikhail Bakhtin, *Rabelais and His World,* p. 18.

through closer scrutiny of *Roustabout*. In his *Elvis! Elvis! Elvis! The King and His Movies* (1997), Peter Guttmacher claims that Presley was suffering from a 103 degree fever during the filming. However, that explanation seems suspect given Guttmacher's unbridled affirmation of all things Elvis. Alternatively, Presley enthusiast Paul Mavin notes in his discussion of *Roustabout*, "Elvis ... is clearly unhealthy looking. Still trim, his pale face, though, is puffy and frequently sweaty, and closeups of his eyes sometimes show someone who's clearly under the influence of some substance."[13] Regardless of which account is the correct one, there's a manifest grotesqueness in the forcible subjugation of the star into yet another substandard entertainment, whatever the source of his visibly compromised condition might have been.

Charlie Rogers is an *American* grotesque. He represents the full, adult fruition of 1950s middle-American terror in response to the construct of the juvenile delinquent. The delinquent is presented in full 1964 bloom of his manhood, violent, potentially deadly, diabolically handsome in his black leather riding gear, terrifying not least of all because of a sexual ambivalence, an ambivalence that must ultimately be deflated. As an explication of the grotesque, *Roustabout* might hinge on a hypothesis. Allusions to Presley's pre-radio, pre-television and pre-recording stardom might suggest a Presley more readily aligned with juvenile delinquency, a hypothetical Presley whose career never took off as it did from state and county fair performer status, a hypothesis that would render Presley's Charlie Rogers a frozen speculation.

---

[13]   Paul Mavin, "Lights! Camera! Elvis!", *Fun in Acapulco* etc., *Wickipedia*, DVD Talk, August 6, 2007.

"I Need a Girl to Make
my Life Worth Livin'"

The relationship between the gangster and the American Dream recur more than peripherally in *Girl Happy* (1965). Rusty Wells (Presley) and his "combo" are introduced playing at a nightclub in snowy Chicago, the American city most famous for its ties with organized crime. Nightclub owner Mr. Frank, a.k.a. "Big Frank" (Harold J. Stone) is so pleased with Rusty's success as a performer that he wants to hold Rusty's act over for several weeks. Intimidated by their employer, Rusty's band members panic, fearing they'll miss their annual spring gig in the more agreeable climate, bikini capitol Fort Lauderdale. With Rusty leading, they make their way to Florida. Ample processions of perfectly proportioned young women's bodies abound, none too short or too tall, none with overbearingly large or incongruously small busts, likewise their derrieres, and none of them fat. In emulating an ideal, they seem the product of an assembly line. To the extent that the title of the movie means anything, this idealization of Fort Lauderdale, or a Hollywood simulation of it, is an ideal location to contract girl-induced delirium.

Big Frank reluctantly allows his 21-year-old daughter Valerie (Shelley Fabares) to spend her spring break at the co-ed hotspot. Rusty persuades Big Frank to pay him and his band to go to Fort Lauderdale and act as clandestine chaperons, basically, to guard Valerie's virginity. Formerly the man thought to be a threat to the virtue of every young women in the Western world, Presley is here cast as leading the sex police. A bouncy ode to that time of year when a young man's fancy turns to matters of raw, animal instinct, "Spring Fever" is performed alternately by Rusty and his Rustyaires, and by Valerie and her girlfriends, each group in their beach-bound convertible. Too gentrified to pass as rock & roll, even with the then-popular girl-group-sound flourishes, it's too sugar-coated to be hit music material.

Arriving at the same Fort Lauderdale hotel where Valerie is staying, Rusty strikes up a romance with a beautiful brunette named Deena (former Miss America Mary Ann Mobley). Rusty takes the initiative despite being warned by nerd Brentwood Von Durgenfeld (Peter Brooks) that Deena 'has nothing upstairs'. Valerie Frank, however, does have something upstairs. Several indications are shown that she's intellectually inclined. When first at the hotel, she briefly wears eyeglasses, a stereotypical indication that she's bookish. Second, she's a university student. Third and of much interest to Von Durgenfeld, she's reading a book about avant-garde composer Arnold Schoenberg. Fortunately, Presley does not attempt to perform a Schoenberg composition. Instead, as Rusty Wells, he introduces himself by sauntering up to Valerie at motel poolside while singing the pleasantly sedate "Fort Lauderdale Chamber of Commerce." Included are lyrics that politely advise Valerie to not be like the young women who display "yards and yards of skin."

Rusty does double duty, safeguarding gangster Big Frank's daughter Valerie and, for the first time, working full-time as professional entertainer, chaperoning Valerie notwithstanding. Presley is again affiliated with recreation as he courts Valerie. They water ski together, go motorbike riding together, go sailing and dancing together, generally engaging in a lot of togetherness together. As was the case when Presley's character romanced Ann Margaret's character in *Viva Las Vegas,* as well when his Vince Everett character did likewise with a Hollywood starlet on a publicity junket in *Jailhouse Rock,* the leisure industry mediates between the sexes during courtship. It's as if man and woman are bereft of the linguistic component of courtship. The only language spoken is smiling.

Given that he's already commenced a romance with Deena, Rusty's dating Valerie points toward his being something of a philanderer. Yet somehow the Presley protagonist is always above such estimations. He's also the pattern for others to be oblivious to the moral and ethical implications of polygamous conduct. At their worst, the tendency of Presley's characters to stray only results in weak comedic complications. University students, people Charlie Rogers' age, didn't hesitate to mock him by singing "Poison Ivy League." Is this, the same audience, his Rusty Wells has no problem affectionately pandering to them. At his Fort Lauderdale motel nightclub gig, he woos them with the good-natured rock & roll song "Startin' Tonight," then the overtly self-serving novelty song "Wolf Call."

Valerie's other suitor is a stereotypically lusty Italian named Romano (Fabrizio Mioni). Though handsome and charming, *Girl Happy* will demonstrate that the Latin Lover is ultimately no competition for Presley. Romano gets rid of Brentwood Von Dergenfeld easily enough by way of an appeal to his hypochondria. Told by Romano that he looks unwell, Brentwood responds by thinking himself seriously ill. It's a plausible stereotype, since intellectuals are deemed a sickly lot and, hence, highly vulnerable to suggestion along those lines. Most of the movie's 90 minutes is devoted to variations on Rusty and his band mates spoiling Romano's attempts to seduce Valerie, Rusty precariously juggling relationships with both Valerie and Deena, and musical numbers that range from lively but unremarkable to plodding and sentimental. For one nightclub performance, Rusty enlists Valerie to prance about to the song "She's Evil." She does so in short shorts while brandishing a placard that states, "I'm Evil." This is popular culture's acknowledgement of the rise of public demonstrations at that time, that they are becoming fashionable and sexy. Valerie shows how activism and expressions of social protest are reduced to a fun affectation of misogynistic narcissism.

Lyrically, the most intriguing of the musical interludes is the gooey ballad "I'm Just a Puppet on a String," wherein Rusty melodically pledges to "do most anything" Valerie wants him to do. Bakhtin illuminates the significance of these lines when he observes that

> [t]he theme of the marionette plays an
> important part in Romanticism. This theme
> is of course also found in folk culture, but in
> romanticism the accent is placed on the puppet
> as the victim of alien inhuman force, which rules
> over men by turning them into marionettes.
> Moreover, only in Romanticism do we find the
> peculiar grotesque theme of the tragic doll.[14]

As such, the aesthetic provenance of *Girl Happy* is not folk culture, but romanticism. Rusty's vocalizing here suggests that true love contains a dualism. It's a veiled confession that his involvement with Valerie isn't something he's pursuing out of freewill, but as one of her thuggish father's puppets. Big Frank is the "alien inhuman force" controlling Rusty. With his immaculate, still-youthful face, crowned by his helmet head of lush, black slicked-back hair, there are moments in *Girl Happy*

---

14   Mikhail Bakhtin, *Rabelais and His World,* p. 40.

where Presley even appears to have been photographed to look doll-like.

That night, frantic to locate Valerie and rescue her from Romano, Rusty and his band give an impromptu performance on the beach to lure her. Instantly, they're mobbed by masses of coeds making out within earshot, including Valerie. All immediately subject themselves to Rusty's musical demand that they "Do the Clam," a song and a dance that managed to escape catching on among the broader public. For all that's silly about this scene, a truth about the militaristic power of popular music is revealed. In more recent years, the decline of dance clubs has eclipsed the once-familiar nightclub sight of patrons flocking to the dance floor, doing so the instant a hit song was recognized, doing so as if dutifully obeying a command. Just what was going on in the minds of most participants at the time remains a riddle wrapped in a mystery inside an enigma encased in a clam shell.

Presley's leadership is childishly emphasized by the off-stage conduct of his band mates. Whenever together but away from him, the musicians are accompanied by the childhood nursery tune "Three Blind Mice." The inclusion of this childhood nursery music also conveys a return to an infantile mentality. Valerie is crushed when she learns, upon being informed in a phone conversation with her father, that Rusty was being paid to act as chaperon. She gets drunk at the strip club to medicate her own abject Elvislessness. Plastered, she takes to the stage and commences reprising "Read All About It," the same tune she'd watched a stripper (Nina Talbot) perform when there previously with Romano. Rusty and company arrive just in time to stop Valerie from turning *Girl Happy* into a contender for the Golden Age of Nudity in American Cinema. A brawl brakes out, and Rusty casually administers a few beatings upon the riff-raff, taking a few knocks while he's at it. The club is busted, and Valerie and a swarm of other young women are jailed for being on the premises. It's the kind of scene that became familiar through more than a few movie comedies and sitcoms of the later sixties and early seventies, the big group arrest and group jailing. The scenario even proved an effective scenario for a U.S. sitcom, *Night Court* (1984–92). Provided you've got plenty of company, it's suggested, incarceration is never a source of serious concern. It's just fun.

Arriving at the police station with his band mates, Rusty says of Valerie to them, "I gotta talk to her *now*." This rationale of insisted-upon immediate gratification, that he wants what he wants when he wants it, is the pretext for the next two labored comedy efforts. First, Rusty tries to get arrested so he can join Valerie in jail. Unknown to him, the cop that Rusty tries to get to arrest him has just told his superior officer that he must avoid arresting anyone that night. Rusty lets the air out of the cop's tire, bends the radio antenna on his motorcycle and, finally, causes his head to be covered with sand after filling the cop's helmet with it. The scene makes it official: Elvis Presley is no longer a threat to society, law or order.

In the second stunt, Rusty enlists the help of some frat boys and a conveniently nearby backhoe to tunnel into Valerie's jail cell. The plan goes awry when Big Frank bails Valerie out just moments before Rusty gets there. With the tunnel having been deliberately collapsed once Rusty gains access, he then dons women's clothing so he can leave the jail with the others. The full fruition of this digression along the path to true love becomes an occasion to see Elvis in drag. Presley appears to have been a good sport about the matter. His verbally maneuvering the police captain into walking into the hole sawed into the floor, in a dubbed-in falsetto voice, is one of the more effective of comic scenes in any Presley film. Juxtaposed against more current sexual politics, the scene asserts drag as a means of confounding established authority.

Rusty then makes a musical attempt to express his desire to reconcile with Valerie when he returns to the motel nightclub to perform "I've Got to Find My Baby." The lyrics are thin on substance. Musically, however, it's one of the all-too-rare instances of a song in a 1960s Elvis Presley movie with some real rock & roll life to it. After springing her from jail and discussing the particulars of her involvement with Rusty, Big Frank figures that Rusty is sincere in his romantic interest for Valerie. He takes Valerie to the club where Rusty is performing. After very publicly passing by Deena and being told by Big Frank to get to work "watching" his daughter, Rusty takes Valerie by the hand and up to the stage where he reprises the theme song, "Girl Happy." Former intellectual pantywaste Brentwood Von Durgenfeld is in the audience, paired off with a skanky stripper. "I've given up on the mental types," he says and, indicating the stripper, pronounces lasciviously, "Not much upstairs, but what a staircase!" Spring break at Fort Lauderdale has taught the intellectual how to regard women as objects.

The path to true love has seemingly run its full, twisted course. Yet it is to the gangster chieftain, Big Frank, that the story owes its happy ending, and it's a dubious happiness at that. As per the characterization of Mario Puzo's Don Vito Corleone of *The Godfather,* to be published four years later, the head hood is the self-made deity pulling the strings and manipulating the affairs of men. Albeit in a much more abbreviated, sanitized schema, Big Frank is also evocative of the idea of the underworld boss. He is what Robert J. Thompson calls "a fixer of problems"[15] in the newer American epic form of the mob story. Indeed, just prior to finally reuniting Rusty and his daughter, Big Frank thinks aloud that the problem between his daughter and Rusty "might be fixable." While the impending shift in genre popularity might simply be the public expressing a preference for a different brand of baloney,

---

[15]   Robert J. Thompson, introduction to Mario Puzo's *The Godfather,* 2002 edition, p. 6.

American popular culture's movement away from westerns and toward gangster sagas was a shift that paralleled a growing moral decline. Even in its most mutated and anti-heroic modes, up to that time, the American western rarely absolved itself entirely of its moral compass. Tales of organized crime as related from the inside of it, however, tend to exhibit a tendency toward being what C.S. Lewis termed being "lost in the abyss of relativism," leaving their audiences to root for and identify with a relatively good Mafia that stands in opposition to a relatively much worse Mafia.

It's a striking lesson in moral contrasts to compare the cardboard Big Frank with the fleshed out underworld boss and nightclub owner Maxie Fields of only eight years earlier in *King Creole*. Walter Matthau's Maxie Fields is a vile reprobate, unquestionably the adversary to Presley's Danny Fisher. Alternatively, Big Frank is threatening, alien and inhuman in terms of his relation to romanticism. However, Big Frank is also the fatherly benefactor to whom Presley's Rusty Wells willingly acquiesces. Presley's previously near-perennially orphaned protagonist finds a place in a family as impending son-in-law to a gangster boss. The co-mingling of criminality and rock & roll was already a determinant feature of *Jailhouse Rock,* as well as the non-Presley movie *The Girl Can't Help It* (1956) and other, earlier movies that championed the new music. Not only with the orphan theme, Hollywood was recycling Elvis Presley.

While peace is preserved between Rusty and Big Frank, there's a more overtly hostile and dangerous quality to the patriarchal figure here than in previous Presley movies. In the end, Presley's Rusty is engaged to be the prospective husband to America's closest approximation of royalty, a Mafia princess. From a society that guarantees life, liberty and the pursuit of happiness for all, all that *Girl Happy* really shows us is the pursuit. As for Rusty, his girl-happy days are largely over. A change in his marital status will necessitate his having to content himself with being wife-happy. For the full span of the movie his life has never really been at liberty. Though never visibly intimidated, he's every bit as much and more in the shadow of impending vengeful disaster as his cowardly three blind mice combo. As *Girl Happy* concludes, it's time for Rusty to go to work watching Big Frank's daughter, as ordered by the gangster chieftain. It's the turn of the "girl" to be happy.

From at least as far back as 1961's *Blue Hawaii,* through American International Pictures' *Beach Party* movies, through *Girl Happy,* much American cinema was becoming a place to go the beach to. Most immediately, as such it was becoming an arena of intensified voyeurism, a place where film footage of those engaged in high jinx on the beach, clad in bikinis, were ogled by fully clad theater patrons scrutinizing them from their seats in the dark. Along with regaling audiences with displays of youthful bodies in a kind of nature, most ideally of all, the beach was the setting for freedoms, some of them real, some of them illusory, all of them compensatory, perhaps, for the greater, spiritual freedoms that were being taken from them.

Echoes of Rock & Roll

B y 1965, the usual formula for the Presley motion picture was a standardized product. The challenge facing those engineering that product was dualistic: how were its most enjoyably familiar aspects to be combined with enough variation on the established formula for the picture to have the allure of novelty? As singing rodeo rider Lonnie Beale in 1965's *Tickle Me*, the footloose Presley is introduced singing on a Greyhound bus during the opening credits. As far as songs sung on a bus go, "Keep On Goin'" is certainly peppier than "99 Bottles of Beer on the Wall." The cheerfully nihilistic lyrics urge the audience, "You gotta keep on goin' on that road to nowhere." Again slotting Presley into the mold of the Hollywood musical leading man, he sings together with traditional, invisible orchestral accompaniment. He is, by his very nature, surreal. As with TV advertising's appropriation of surrealism, the opening presentation of Presley congenially wrenches the audience into a universe other than parallel, one in which the commodity publicized is the safe oasis from the strangeness of that which surrounds the commodity. The commodity here is Presley himself, in this case as a Beale cutlet, the name "Beale" being a possible reference to the most famous street in Presley's native Memphis.

An impoverished rodeo star, Presley's Lonnie Beale spontaneously takes on a singing gig at a roadside bar to earn his food. After he sings the hedonistic "If it Feels so Right, How Can it be Wrong?", a question that could be easily answered at any free clinic, Lonnie is jumped by a lusty, busty blond. This sparks an instantaneous scrap with her boyfriend, who basically volunteers to have Lonnie beat him up. Lonnie's winning combination of vocals and violence catch the eye of Circle Z Ranch proprietor Vera Radford (Julie Adams), who offers him a job. Lonnie consents, only to discover on arriving at the Circle Z that it's a guest ranch for actresses, models and "career women." Generally speaking, fat women, even moderately plump women, don't exist in Presley movies, or make only rare, peripheral appearances. The Presley protagonist is again closely associated with large accumulations of shapely female flesh. The relentless pounding in of this form of erotic representation further encourages a polygamous mindset among the male audience while undermining the self-esteem of the female audience. Implicitly, one woman is not to be regarded as sufficient to satisfy the sexual expectations of one man.

Lonnie is assigned a room with comic sidekick Stanley Potter (Jack Mullaney). In the world of musical comedies, it becomes necessary to delegate. Given his other performing virtuosity, perhaps, in the right role and with the right director, Presley might have exhibited comedic acting ability as well. That he was never given such an opportunity wasn't a limitation uniquely imposed on his own stardom. While most of Presley's movies in the 1960s were closely affiliated with the musical comedy genre, being funny wasn't part of his job description. Was this a reflection of the notion that his aura as King of Rock & Roll merited a kind of religious veneration, one that, with few exceptions, was prohibitive of his portraying someone to be laughed at? In that Hollywood leading man roles, in general, have tended to be and continue being weighted toward solemnity, they also point to something prescriptive about manhood. For all that is idealized as being great about the manhood of most Hollywood leading man roles, it is an idealization that usually leaves little or no room for their showing greatness of humor. Instead, what is more often emphasized is the leading man's skill at inflicting damage, pain, death or seduction.

The Circle Z constitutes a homegrown harem for Presley. It's a plot device that serves multiple purposes. Women characters with the most desirable physical attributes are pitted against each other and, by extension, against the female audience. As Vera Radford tells Lonnie, "If it appears you're giving one too much attention, they begin scratching and clawing like wildcats." Every woman is an animalistic rival vying against every other woman. Gender relations are thereby shown to operate in a manner comparable to the competitive dynamics of the free market. Despite, or perhaps in part because of, his down-home earthiness, saying that his uncle put him on a saddle before he could walk, Lonnie is an embodiment of American glamour. As noted in the discussion of *Flaming Star,* above, glamour is etymologically connected to witchcraft, and is, according to critic John Berger, the chief quality that advertising associates with what it promotes: the quality of being *enviable.* Proceeding from Berger, then, the determinant nature of advertising could be called demonic. Talented, young, handsome, famous on the rodeo circuit, surrounded by beautiful women in a job that is more recreation than occupation, the only thing missing from Lonnie's life from the standpoint of crass materialism is riches, something that will also be resolved before this Presley installment concludes. Further accentuating Lonnie's enviable qualities is Vera's jealous right-hand man and swimming instructor Brad Bentley (Edward Faulkner). Brad postures as a muscle man without having the build for it. He and Lonnie demonstrate an immediate mutual animosity toward each other.

The lone female resistance to Lonnie is calisthenics instructor and Britt Eckland lookalike Pam Merritt (Jocelyn Lane). The closest thing to an explanation for Pam's hostility toward Lonnie is her dismissal of him as a "Sagebrush Lothario", a high concept reference for a Presley movie. Pam's grandfather is rumored to have hidden a treasure in a nearby ghost town, and the complications related to locating and securing the treasure is the fodder for much of the film's goings on. The central theme of *Tickle Me,* however, is that of a romantic narrative grounded in class struggle. The real conflict, that which must be overcome, is the problem of how a good ol' boy is going to win over a woman who speaks as if on loan from the most ivy of Ivy League universities. As with Daisy Buchanan in Fitzgerald's *The Great Gatsby,* Pam *sounds* like money. Her low opinion of Lonnie goes lower still as Lonnie plays instructor to the female guests at the ranch. She sees him cozying up to one of them in an archery lesson, leading another on a horseback riding lesson, applying suntan lotion to a third.

When Lonnie sings the hypnotic ballad "(Such an) Easy Question," every woman congregates around him in reverent adoration like a flock of robotic Stepford Wives. It's at this point that a transformation occurs in Pam's attitude toward Lonnie. As he croons, complete with the embellishment of an invisible echo chamber, Pam's harsh countenance softens, and she too moves in on him. She soon transforms from being an uptight, petulantly precocious schoolgirl to someone at the dawning of an awareness of herself as a sexual being. Thraldom strikes again.

Pam is kidnapped by masked thugs. Presumably, they want to get the lowdown on the whereabouts of her grandfather's treasure. Lonnie and Stan rescue her. Local Deputy Sheriff Sturdivant (Bill Williams) shows up to investigate. The whole lame development has the quality of filler to it. Lonnie then follows Pam via Jeep to the nearby ghost town of Silverado, where Pam's grandfather's fortune is rumored to be hidden. Together in the abandoned saloon, Lonnie and Pam share a flashback to an Old West that never was. Affecting different Old West characters, they don't even have their own respective imaginations. As "the Panhandle Kid," Lonnie rescues Pam from Brad Bentley's double dealing "High Card Harry." Pam is a mute chanteuse, or possibly just a working girl, and disputed piece of property for whom Presley/Lonnie/Panhandle Kid asserts his martial superiority over Brad/Harry in this painfully dumb fantasy. In terms of what it contributes to the story, the pointless digression aligns Pam's identity with that of a barroom prostitute. With her identity so leveled, she becomes far more vulnerable to musical propositioning. Lonnie concludes the flashback sequence by singing the undistinguished "Put the Blame on Me." Just as Presley's voice also sounds like money, in keeping with soundtrack album sales for his every movie, his voice *is* money. Again, an echo chamber is employed. It's as if we are expected to believe that Presley's vocal abilities broach the realm of the superhuman, or even the non-human. An echo chamber was effectively used in his 1956 hit song "Heartbreak Hotel." The use of this device in *Tickle Me*, however, is the furtherance of how canned, processed and artificial Presley had been made to appear in one more suffocating contrivance of a movie. In keeping with the ongoing challenge of how to revamp Presley as product, in this instance his singing sounds like a mechanical love moan.

Lonnie finally kisses Pam when the two read her grandfather's dog-eared treasure map. Almost immediately thereafter, Lonnie loses Pam when she finds him capitulating to a kiss from aggressive boss lady Vera Radford. That Presley is consistently subjected to sexual aggression from women in most of his movies suggests a reversal of what, up to that time, had been more conventional sexual interaction between the sexes. While usually facing various challenges in winning over the woman he's especially interested in, the Presleyan protagonist's irresistibility to women is such that a response of male passivity to female sexual assertiveness is promoted as the social norm.

"I Feel Like I've Known You Forever," Lonnie croons in a conciliatory, masculine mode at Pam's window that night, but to no avail. Apparently, she doesn't feel she's known him that long. As if to redeem himself from his lip-locking dalliance with Vera Radford, he returns to the rodeo circuit. A montage shows Lonnie doing as badly as a rodeo star as he is at trying to reconcile with Pam. After a brief incubation period following Lonnie's efforts to reconcile, however, she's haunted by memories of his singing as he eventually recovers his bronco-busting prowess.

Lonnie returns to the Circle Z a better bronco buster, but still a financial failure. He and Stan follow Pam to the Silverado ghost town. A cloudburst forces the three of them to take refuge in an abandoned hotel. Harassed by men in monster masks as the perfunctory dark and stormy night rages outside, nature itself sides with their persecutors. Presley's Lonnie overcomes the ghoulish foes with the use of karate, and then unmasks the villains. One of the malefactors is Chef Adolph from the Circle Z Ranch, someone who's appeared only momentarily and isn't given even a single line of dialog for the duration of the movie. And with a name like Adolph, what need is there for him to have any lines, really? This lame variation on "the butler did it" is the Hollywood equivalent of laying the blame at the foot of the real working class, as is true of many British murder mysteries, most notably the early works of Agatha Christie. This unmasking is what Stuart Galbraith IV has correctly pointed out is *Tickle Me*'s affinity with the Saturday morning TV show *Scooby-Doo* (1969–present).[16] Each week an animated cartoon gang of young people and their cowardly animated cartoon dog

---

[16]   Stuart Galbraith IV, *Tickle Me* @ DVD Journal, *Wickipedia,* 2010.

Scooby-Doo debunk ersatz ghosts, monsters and the like, every installment climaxing with a literal unmasking of the villain. The guilty party can always be counted on to be the new character in the piece whom the gang is not acting on behalf of. That is, the only possible suspect always turns out to be the guilty party. This infallible triumph of a childish rationalism indoctrinates even the dullest of minds to believe in the atheistic materialism that implies that, ultimately, people can and will demystify everything.

Concluding the haunted hotel episode, Stan falls into the cellar and accidentally discovers Pam's grandfather's hidden fortune in gold coins, which pour forth like a jackpot from a loaded slot machine. Deputy Sherriff Sturdivant, who turns out to have been in cahoots with Chef Adolph, makes a play for the loot but is subdued by Lonnie and Pam. The final adversity facing Lonnie, his financial poverty, is abolished as he and Pam drive off together as man and wife, oblivious to Stan who's stuck in a metal washtub tied to their Jeep. The shrew has been tamed with an ample class surplus and clown in tow to provide free comic relief.

Tickle Me, a movie with an even more irrelevant title than *Singin' in the Rain,* and certainly nowhere in the same league as that 1952 feature as an entertainment, depicts the resolution of class antagonisms, not by way of the eradication of class distinctions, but through the absorption of a leisure-bound, blue collar good ol' boy into a well-moneyed marital arrangement. Contrary to Presley's Ross Carpenter role in *Girls! Girls! Girls!,* and the ongoing antipathy of most other Presley heroes toward receiving charity, this Presley protagonist, Elvis the de-mystifier, has no apparent objections to being kept. The significance of Presley as perennially associated with fun, in this case even in the climactic encounter with would-be monsters in a haunted house, has the quality of an amusement park diversion. It is to the status of an amusement park that this movie aspires and none-too-effectively. The habitual presentation of Presley as always employed by one or more leisure or entertainment businesses, in addition to his always being a singer, has an almost prescient quality to it. It reflects what author and pastor Tim Keller has accurately identified as the dramatic ascendancy of recreation industries that has taken place since the end of the Baby Boom circa 1960. As with so many other Presley movies made in the 1960s, *Tickle Me* shows the other side of the double-headed coin embossed with the King of Rock & Roll. He's also the king of providing ways to kill time.

MIDDLE EAST ELVIS

In what might be a more politicized variation of playing himself, Presley's *Harum Scarum* (1965) has him playing movie star and singing karate expert Johnny Tyronne. The movie begins with Johnny in sheikh's garb, sword-fighting various opponents and subduing a leopard with karate chops. It's a movie within a movie, the premiere of Johnny's latest before a gathering of well-heeled, Arabic-dressed types. The promotional slogan for *Harum Scarum* promises "Elvis brings the Big Beat to Bagdad [sic] in a riotous, rockin' rollin' adventure spoof!!!" The misspelling of the name of the Iraqi capital is Hollywoodese for part of the world about which Western audiences knew next to nothing. Nearly half a century, two Persian Gulf wars and the advent of CNN later, among most of today's Western audiences, little has changed. Opening with the tune "Harem Holiday," viewers are musically re-initiated with the familiar proposition that a Presley movie means it's a time to relax, check your brain at the theater auditorium door and be pleasantly indoctrinated. Whereas *Harum Scarum* is among Presley's silliest film vehicles, it's a silliness that instructs males on treating females as commodities, that venerates imperialism, possibly even anticipating American military adventurism in the Middle East near the end of the twentieth century and into the twenty-first.

In the Presley-sung theme song that accompanies the opening credits, the lyrics to "Harem Holiday" isolate the basic elements of the pop culture ideal of masculinity. "Gonna travel, gonna travel wild and free, because this great, big world is callin' me. Every pretty girl is gonna know I'm around, they're gonna know I'm in town on a harem holiday ... Twenty women, twenty women by my side, I'm gonna kiss them all because I've gotta keep 'em satisfied. Gonna have the best time money can buy, I'm gonna be flyin' high on a harem holiday." Travel, absence of inhibitions, heeding the voice of the world, attractiveness and notoriety among many women, particularly pretty ones, a capacity to satisfy all of them, and good times wrought through much money: therein is sounded a hedonist's creed.

After a Rudolf-Valentino-meets-Elvis-type rescues a beautiful woman from the aforementioned leopard attack with a well-timed karate chop, Johnny and the woman embrace. He concludes the movie-within-a-movie with the bland songlet, "My Desert Serenade." Immediately thereafter, Johnny consents to sing for the premiere audience with the equally bland "Go East, Young Man." That's three Presley-sung tunes within the first ten minutes of the movie. The first one asserts the main sexual-political agenda; the subsequent two function as a kind of romantic subterfuge that either repress or suggest foreplay to that agenda. Following the demonstration of his singing wherewithal, Johnny is swarmed by admiring Middle Eastern presidents and potentates. He's invited to the mythical Middle Eastern kingdom of Lunarkan, a land two thousand years behind the west, someplace where no American has ever set foot. That is, it has been untouched by the so-called civilizing influence of America, and is presumably a place untouched by Judeo-Christian moral prohibitions and inhibitions. Johnny is told by an American ambassador that, if he'd go on a goodwill mission to Lunarkan, it would be "most helpful to the state department." He dutifully accompanies the suave Prince Dragna (Michael Ansara) and the curvaceous Aisha (Fran Jeffries), a semi-dominatrix type, to Lunarkan. While en route, Johnny extends his goodwill to do some smooching with Aisha. Before things get too amorous or another singing opportunity occurs, he's knocked out by a spiked drink.

Regaining his consciousness surrounded by beautiful harem girls, Johnny questions his circumstances by singing the semi-samba number "Mirage." The combined visuals, setting and lyrical context all suggest a TV-advertisement of Presley as polygamous subject of adoration and enchantment, pampered within a hallowed hallucination. He's been kidnapped by the minions of Sinan, Lord of the Assassins and a huge Johnny Tyrone fan (Theo Marcuse, in all his menacing baldness). He tells Johnny, "I have need of your talented hands to eliminate a person of great importance." That person is Lunarkan's reigning King Toranshah (Phillip Reed).

Indications of an antipathy between America and Islam underscore snippets of dialog culled from a long tradition of Hollywood camel operas. Sinan refers to Johnny as an "American unbeliever." Mention is made that King Toranshah must stay confined to his palace during Ramadan. He defeats his beautiful daughter Princess Shalimar at chess (former Miss America Mary Ann Mobley again, fresh from the set of *Girl Happy*). A distinctly Hollywood touch is evident in Ms. Mobley's decidedly non-Islamic display of her ample cleavage.

After Johnny makes a valiant but unsuccessful attempt to overpower his captors, who greatly outnumber him, Sinan has Johnny flogged as what he calls "a foretaste of things to come." Unlike when Presley had the lash taken to him in *Jailhouse Rock,* this time his whipping isn't shown on screen. Here he looks none the worse for wear afterward, but acts only slightly more wounded than any actor might in a standard "Thanks-I-needed-that" moment. King Toranshah himself, against whom Johnny is to deploy his talented hands, is then favorably introduced by way of his facility for chess, his faithful dog at his side, his gentle manner toward his daughter, his bank manager's diction and his immaculate fake beard.

In his first, short-lived escape from hands less talented than his, Johnny meets the Princess and woos her with the musical blandishment "Kismet." The musical seduction illuminates a facet of many a Hollywood musical, not just Presley's: singing greatly accelerates the processes of romance and courtship. What might otherwise take several pages of dialogue and multiple scenes to establish can be accomplished within the span of a two-minute song. Musical interlude aside, only a montage can expedite such matters with that kind of efficiency. As such, music functions as a kind of magic, one that in the case of Presley's movies invariably glorify him as the supreme magician. Also, as discussed in the critique of *King Creole,* evident too is another manifestation of accelerated intimacy, a false intimacy.

Promising ten thousand dollars cash and much foreign aid to help him escape, Johnny enlists the help of an opportunistic thief named Zaccha (Jay Novello), his three dancing slave girls, a bongo-playing male slave, a lovably larcenous dwarf named Baba (Billy Barty), and, again reflecting Presley's irresistible rapport with children, two small orphans. Johnny takes them all under his wing. As "The American," Presley appears to embody that great U.S. credo, "Send us your poor, your sexy slave girls, your huddled kleptomaniac midgets yearning to breathe free." As lone representative of America, Johnny does his patriotic duty to free the defenseless, the common people and, quite literally, the little people. All the while, he's also preserving a dictatorship. Lunarkan is a backward but allegedly goodhearted nation state. They need protection from the impending menace of a home-grown evil that has somehow accessed information about Johnny Tyrone's talented hands.

Johnny's unlikely team joins up in a Lunarkan marketplace when he sings the exuberant "Shake that Tambourine." Market patrons are captivated by Johnny's performance. It's a lively tune, one that the star sells admirably. Elvis Presley launching into music and dance with the accompaniment of comely dancing girls in a Middle Eastern, Islamic public square is also more than a little surreal.

Little Baba makes his way through the crowd helping himself to the money belts of those transfixed by Johnny and the dancers. It's a blunted parody of a recurring episode, one first seen at the five and dime heist in *King Creole*. Reiterated here is how Presley's Danny Fisher sang to serve as a decoy. He enables a gang of young toughs to rip off department store merchandise. As it was in *King Creole* (discussed in the chapter "Magnum Elvus"), generally, this is popular culture making a confession. Specifically, Elvis Presley, his singing, and possibly rock & roll at large, are all less culture than they are distractions, distractions designed to divert people's attention from recognizing that something criminal is going on. But what is the crime? That they take money for the often-slipshod quality of the goods they provide?

In its own boneheaded way, the script of *Harum Scarum* appears to have been gleaned from the same directives of Cold War–era American foreign policy. Hollywood employs Presley to sow ideological seeds. Foreign countries are shown as populated by aspiring murderous despots, exploiters of foreign aid, slaves and orphans, as well as other small folks engaged in various antics, all of them in need of a specifically American rescue. Either propping up or destabilizing regimes depended on whether or not they were sympathetic toward or incompatible with American or Soviet interests were standard Cold War procedures. In *Harum Scarum,* Elvis Presley approximates a singing CIA covert operation.

Johnny, Zaccha, Baba, the dancing girls and the orphans assemble in a generic-looking room wherein is sung *Harum Scarum*'s closest approximation of a rock & roll song, "Hey, Little Girl." Adhering to the formulaic Presley movie element of his appeal to little children, he flirtatiously opines "Hey, little girl, you sure look cute to me," as an orphaned little waif boogies artfully before him and the others. Was this an expression of a more innocent time, or the anticipation of a perverse future? Whatever might be said speculatively about the little dancing girl, including her musical accompaniment, she's a pre-teen version of a rock & roll female orphan.

Deke Rivers of *Loving You* and Vince Everett of *Jailhouse Rock* provide the most clear-cut, but hardly singular examples in Presley's earlier movies of the presumed failure of the conventional family. They're troubled in the absence of parental authority. Yet that absence is also shown to produce a youth who is special, even exceptional and superior. Parenting, it's intimated, is redundant at best, and possibly even a hindrance to optimal self-realization. The assault by rock & roll on the nuclear family, among its more ruinous aspects, is something for which rock & roll is presented as being capable of fully compensating the alienated individual. *Harum Scarum*'s "Hey, Little Girl" re-articulates the same idea for successive generations.

Perhaps the most pervasive personal and spiritual wreckage wrought by rock & roll is what's been termed the orphan spirit. According to the theory about the orphan spirit, the absence of love and affirmation from either or both a male and female parent during childhood and possibly adolescent development is what engenders an orphan spirit, an individual who lacks a clearly defined sense of identity. Those affected act out in various clearly identifiable ways, groping for a sense of self among all manner of excessive forms of behavior, addictions, consumerism, overwork or indolence, identification with corporate brands, either extreme conformism or rebelliousness against authority, including extreme conformity to rock & roll rebellion, promiscuity, and any other form of compulsive conduct.

In a solitary moment, the Princess gazes meditatively on a pool of water. Johnny appears as a shimmering image on the surface of the water and sings the undistinguished ballad "Golden Coins." She looks on transfixed as he rhapsodizes, "All my treasures are yours my love." Sweetened with generous helpings of syrup, Her Majesty Miss America surrenders to a sexual fantasy of Elvis Presley. She then mistakenly suspects that Johnny is in league with Sinan. When she blows the whistle on Johnny and his associates, Johnny and his surrogate family are imprisoned long enough for him to sing "So Close, Yet So Far (from Paradise)." The title lyric bespeaks a displaced religious impulse. It's corny, but Presley negotiates a compelling crescendo or two out of it. Paradise, it's lyrically suggested, is not a place but a woman.

Too cute to be captured, the diminutive Baba springs Johnny and his cohorts from prison. Johnny manages to gain an audience with King Toransha and the Princess long enough for him to explain things. Thinking that King Toransha has been killed, Prince Dragna, who masterminded the scheme, is eager to cash in on Lunarkan's oil deposits. Dragna pays off Sinan. Craftily, Sinan double-crosses Dragna, telling him he'll only be kept on as a puppet leader, Lunarkan's live-action version of Howdy Doody.

With the King, Princess, slave girls, Zaccha, little Baba, the kids and Zaccha's mercenaries in tow, Johnny implements a plan of attack to overwhelm Sinan's assassin forces. Predictably, Johnny assumes immediate control and those with him obey him unswervingly. A night-time battle sequence is farcically played out to comical orchestral accompaniment. Were it not for that musical cue, Zaccha's shameless mugging for the camera, and the very idea of a little person as a "freedom fighter," however, it would be impossible to read this alleged spoof as anything other than an inferior action-adventure movie sequence. After stating that "A king who would not fight for his kingdom does not deserve to have one," King Toranshah goes to fight his evil brother, but ought not his majesty offer wine when serving cheese?

Sinan is gunned down by machine gun fire when the comedic quality of killing men in battle with swords wears thin. How the modern instrument of death made its way into a land completely untouched by the Western world is anyone's guess. A merciful King Toranshah determines to have his would-be usurper of a brother, Prince Dragna, and the Prince's co-conspirator Aisha sent into exile. "Just don't exile him to America," quips Johnny, and the forces of Elvis all enjoy a good laugh after a fun night of mowing down insurrectionists with machine guns.

Cut to a Las Vegas hotel lobby sign promoting Johnny and "his Harem of Dancing Jewels from the Near East." Johnny reprises the opening tune "Harem Holiday" while surrounded by a score of beautiful dancing girls in harem attire. The Presleyan promotion of polygamy-mindedness is again reasserted by his being in the decorous presence of loads of pretty women, simultaneously championing polygamy in song. Women are shown as something to accumulate and display. Equivocating women with commodities, money or both, is reinforced by way of the simultaneity wherein Zaccha and Baba play in the casino as Johnny sings and is swarmed by women dancers. Zaccha places a coin that Baba found in a slot machine. The slot machines registers a jackpot as the word "aristocrat" comes up three times. Having been absorbed by America, the two thieves effortlessly acquire riches, ennobling themselves in much the same way that multiple women are shown being drawn to Presley. Having recited his wholesomely orgiastic song lyrics, Presley then steps off the stage and into the audience, a capacity crowd that includes King Toranshah, Princess Shalimar and the rescued orphans. He exchanges meaningful glances with the King as if to receive his permission. The movie concludes with Elvis giving the Princess a long, languishing kiss on the lips.

After Presley's character has been the focal point of a herd of showgirls, after he's proclaimed with full orchestral accompaniment that he's going kiss every pretty girl in Las Vegas and "keep 'em satisfied," by reprising the opening song, he kisses the Princess. Doesn't that make her rather common though, subordinating her to his taking on the mantle of Middle Eastern sexual potentate? That is, after all, what a member of a harem is there to accommodate. Here, Presley proclaims that the sexual revolution has begun, and more than just symbolically. The monarchy has been dethroned and relegated to the status of Elvis's common chattel. The sexual availability of women will be the coin of the realm that picks up the tab.

The concluding reprise of "Harem Holiday," wherein Presley's body movements are minimal at best, is strikingly ambivalent. The women dancers surrounding him do almost all the moving. Partially expressed again is man's sexual domination of women. They're there to perform for Presley as he crows about how he'll pursue his own pleasures. Yet the question worth asking is: who's in charge here? The star's power to indulge his anti-monogamous sexual interests is celebrated. However, he's physically immobile compared to the dancing harem girls around him. Singing aside, he's powerless.

Although a very different movie in many respects, this conclusion has an intriguing parallel to the conclusion of *G.I. Blues* (1960). Both movies end with production numbers featuring an Elvis Presley who is bodily restrained. Whereas in the earlier, more plainly propagandistic effort, he's bound by his stiff-looking uniform and the troops marching alongside, in *Harum Scarum*, it's the surrounding dancing girls who are the kinetic straight jacket boxing him in. In keeping with

Hollywood's ongoing erasing of Presley's rock & roll identity, a stationary, singing Elvis is no Elvis at all. The overt political naïvety of this production appears inclined toward inculcating mass audiences to accept that liberal democracy can absorb Islam limitlessly and with total impunity.

ELVIS DOES HISTORY

Turning a profit from a compulsion can cause those with the compulsions to be deemed winners. However, there's something dichotomously authoritarian about thinking of people as being either winners or losers. In *Frankie and Johnny* (1966), Presley's character Johnny is identified a loser, not because he gambles compulsively, but because when he gambles, he loses. Gambling is possibly the purest expression of the leisure business as business. To make a profession of gambling though, most professional gamblers must rely on the sharpness of their wits insofar as their livelihoods depends on their capacity to manipulate odds and chance. As Johnny, Presley presents no other morally questionable attributes, but he's mentally deficient in limiting his gambling to roulette, a form of gaming requiring no skill and that rarely offers a return. *Frankie and Johnny* presents elements both familiar and nearly novel to a Presley movie.

Familiarly, Presley's character plays for a living, as showman and as gambler. Slightly unusual is the introduction of his character as already being in a committed relationship (*Love Me Tender* and *Blue Hawaii* being the only other exceptions in this respect) this time with the lovely Frankie (Donna Douglas of TV's *The Beverly Hillbillies* fame). Exceptional too is the fact that Presley's Johnny is not irresistible to all women here, a touch that distances Johnny from the standard Presley screen identity.

That touch could be due, in part, to *Frankie and Johnny* being a story loosely based on musical folklore and historical truth. To get to the core of this folkloric confection, a conceptual framework suggested by the strange bedfellows of William Shakespeare and philosopher Friedrich Nietzsche proves a workable hermeneutic—as the following will show.

The movie offers no indication that Frankie and Johnny are either married or intending to marry. Curiously, for a movie set in the nineteenth century, there's no reference to marriage anywhere in the movie. It's a detail exempting Johnny from appearing as another of Presley's lovable philanderers. He and Frankie occupy separate bedrooms aboard the gambling riverboat the S.S. Mississippi Queen. The costumes and a reference to the worthlessness of Confederate currency indicates that the movie is set some time in the latter nineteenth century. The traditional American song "Frankie and Johnny" recounts the allegedly true story of a pair of young lovers. A woman caught her man cheating on her and she killed him. It's the cinematic embellishments, the candied gauze of a plot surrounding the central non-fiction, in which resides the exposition of popular culture's use of adaptation as a process of falsification, the denial of death and the gaseous exoneration of mankind through Elvis Presley.

Johnny is introduced as having gambled himself into penury. Riverboat boss Mr. Braden (Jerome Cowan) instructs his henchman Blackie (Robert Strauss) to throw a patron off the riverboat for trying to use Confederate currency. Further emphasizing his ruthlessness, he mutters that, if Johnny's doesn't start singing, his legs will be broken. After Frankie and Johnny perform the quasi-Dixieland number "I'm Gonna Make Petulia's Two Lips Mine," Johnny and his sidekick, piano player Cully (Harry Morgan) go ashore to consult a gypsy fortune teller. It's revealed to the audience that the fortune teller, Madame Zolita (Naomi Stevens) is a charlatan. She tells Johnny that gambling with a redhead at his side will break his losing streak. The most immediate complication is that Johnny's sweetheart Frankie is a blond. Just as the original account of Frankie and Johnny is a tragic one, this opening adheres to a familiar predicament in Shakespearean tragedy. The path that Johnny is to take is foretold to him by a supernaturally oracular agency, albeit a false one. In tragedies such as *Hamlet* and *Macbeth,* the tragic hero's plight is predetermined by his appeal to supernatural pagan agencies.

This tragic scenario has precedents even earlier than Shakespeare, as can be seen in Sophocles' *Oedipus Rex* and the Biblical plight of King Saul in 2 Samuel, when Saul consults the Witch of Endor in his bid to kill David.[17] Sometimes, as with *Hamlet,* the tragic hero indicates he's trapped between the natural and supernatural order of things. In Shakespearean tragedy, the bard would always have it that the natural order, the status quo, must always win out. Tragic heroes are invariably destined to meet either doom or some other great loss. What is the protagonist's tragic flaw in *Frankie and Johnny*? That he gambles? That he has the semblance of someone who cheats on his lover? That he stars in bad movies? In *Frankie and Johnny,* American pragmatism recognizes that the fix is in. The hero will make his own luck.

Arriving on the riverboat is sultry redheaded showgirl Nellie Bly (Nancy Kovac). She immediately brings good luck to Johnny at the roulette wheel, but is lured away at the sight of the oily Braden. In turn, Braden has dumped the cute and accommodating Mitzi (Sue Ane Langdon, who was Madame Mijanou in *Roustabout*) upon being told by Blackie of Nellie's arrival. Braden makes the piggish boast to Johnny that Nellie is "private stock, all 120 pounds of her." Cully works Nellie Bly's

---

[17] 1 Samuel 28, although unlike the works of Sophocles and Shakespeare, I do not regard the bible as fictional.

name into his new composition, "The Ballad of Frankie and Johnny." As Johnny rehearses the ballad, the action dissolves into an enactment of the lyrics. As if articulating a timeless, amoral archetype, the lyrics commence: "This story has no moral; this story has no end; this story only goes to show that there ain't no good in men!"

Following a spectacular win and equally spectacular loss in the casino, Johnny goes to his bedroom, next door to Frankie's bedroom. He engages in his other, less expensive compulsion, singing. The song "Beginner's Luck" dissolves into a pastoral fantasy, one in which Johnny rests his head in Frankie's lap as they have a private picnic. When song lyrics expound on not much of anything, as is the case here, the rhetorical function of those lyrics deflect the focus onto the singer and his harmonious naval gazing. With "Beginner's Luck," however, Presley's Johnny simultaneously woos his sweetie. His inwardness absorbs her as he makes love to her in song and, by extension, to the female movie audience.

When the riverboat docks in New Orleans, Johnny leads a marching band. Everyone is decked out in celebratory red and white uniforms as he sings, not to anyone in particular, the vaguely rousing "Down by the Riverside" and "When the Saints Come [sic] Marching In." The riverboat ladies go ashore to obtain costumes for a masquerade ball. Mitzi, Frankie and Nellie all buy or rent Madame de Pompadour costumes, each without the others' knowing. When the costumer tells Mitzi that no man will be able to resist her, she says that her problem is just the opposite, identifying herself as a woman of easy virtue, and possibly a nymphomaniac.

It's a matter of some significance that these costumes are identified with Madame de Pompadour, rather than Marie Antoinette, to whom these costumes might more readily be attributed. Madame de Pompadour was a courtier and mistress to Louis XV. Mitzi, Frankie and Nellie are all potential mistresses to King Elvis. To consider costumes as an expression of alter egos suggests that all of these women are adulteresses. Among them, the character of Mitzi functions as a kind of folkloric fifth business. "Fifth business" is the term for the minor character in an opera who is essential to the execution of plot machinations. It is Mitzi who, in the stage number, informs on Johnny to Frankie, telling her that he is warming up to Nellie. In turn, Frankie, as per the title song, guns down of Johnny. The three female characters, all wearing identical costumes, enact various weak comedic and romantic complications at the riverboat masquerade ball. From the high-class "private stock" Nellie, to the more principled Frankie, to the sexually frustrated Mitzi, at heart, and much more so in appearance, each is visibly indistinguishable from the others.

Johnny appears in a completely black cowboy outfit with white western trim, but no hat, and gives the audience a musical pep talk. "Everybody Listen to Me," begins the lively tune, complete with backup vocals by the trusty Jordanaires and the anachronistic twanging of an electric guitar. "This world's a wonderful place ... shout it out!" His gestures, shown from the waist up, bear traces of his dynamic 1950s dance style. Braden and Frankie demand of Cully that he tell them where Johnny is. Braden suspects that Johnny is making time with Nellie, while Frankie, with sledgehammer-subtle irony, says she'll kill Johnny if he cheats on her. As plot developments continue aligning themselves with song lyrics, Nellie tells Frankie that Johnny only wants her to be his lady luck at the casino. Nellie just wants to make Braden jealous so he'll propose marriage. The two de Pompadours hatch a plot inspired by the third de Pompadour, a drunken Mitzi, to test Johnny's fidelity to Frankie. When Frankie, pretending to be Nellie, sides with Johnny by the roulette wheel, he wins. Yet he's also cautioned the roulette wheel operator to keep his hand off a hidden magnet button. He knows he's been playing a rigged game. Upon winning, Johnny kisses the de Pompadour he's been misled to think is Nellie. He recognizes by her kiss that he's been accompanied by Frankie, who slaps him and walks out on him for his little infidelity, an infidelity in intention only, not in action. The gypsy fortuneteller's advice that Johnny needs to be accompanied by a redhead to break his losing streak in the casino is invalidated. More irrational still is how this development reveals that Johnny must have been deliberately losing all along, fully aware of the presence of the hidden magnetic all the while he gambled. It suggests that those men designated "losers" occupy that role of their own free will and that the superior man, Johnny, makes his own luck. Nellie, in a snit after seeing Braden paw Mitzi, then approaches Johnny, who kisses her, thinking that she's Frankie and has changed her mind. Seeing this, a jealous Braden undertakes to beat the living Elvis out of Johnny. Johnny holds his own, however, and the bout concludes with Mitzi knocking Braden out by smashing a bottle of champagne over his head.

Seeking reconciliation, Johnny goes to Frankie's hotel room, casino winnings in hand, only to have the still-angry Frankie dump his cash on an instantly frenzied crowd in the street below. Johnny wanders onto the street to sing the bluesy "(I've Got) Hard Luck," accompanied on the harmonica by a Black street urchin. For a time, Johnny seems affirmed as a loser. Aside from Presley's duet with a distant, anonymous Black woman at the opening of 1957's *King Creole* and his being backed up for "Trouble" by a Black jazz combo in the same movie, this is the only instance when a Presley movie shows him musically collaborating with Black people. Presley was widely criticized for his under-acknowledged debt to African Americans for appropriating their sound and their rhythms. Moreover, the scarcity of Black people in Presley's movies given the musical kinship between him and Black America suggests that, despite being America's foremost ambassador of cinematic fun since Walt Disney, it was expected that that audience be predominantly White, possibly with a racist disdain for seeing Blacks.

Braden laments his loss of Nellie and takes comfort in getting drunk with Mitzi. Johnny returns to sing his apologetic "Don't Stop Loving Me" to Frankie. Hoping to solve his boss's romantic problems, Braden's minion, Blackie, puts real bullets in the stage gun that Frankie is to shoot Johnny with. For a second time we're shown an identical performance of the ballad: "This story has no moral; this story has no end; this story only goes to show that there ain't no good in men!" However, even the most amoral of stories has a moral; for example, a story that endeavors to maintain an amoral stance respective to murder, through its failure to condemn murder, condones murder through its failure to judge. Even amorality is a moral stance. As philosopher Immanuel Kant maintained, to think is to judge. The "story that has no end" manifests a basic tenet of the Zoroastrian religion, which originated in sixth century B.C. in Persia, one from which Nietzsche appropriated the concept of eternal recurrence, the spiritual framework which, for argument's sake anyway, he advocated to supplant Christianity. Because Zoroastrianism rejected all forms of asceticism, a compulsive gambler such as Johnny is presumably free from being subjected to any moral judgment. Manifesting Nietzsche's Overman, Johnny isn't subject to what Nietzsche called the "slave morality," a morality comprised of the conventional virtues and values propagated by the weak to subjugate the strong. Johnny is enabled to escape tragic destiny by way of his stepping outside his mortality and into a Zoroastrian-style schema of eternal recurrence. His escape from tragic destiny is not the result of a "good" disposition, but is an outgrowth of chance, the element upon which, as a compulsive gambler, he stakes his life.

A suddenly sober Braden proposes to Nellie, learns of Blackie's scheme, and races to halt the show and save Johnny's life. He arrives just short of being in the nick of time. Frankie has fired the gun. This is the standard stuff of tragedy. Impending disaster looms large, as do the forces that might prevent that disaster. Tragedy has long been lauded for its cathartic qualities. It's emotionally cleansing to sit through a good stage tragedy. Ordinarily, however, the audience is aware of something that the tragic hero or tragic heroine isn't aware of, something pertinent to the protagonist's downfall. The catharsis isn't just the cleansing properties of a good, communal cry. Whether the protagonist has been subjected to a fate that's good or ill, the audience has been set free from its helplessness to intercede for the doomed central figure of the drama they've been watching.

The cathartic qualities of tragedy can elicit a sense of helplessness among its audience. "Don't kill that man Oedipus; he's your father!"; "Don't have that duel with Laertes, Hamlet; his sword has poison on it!"; "Stay home on the Ides of March, Caesar; they're waiting to kill you!" All these scenarios evoke the audience's desire to witness an escape from tragic inevitability. What makes these scenarios all the more tragic is that they are always or almost always avoidable. However, it's not Johnny but Frankie who's the most tragic figure of the piece. Subject to the tragic flaw of jealousy, she's committed murder, lost her lover, and is likely to be incarcerated for the rest of her life, as both the song and historical accounts appear to verify. At this juncture Elvis as Overman becomes most apparent. A hysterical Frankie tries to bargain with Johnny for him to survive. Briefly, Frankie is unaware that the cricket medallion that she gave Johnny for good luck stopped the bullet and saved his life. Frankie pleads that she won't even object to his gambling anymore. This is the incursion of movie fiction into the storied reality. Not only has Johnny cheated death and made Frankie totally submissive to him, he emerges triumphantly unchanged, unscathed and unrepentant. Nellie consents to Braden's proposal. Johnny, still unbound by any marital commitment, steps out from behind the theater curtain and, in a sense, out of the story that claims to have no moral. He then confirms this story indeed has no end by singing, "Hey Everybody Let's Go On with the Show." Free from death because of protection provided by a metal cricket, Johnny is also free to resume the monotonous pursuit of his compulsive gambling.

SON OF I AM A FUGITIVE FROM THE GREAT SOUTHERN HAWAIIAN FRUIT COMPANY

I n terms of sheer adulation of its star, *Paradise, Hawaiian Style* (1966) is probably the most idolatrous of all Elvis Presley movies. Opening with the descent of his airplane onto the Big Island, Presley's Rick Richards laments to a stewardess that he lost his last job as a pilot due to too much slap and tickle with a female coworker. Now no one will believe he's changed his lusty ways. Therein resides the specific element of product differentiation that distinguishes Presley's Rick Richards from his other roles. Rick Richards is the most conspicuous womanizer of all of Presley's screen personages. He visits friend and fellow pilot Danny Kohana (James Shigeta) to suggest a joint partnership in a charter helicopter service. Structurally, in part, this is a tale of Elvis-meets-business-partner, Elvis-loses-business-partner, Elvis-gets-business-partner-back-again. Strangely, the narrative is less story than something subordinate to the enactment of a ceremonial procession. Buttressing the goings-on is the window-dressing of Rick's business and pleasure ventures with numerous beautiful young women, as well as a generous peppering of travelogue cinematography featuring Presley's true costar, Hawaii itself (again). These components frame the canonization of Presley, enduing him with the status of an idyllic pagan deity.

Opening credits are accompanied by aerial shots of Hawaii and Presley singing "Hawaii, U.S.A.": "Gee, it's great, to be in the 50th state. Gee, what fun, just to surf and to swim in the sun." It's a commercial. The movie's second song, a novelty song, "Queenie Wahine's Papaya," he performs to a group of small children. Central among those children is Danny's daughter Jan (the calculatedly cute Donna Butterworth). Musically introduced in the movie as a paradisiacal Presley identity, and later repeatedly reaffirmed as much, Presley is something of a Peter Pan figure. His first musical duty is to appeal to children and, by extension, the child in each of us, or perhaps endeavoring to reduce everyone to a level of childishness.

Persuading Danny to re-team with him, Rick Richards proceeds to drum up business by renewing a romance with an old flame, Lehua Kawena (Linda Wong). She's an island hotel employee, one who might steer business his way. Having been stood up by him two years earlier, soon they're embracing and kissing each other with total abandon. Physical amour erupts without the standard assistance of any wooing serenade. This is one of the paradisiacal aspects of Hawaii for men. Men don't have to be able to sing or look like Elvis to instantly pick up beautiful women there. Intimacy is greatly accelerated as musical preliminaries have been dispensed with. Lehua consents to an oral contract. If he scratches her back, she'll scratch his. Much screen time is used up repeating identical sequences with three more women at three different hotels. An exception occurs when the oral contract is enacted musically by Rick and lady lounge singer Lani Kaimani (Marianna Hill) as they melodically pledge to "Get rid of [their] itch together." The overarching monotony of these Rick & roll sequences shifts the movie from the narrative form toward the ceremonial, less a story than a visual and auditory ritual.

Accentuating Rick's heaven-on-earth existence, he interviews another throng of beautiful women to be the secretary of his and Danny's helicopter service. Determined to keep Rick's mind on business, Danny hires Judy Hudson (Suzanne Leigh), an upper-class Brit, who he de-privileges first by dubbing her "Friday" and later by finding an official business reason to do close-up photography of her in a barely-there black bikini. Danny persuades her to wear a wedding ring to fend off Rick. Seemingly deterred by the ruse, Rick takes to the air in his chopper, this time to meet the lovely Pua (Irene Tsu). They take a slow trip down a lazy tributary in a canoe. The abundant manpower suggests that Hawaiian labor is extremely cheap. The shores are lined with hordes of natives standing and waving, some throwing floral leis at them as Rick sings the inanely catchy "Drums of the Island (You're Beating in My Heart)."

At this juncture, the movie forgets itself. Presley is no longer playing a role in a movie. He's the universally loved, universally worshiped entertainer Elvis Presley, wildly thronged by hordes of worshipers in a pagan reinterpretation of Christ's triumphal entry into Jerusalem.[18] To the extent that this might still somehow possibly be Rick Richards, who or what is it that the natives are paying homage to? This is the construct of Presley as golden-voiced polygamist who seduces nearly every woman he meets. It's not just Presley, his singing or even his looks being exalted, but the abandonment of monogamy and self-control.

As Rick and Pua step on shore, they're swarmed by armies of hula dancers. The interracial marriage between the Asian Danny and his Caucasian wife indicates that the movie contains a socially progressive element. Not so progressive is Rick's

---

[18] Zechariah 9, Matthew 21.

policy of indiscriminately hitting on women of all ethnic backgrounds alike. The hallowed grovel-fest, with Presley's Rick at the epicenter, trumpets the superiority of the White sexual conqueror.

However, all play, none of it in the guise of work, makes a dull boy an even bigger dullard. Rick returns to his office to take on his next assignment, a weak musical comic interlude. He and a shapely tank top–clad brunette, Joanna (Julie Parrish), fly an assortment of dogs to rendezvous with their adoring elderly owner. While en route, Rick sings of how he'd like to be a dog ("It's a Dog's Life," not to be confused with Iggy Pop's "I Wanna Be Your Dog"). Joanna spills a box of dog biscuits in the helicopter, and the spill sparks a feeding frenzy among the pooches. Rick's helicopter flying becomes dangerously erratic. Featuring a residue of rock & roll-ish guitar licks, the tune is as close to rock & roll as this movie ever ventures. For all that's lame about the scene, as music, as comedy, as a plot point, whether by conscious design or not, it seems to mock rock & roll while relegating Presley to a self-mockery.

His Rick Richards digresses into 1966 cheesecake photography as he takes some pictures, for business reasons of course. The bare-as-could-be-dared, black-bikini-clad, even more definitively de-privileged secretary Judy/Friday poses. The scene is a thoroughly gratuitous incursion of titillation that does nothing to advance the narrative, such as it is; it only grants Rick and the movie audience another opportunity to appraise Judy's goods.

Rick returns to the skies with little Jan. By way of another childish novelty song, "Datin'," he shares with her and the movie audience a genteel lesson on the birds and the bees. Indeed, when dating for the purposes of establishing a marital relationship is dismissed, dating and those who indulge in it can be reduced to mere conduits of fun for fun's sake.

Continuing the hodgepodge procession, on a sound stage decked out like a beach, Rick sounds out "[A] House of Sand [is an Empty Work of Art]." Suitably, the lyrics are also empty. A half-dozen sexy young women in bikinis encircle Rick, Jan joining them, possibly to clean up appearances a bit, possibly for educational purposes, a suggestion of what every little girl should aspire to. The musical accompaniment includes some tinny electric guitar flourishes, as if to satiate the groundlings with a little reminder of rock & roll: worshiping Elvis, a visual jolt to the hormones by way jiggling women's anatomy and, oddly enough in this case, posturing at making some kind of claim about art. Here, rock & roll is championed as culture and the compensation for those who've been deprived of art.

The standard inclusion of an altercation occurs when an aggressive boozer tries to put the moves on secretary Judy at a buffet restaurant. This time Presley's character dispatches the offender with a smorgasbord combination of boxing, karate and judo moves. The buffet dinner is thereby accompanied with buffet-style violence. Danny attends to complaints about Rick's dangerous flying, caused by the dog biscuit fiasco. As it turns out, the convertible that Rick forced off the road with his helicopter was driven by a Mr. Belden (John Doucette). In a land where all and sundry appear to drive convertibles, Belden also holds the distinction of being chief executive for the aviation bureau. For inadvertently buzzing Belden by chopper, Rick's flying license is suspended.

When Judy tells Rick that she took a couple of calls for him, he asks whether they were business- or pleasure-related. She replies that she's "beginning to wonder if there's a difference." For Rick there really is no difference. As a compulsively satyric figure always acting on such impulses, he's the antithesis of a free man whose paradise is his prison too. Absence of freedom, manifested through the absence of self-control, is shown to be desirable. Experienced through the kaleidoscopic perspective of the Presley protagonist, the Hawaiian paradise presented is an exotic, often airborne excursion into the world of a man abandoning himself to carnal appetites, albeit in a G-rated way.

Unaware of his suspension, Rick flies the abrasively cute Jan to a beach. As per another of the usual Presley movie formulas, Presley's instant and irresistible rapport with children is stressed. Lani's father offers her to Rick in marriage, pointing out to him that she is of royal blood. Could it be that, because he's already King of Rock & Roll, that Rick humbly declines? Lani joins Rick and Jan on a flight to a more secluded part of the island, along the way indulging the audience with some promotional postcard-style cinematography.

After a swim, wanting Rick's amorous attention, Lani tosses the helicopter key away. Stupidity figures prominently when she turns out to not have any idea where she threw the key and, rather than scan the surface of the sand, the three of them commence digging for it. Angrily, Danny flies to their rescue with a spare key for Rick on hand. On returning to the office, Rick discovers his pilot's license has been suspended for a month. Danny, taking daughter Jan with him, doesn't return. As if to state that, where Presley is concerned, one good rescue deserves a better one, despite his suspension, Rick heroically flies off to search for Danny and Jan. Much of this plays out like plot development in the near-total absence of a plot. Rick finds that Danny, too mad at Rick to remember to gas up, has crashed his chopper on a rock. Jan is unscathed, but Danny is hospitalized with a broken leg.

Rick and secretary Judy visit a bistro together where little Jan, like a seasoned lounge lizard, belts out a Hawaiian-ized rendition of "Bill Bailey, Won't You Please Come Home?" As Jan, Donna Butterworth's proficiency at vocals are slick and well-rehearsed, as per her overall performance. Perhaps Ms. Butterworth had a stage mother comparable to Colonel Parker's dominance of Presley.

Rick is confronted by all four women business partners in a restaurant. As with Jan being a processed child, although differing from one another in the particulars of their pretty faces, they are all of approximately the same height, similar hairstyles and figures. Woman is standardized. Rick escapes them when, without warning or explanation, a mob of hula dancers pulls him onto the stage where he sings the senseless "Stop Where You Are." Every time he utters the refrain "Stop," sound ceases and the action momentarily freezes. This brief, silly disruption in the basic formal properties motion, exemplary of what happened when 1960s popular culture tried to get artsy, re-emphasizes the idea that *Paradise, Hawaiian Style* is not so much a screen narrative as it is an idolatrous procession or parade. Most simplistically though, Hollywood is where Presley's Rick Richards got into trouble, and Hawaii is what rescues him.

After the musical digression, that is, when Presley re-inhabits the character of Rick Richards, he's simultaneously confronted by all four of his lady business contacts. A crisis, the inevitable crisis that this subplot was set up for, is averted when Rick buys them all off by promising each of them a cash percentage of the helicopter business. It's the typical, fallacious economic moral of the movie: no problem is so great that you can't buy your way out of it. Punctuating the business negotiation is the exoticism of an island drum performance, one accompanied by a group of male natives in traditional attire, performing percussive accompaniment by rhythmically slapping themselves. Rick negotiates the reinstatement of his flying license from aviation executive Mr. Belden. Regarding Rick, Belden says "a man [who] risks his entire future to save a friend can't be all bad." Although his secretary Judy has deemed him "bitter and arrogant and just plain selfish," he redeems himself by way of being a businessman's estimation of him as a friend indeed.

Finally, Rick negotiates a female partner for himself. Despite her previously expressed open contempt for him, he takes Judy to his side. Although she's been pretending to be married all along, he boasts to Danny that he "can spot a single girl with [his] eyes closed." That is, he has inherently reliable intuition as to whom he can ethically put the moves on. De-privileged once more by showing her stated opinions meant absolutely nothing, she immediately acquiesces to Rick's advances. The casualness with which a spouse is chosen proceeds with all the care with which a pack of gum might be purchased.

Paradise, Hawaiian Style is a naked attempt to emulate the commercial success of 1961's *Blue Hawaii*. It too concludes with multiple variations on the triumph of the deal. The deal here is the renewal of the Presley protagonist's business partnership, and the limiting of his romantic interests to one woman. However, his rationale for choosing Judy over all his other romantic interests appears to be entirely arbitrary, unless race is of any significance to Rick Richards. Concluding the movie's overall proceeding by an implied marriage is a standard plot device for completing a narrative. Simultaneously, the almost completely random casualness with which the hero makes what is one of the most critical choices in life also cheapens marriage, promoting an approach likely to predestine a marriage for failure. While it wouldn't be until years later that divorced protagonists would become a commonplace in American movies and television shows, inherent to this cultural attitude toward marriage is a movement toward the normalization of divorce, a less than paradisiacal experience among most who experience it.

Just as Rick and Judy are about to kiss and seal the deal of deals with a kiss, he's hauled off by a horde of natives to sing his ultimate love song to Hawaii itself, "This is My Heaven." Danny and Judy look on adoringly. Presley then launches into a reprise of the opening ear worm, "Drums of the Island (You're Beating in my Heart)," as a huge assembly of hula dancers in island garb rhythmically slap themselves, all to the beat of a huge percussion section in front of a giant rock face with conch blowers atop of it, a waterfall flowing as fountains gush gloriously and an intervening chorus chants "Hawaii! Hawaii!", all of it with Presley standing at the epicenter, striking a pose readily recognizable as belonging to his previous rock & roll identity.

The religious concept of paradise is brought into agreement with the singing, swinging leading man acting out his hedonistic impulses. Aside from Presley, who is this a paradise for? Judy notwithstanding, it's not a paradise in which women fare too well. Presley is decorated with women. Even at his most magnanimous, as his jilted female business associates discover, there's only so much Elvis to go around. Fans must content themselves with his celluloid image and buying his soundtrack recordings to revisit memories of that image. The paradisiacal Presley masculine ideal, to be wildly desired by all women; admired, envied or emulated by all men and loved by all children, does not find its lone expression in Hawaii. More than anywhere else in America, however, Hawaii is the natural habitat for that ideal. That which is the most plausible amid all this implausibility is that it was the King of Rock & Roll who, knowingly or unknowingly, contributed much toward inspiring what has since become international sexual pandemonium.

BEYOND GOOD AND ELVIS

Spinout, the 1966 Presley racing car movie musical, was promoted as featuring its star "With his foot on the gas and no brakes on the fun!!!" As singing race car driver Mike McCoy, Presley's romantic attention is sought by three women in particular: poor little rich girl Cynthia Foxhugh (Shelley Fabares, recycled from 1965's *Girl Happy*), psychologist and author Diane St. Clair (Diane McBain) and Mike's drummer Les (Deborah Walley), about whom is related the implausible running joke that she can't get recognized as a woman, not a claim that even the briefest of glances at Ms Walley would vindicate. The sum total of Mike's interests is limited to singing, racing and remaining unmarried, evidently, so he can kiss as many 'girls' as possible.

In the sexist theme song to *Spinout*, Presley likens driving a car to being seduced by a woman: "When the motor's warm and she's purrin' sweet, let me warn you, you're on a one-way street." After the opening credits, Presley is introduced performing in a modestly-sized nightclub. The song he performs, "Stop, Look, and Listen," again cautions against female seductiveness. "When you see a girl a girl struttin' by, givin' you that evil eye, and she got a kind of dreamy look, just enough to get you shook, now boy, don't you lose your head, you better, stop, look both ways, listen!"

That tune is immediately followed by yet another even more lyrically pointed accusation against women in "Adam and Evil." One of Presley's band members, Curly (Jack Mullaney, Presley's comic sidekick from *Tickle Me*), does some comic mugging while wearing a turban. He launches into some mock snake-charming as a lead-in to the song, as if to signify that the evil expressed in the moral sensibility in the song can somehow be made subordinate to pagan mysticism. In this instance, however, Presley proclaims his capitulation to those wiles. "Now Adam and Evil, they go hand in hand. Eve taught him sin, that's the way it all began." From there, Presley's Mike McCoy jubilantly sings, "If trouble is a woman," trouble here he comes; that he "shouldn't take forbidden fruit, 'cuz [he] believes [he'll] be headin' straight for heartache"—but "baby," he continues, she's "the devil [he] can't live without." He then asks, "Who cares about tomorrow?" She's the one he needs tonight, and "Baby, if you're evil, hold [him] tight."

Disguised as a novelty song, "Adam and Evil" is possibly the most aggressive musical attack on Judeo-Christian sexual morality presented in any Elvis Presley movie. The live-it-up-now, pay-later sexual ethos has since become a far more pervasive social and cultural norm. After Mike and his band play their closing gig at a Santa Barbara nightclub, the smug intellectual Diana St. Clair spies on them as they camp out in the not-too-distant woods. Woman's voyeurism will initiate the triste with Mike.

He approaches her and, within moments, has his hands on her waist, but is prevented from kissing her by binoculars dangling from her neck. He then woos her with song: "You're all that I want; you are my heart, my soul, my dream come true; All that I am, I am because of you." The lyrics are absurdly over-determined. Given how obviously game she is for his attention, the musical token of ritual seduction is redundant to the point of prompting the question of why he's singing. It's as if singing is a declaration of his victory, like Johnny Weissmuller beating his chest and doing a Tarzan yell after killing a lion with his bare hands. Diana tells Mike that he's the ideal embodiment of his own overblown reaction to her, that he's "the perfect American male" and she intends to marry him.

Bazillionaire and racing car magnate Howard Foxhugh coerces a resistant Mike and his band to play a tune for his daughter Cynthia on her birthday. In ballad mode, Mike charms her with "Am I Ready (To Fall in Love with You?)" At the song's closing, he comes within a hair's breadth of passionately planting a kiss on her lips. The moment the song ends, he immediately pulls back and disinterestedly orders his band mates to pack up. Albeit in a different presentation, the scene reiterates a characterization of Presley first seen in *King Creole*: Elvis as a kind of musical prostitute. Unjustifiably assuming the moral high ground, he then reprimands Cynthia for being "pathetic." Scolding her, he says it was only through her father's influence that a man would express an interest in her. Cynthia readily agrees with Mike's assessment of her, sobbingly saying that she's ugly too. A then-sympathetic Mike kisses her pouting lips. Pop Foxhugh has an alternative motive for having coerced Mike. He wants Mike to drive his new "Fox Five" racing car in a local competition, publicizing his new product. As Mike and Cynthia lock lips, strains of Wagner's famous wedding march theme are heard, as when Diana earlier told Mike of her own intention to marry him. The Wagnerian musical touch suggests that kissing on the lips is exclusively reserved for marriage.

Cunning Howard Foxhugh exerts his influence to have a policeman evict Mike and the band from their campsite. Les (later confessing her name is short for "Lester") is the most defiant toward the affable young officer. "Okay flatfoot, cut the soft sell. What's the charge?" she demands. The cop's name turns out to be Tracy Richards, a formalized inversion of the name of comic strip detective Dick Tracy. They discover that both of them are gourmet cooks. Mike then smooth-talks an elderly couple living in the mansion next door to the Foxhughs, persuading them to rent their mansion to him and his band. The man who most often persuades with song shows he can make a sale without musical accompaniment. Obstacles invariably arise. Ultimately, however, the Presley protagonist always gets his way. Here, however, he's been manipulated by a childish bit of reverse psychology, the persistence of the rock & roll mentality. "The simplest way to get you to stay was to tell you to go," Cynthia later tells him. Anxious to cordon off Mike from Cynthia, Les persuades Mike to test-drive the Fox Five racing car. After briefly warming up to Howard Foxhugh, Mike angrily declines the rich man's offer to have him race in the Fox Five. He fumes that he's "good enough to drive [Foxhugh's] car. [Yet] he's not good enough to marry [Foxhugh's] daughter." Cynthia and her father's young 'yes' man, Phillip (Warren Berlinger), joins Mike's backyard babe-fest party. As musical enchanter who's traded in his flute for a guitar, with a procession of nine buxom bikini models following him, Mike sings "In My Little Beach Shack." Any doubts the audience might have about the relevance of the tune are quickly allayed upon Mike's leading the procession of bikini-clad young women into an actual little beach shack, a tent really.

As Officer Richards comes around to sample Les' gourmet cooking, Diana cuddles with Mike. Mike's band mates Curly and Larry (Jimmy Hawkins), in the interest of keeping the band together, distract Mike from Diana and Cynthia. They have even larger gangs of young women to surround and worship Mike in mid-1960s mass cultural Dionysian manner. Whether dressed in bikinis or something more substantial, shapely young women surrounding Presley is a frequent staple of his movies. An even bigger party occurs in the backyard of the mansion that Mike and his band are and shimmying, female flesh. Afterward, Les, who's still involved in an ongoing battle to be recognized as a woman, turns up in an evening gown. After smooching with Mike, it seems she's the dark horse he'll unexpectedly pair off with. Cynthia and Phillip cozy up to each other. When Foxhugh strikes up a conversation with Diana, she learns he's a fan of her books.

Mike then performs the musical epicenter of the movie, the perfect summation of what motivates him in this and several other Presley movie ventures of the 1960s: "(I'm just wild about a) smorgasbord ... a little kiss here, a little kiss there," he sings. As a title, "Spinout" is a bit of subterfuge. Although candid about the actual cinematic agenda here, however, "Smorgasbord" probably wouldn't have worked as a movie title. Whereas kissing suggests a physical shorthand for sexual conquests, the identification of women as items in a smorgasbord again relegates woman to the status of an object to be consumed. Just as, etymologically, the term "consume" means to use up, this specific, popular culture agenda asserts that an individual woman is only of interest until the novelty of her wears off.

Are we to believe that Presley's Mike McCoy does all this kissing and carrying on while remaining a virgin? Moral constraints of the cinema of that time, coupled with the making-wholesome of the Presley image, enforced a particular code of conduct on his roles. The paradox of the Presley protagonist surfaces, how to be a virtuous polygamist: convert to Mormonism? The irresistible polygamist must limit his sexual activity to kissing.

Foxhugh, Officer Tracy and Phillip demand that Mike tells them who he intends to marry. As if out of desperation to work the theme of auto racing into the plot, Mike replies he'll let them know after the race. At the race, the previously wimpy Phillip steals Mike's racing car. Cynthia spontaneously joins the race. Both developments take place with no apparent rhyme or reason: they simply involve as many of the central characters as possible in the tiresomely wacky procession that is more chase than race, a popular facet of many a 1960s Hollywood movie. Mike hot-wires a car with a dead battery and cruises to victory, beating not just Phillip and Cynthia, but also the snooty Foxhugh, who Mike said must be taught a lesson. A pop culture-venerated youth must teach the middle-aged.

Mike announces that he's going to marry Cynthia *and* Diana *and* Les. Action then shifts indoors and he addresses the audience directly, telling us as he kisses each woman that he did marry Cynthia- to Phillip; that he did marry Diana-to Foxhugh; and that he did marry Les—to Officer Tracy. Evidently, in addition to being a singing race car driver, Mike is also a justice of the peace, or perhaps an overly affectionate priest. He heroically maintains his initial objective of staying single, free to further his ambition to become the world's most prolific distributor of mononucleosis. Continuing his enjoyment of life's smorgasbord, he winds up the proceedings with a performance of the upbeat "I'll be Back" in the same nightclub in which he started out, this time populated by the three pairs of newlyweds. That is, the movie concludes with the guarantee that, for as long mass audiences are willing to pay for it, there'll be more of this stuff coming down the pipeline. Mike's band includes a new, female drummer. Individual women, it's implied, are readily replaceable.

As per the previous chapter on *Frankie and Johnny,* the writings of Nietzsche suggest added depth to interpreting *Spinout.* The Nietzschean idea I refer to that is key here is his characterization of "frenzy":

> If there is to be art, if there is to be any aesthetic doing and seeing, one physiological condition is indispensable: frenzy. Frenzy must first have enhanced the excitability of the whole machine; else there is no art. All kinds

of frenzy, however diversely conditioned, have the strength to accomplish this: above all, the frenzy of sexual excitement, this most original and ancient form of frenzy. Also the frenzy that follows all great cravings, all strong affects; the frenzy of feasts, contests, feats of daring, victory, all extreme movement; the frenzy of cruelty; the frenzy in destruction; the frenzy under certain meteorological influences, as for example the frenzy of spring; or under the influence of narcotics; and finally the frenzy of will, the frenzy of an overcharged and swollen will. What is essential in such frenzy is the feeling of increased strength and fullness ... A man in this state transforms things until they mirror his power—until they are reflections of his perfection. This having to transform into perfection is—art. [19]

Frenzy is not art itself. Nietzsche called frenzy a precondition for art. Beginning with Presley's explosive 1950s rock & roll debut, he was seemingly a purveyor of frenzy. Equally unquestionable is that Presley generated a massive frenzy of public sexual excitement, one of "the frenzy of the will, an overcharged and swollen will." Moreover, audiences caught up in a truly rousing, rock & roll performance, or even a recording of the same, experience a "feeling of increased strength and fullness." The mirror of Presley's power, however, the reflection of his would-be perfection and the various other hysteria-inducing rock & roll music acts that followed were types of mass mania. Presley's movies of the 1960s, including *Spinout,* almost

---

[19]   *The Portable Nietzsche,* "Twilight of the Idols", translated by Walter Kaufmann, p. 518.

invariably featured "contests" and "feats of daring." Yet we can go little if any farther in understanding if limiting our view to a Nietzschean prism, the frenzy of Presley and rock & roll failed to precipitate any commensurate art form or art movement, aside from music largely devoid of any reflective consequence.

The Elvis Presley who electrified the youth of the Western world and drew legions into a vicarious form of thraldom revealed that the artificial semblance of frenzy he presented was just that—artificial. The hysterical masses, tantalized in the 1950s by a menu promising unlimited sexual frenzy, were told to content themselves with "a little kiss here, a little kiss there." As such, Presley's masculine sexuality was an approximation of a facet of female sexuality: the tease.

ELVIS MEETS THE
COUNTERCULTURE

As musical navy frogman Ted Jackson in *Easy Come, Easy Go* (1967), Presley is restored to active military duty. Of the ineffectual boredom-killer, Leslie Halliwell says it's an "empty-headed star vehicle, almost indistinguishable from many of the others."[20] For the most part, however, it's not the plots of Presley's movies that are indistinguishable from one another. It's Presley himself: the manner in which he's showcased in his movies, his at-times-visible and growing disinterest toward being situated in productions crafted from inferior scripts, productions husbanding him to singing inferior songs, that's what verges on being indistinguishable among many of his movies. The magnitude of Presley's stardom would make any questions about the possibility of his being an underachiever seem absurd. The overall quality of most of his movies of the 1960s indicates otherwise. Although empty-headed, however, *Easy Come, Easy Go* has a storyline distinctly different from Presley's other movies. Of particular interest pertaining to this feature is its significance as the first cinematic documentation of Presley encountering the 1960s counterculture.

---

[20]   *Halliwell's Film Guide,* Leslie Halliwell, p. 327.

Familiar as a standard Presley movie component is the sensibility expressed in the lyrics of the opening theme song: "Easy come, easy go ... Crazy love is in the air ... delightful, mmm, day and night-full, so many girls in every port." The lyrics then move in an even more sexual-consumerist direction: "Kissing, kissing, pound for pound, delicious." Presley's Ted Jackson performs the tune for a speedboat full of his fellow swabbies as they sail away from an impressive display of American battleship muscularity.

Once docked, he and his naval buddies pay a daytime visit to the nightclub of his old pal, the non-naval, anachronistic beatnik Judd Whitman (Pat Harrington). In the club, the Easy Go-Go, Ted and his pals encounter a go-go dancer shaking to the sounds of the house band. As if anticipating an inquiry from Ted about her sexual activeness, hepcat Judd informs him that "She doesn't swing." Undeterred, Ted presses Judd to connect him and his shipmates with some female companionship. Judd obliges by bringing out a wheel of fortune which, instead of featuring large digits, is adorned with photos of young women in bikinis, each one featuring the name and phone number of the woman depicted. This moves Ted to pick up an instrument to sing, "(Step Right Up, Let the Wheel of Fortune be Your) Love Machine."

The sight of Presley in uniform while strumming an electric guitar, musically encouraging his chums to choose a woman with little more discretion than is used choosing a casaba melon, is the most emblematic image of the military-industrial Elvis. It's a moment simultaneously harnessing rock & roll's most identifiable symbol, the electric guitar, to Elvis Presley in military uniform. All the while, he's shilling for a gambling device that merges erotic pleasure with a male-dominated marketplace operation of chance. It's a jarring agglomeration of symbols, unsettling, perhaps, in that it presents no real contradictions. There's no real conflict between the manipulation of chance for personal profit and sexism, militarism and rock & roll. Here too can be seen an example of how cultural Marxism, including Critical Theory, definitely wouldn't get it right. As bluntly ideological as anything ever put on film, yet contradiction-free, the scene manifests an unbroken continuum between military politics and the subjugation of women.

The following day when back aboard their battleship, Ted and his swabbies sight a cabin cruiser, one helmed by three young women in bikinis and a young man. Ted dons his scuba gear, plunges into the ocean and discovers an unexploded mine which, for some unexplained reason, is lodged off the California coast. That's followed by a lengthy, underwater disarmament sequence. When clumsily handled, as is the case here, the suspenseful takes on the semblance of killing screen time. Eventually disarming the mine, he discovers a treasure chest. He then boards the bikini-filled cabin cruiser, scolds those aboard for not vacating a restricted area and, while doing so, confiscates the film that was shot underwater by the young man, Gil Carey (Skip Ward).

Back in uniform, Ted visits hydrophobic Captain Jack (Frank McHugh), the elderly owner of a marine salvaging rental business. Captain Jack refers Ted to Joe Symington, who inherited all the local lighthouse records from a seafaring father. Ted drives up to Joe's house in his obligatory convertible. It turns out that Joe is actually Jo, as in Josephine Symington (Dodie Marshall), who owns the lighthouse records and is also the same woman who go-go danced at Judd's club and "doesn't swing."

At Jo's, Ted encounters the aged Madame Neherina (Elsa Lanchester, most memorable for her title role as 1935's *The Bride of Frankenstein*) leading a yoga class. The Madame gives Ted a musical chastisement. Together they perform a childish novelty song, "Yoga is as Yoga Does" ("There is no in-between, you're either with it, on the ball, or you've blown the scene").

This sadly uncritical spoofing of yoga, a practice that has had a huge resurgence in popularity in recent years, reflects a sorry spiritual naïvety on behalf of the secular West. Combining meditation techniques with various physical poses and stretching exercises, whether they know it or not, yoga practitioners are endeavoring to detach themselves from the physical world to experience personal union with one or more of 300,000,000 Hindu deities, many of whom have malevolent qualities. To the extent something authentic is being accessed, can someone participate in yoga without any risk of incurring spiritual harm?

Ted is given a crash course on what it means to be "with it." Jo escorts him into the next room, one wherein a young couple, locked in a loving embrace, have a huge vat of spaghetti dumped over them as they kiss. A crowd of young onlookers applauds the spectacle. "It's a form of art," Jo tells Ted; "it's a sincere attempt to break loose from convention." Three young women, clad only in bikinis and wet paint, are then guided by a young man who helps roll them across a large, blank surface. A similar stunt was enacted by artist Yves Klein seven years earlier. Klein died soon after attending the premier of the 1961 documentary *Mondo Cane,* wherein he was mockingly shown engaged in his eccentric artistic practice. As the arbiter of common sense, Ted doesn't get it. The scene reinforces the common idea that modern art is more or less just a fraudulent sham, one that emerged as something perpetrated by exclusionary confidence tricksters, including the likes of yogi Madame Neherina.

The inclusion of yoga and the two performance art pieces suggests a documentation of Elvis Presley in attendance at a happening, a spontaneous or improvisational performance especially in vogue in the 1960s and involving audience participation. But is it *Art*? No more so than any other standard 1960s Presley film fare. Authentic happenings didn't have the status of mass culture commodities. In part, they repudiated the commodity status of art. The sight of Presley being confronted by a popular culture rip-off of silly, bad avant-garde cultural practices points to the ease with which most any aesthetic practices can be co-opted. The mantle of coolness thought synonymous with youth resides with a generation younger than Presley is here. Presley is surrealistically dictated to here by an actress who, 31 years earlier, portrayed the Bride of Frankenstein. Additionally, the rhetorical coherence of this attack on the counterculture suggests a contrasting recognition of Presley as a mass culture approximation of Socratic irony. The more authentically with-it Presley readily proves that younger, superficially hipper others are really his cultural inferiors.

Ted-vis tells Jo he's researching a naval history book, which persuades her to show him the naval record of a ship that sunk off the coast carrying Spanish pieces of eight. Ted's friend Judd, a walking repository of hipster clichés that were already old when this movie was first released, is brought in on Ted's plan to salvage the treasure. Ted performs the pseudo-rocker "You Gotta Stop" at the Easy Go-Go. Judd agrees to help finance the job if Ted performs at his club should the plan fail. In need of a third person to carry out the salvaging, Judd recruits Jo to join them on a motorboat ride. The beautiful, wealthy cabin cruiser owner, Dina Bishop (Pat Priest) looks on from the marina in her standard-issue bikini. When the idealistic Jo discovers that Ted isn't really a naval historian, but rather a fortune hunter, she calls him a "get-rich-quick creep." She agrees to join them, however, and plans to share the money to set up a new center for the arts for those Ted calls her "kook friends." He asks her if she'd like him better if he "hated money, grew a beard and stood on [his] head." As promising a concept as that might have been, together with a few tunes thrown in, the idea was never undertaken. "I've got principles," Jo tells Ted; "that's something you couldn't understand."

Then Gil, hip to Ted and Judd's plan, lies to Captain Jack, telling him that Ted and Judd sabotaged Dina's cabin cruiser.

Meanwhile, well-to-do Dina makes advances toward Ted, who tells her of his shoe-less childhood. Mass culture imitates Presley yet again. She offers to join his "fishing trip," boasting that she has no principles. "Gil," she tells Ted, "is just a poor boy who wants to become rich," while for her, "everything is just fun and games until the right millionaire comes along." Ted says he'll take a rain check on joining her. She indignantly replies that she doesn't give rain checks, and they part company. When Ted visits Captain Jack again, he discovers that, as a result of Gil's false accusations, Captain Jack is revoking Ted's rental of salvage equipment. Ted and Gil brawl a while. Naturally, Ted prevails. He goes to Jo's to tell her of the revoking of their equipment rental. A party is taking place at Jo's. She interrupts the dancing to announce: "I want tell you something *beautiful!*" in the most vapidly conflated 1960s sense of the term "beautiful" imaginable. She tells the crowd that they're going to have the money for the arts center. Ted tells Jo about how Gil suckered Captain Jack into renting the salvaging equipment to Dina. Undaunted, Ted proceeds to musically unite the crowd by singing the pseudo-gospel "Sing You Children, Sing." In a nod toward 1960s co-operativeness, the crowd sings and claps along. The song is lively enough. Along with most of what Presley sang in his movies by this point in his career, however, something doesn't quite ring true about it. It's an instance of a gospel song that neither mentions Christ nor glorifies God—a gospel song that isn't a gospel song. What's exalted here, besides Presley, is an inanely-led collective and its capacity to moo for the sake of mooing.

Ted, Jo and Judd return to Ted's convertible only to discover that it's been dismantled and turned into a mobile by Zoltan (Diki Lerner), one of the hippy artists on hand. In turn, they borrow Zoltan's ridiculously flamboyant vehicle, another swipe at '60s counterculture. Gil and Dina kidnap Captain Jack, enlisting his aid in helping them to retrieve the treasure.

When Ted and company catch up with them, he and Gil spice up their fisticuffs by duking it out underwater. Upon having his oxygen line stuffed inside his wet suit by Ted, Gil puffs up like a balloon and floats to the surface. Ted, Jo and Judd raise the treasure, are congratulated by Dina, thanked by Captain Jack for their helping him overcome his fear of water, and then scorned by Gil, who despises "a good sport." An expert appraises the coins as being worth a mere 3,900 dollars because they're only copper covered with a patina of slime. In an instance of true, 1960s communal-ism, Ted, Judd and Captain Jack chip in their shares together with Jo to establish the new arts center. Judd volunteers to spring for beer and pizza if Ted will make good on his promise to perform at Club Go-Go again. "You've got a deal, partner!" enthuses Ted, then appears before a full house at the club, electric guitar in hand to perform the semi-samba closing number, "I'll Take Love." It's a conclusion with promises of unseen beer and pizza, a renewed business partnership and, though on a drastically more modest scale, as per *Blue Hawaii* and other Presley features of the decade, the triumph of the deal. Ted and Jo kiss, a typical constant in Presley pictures that he's been uncharacteristically deprived of up to this point. Perhaps Jo will swing after all now that it's been made abundantly clear that living free depends on charity. *Easy Come, Easy Go* presents two parallel narratives. Most overtly it relates a flimsy competition, one wherein Presley's Ted Jackson, pal Judd and would-be bohemian Jo try retrieving sunken treasure before rich, unprincipled Dina and her lackey Gil. The other narrative presents a competition too, one to determine with whom cultural supremacy and superior cool resides, Presley or the emerging counterculture. Presley, though still youthful here, clearly belongs to an older generation. He's dated, not just by his military background, but through allusions to a previously existing business partnership with the beatnik Judd. That Presley's Ted Jackson and his cohorts should donate their find to establish the new arts center suggests a happy compromise. Yet throughout the movie, the music is Presley's. At least, it's what he's been designated to perform. Musical representation of the counterculture here isn't really counter cultural at all, but the abominable "Yoga is as Yoga Does" that Elsa Lanchester performs with Presley. The only legitimate grounds on which Presley ought to compete with the flower power generation, their music, is absent from the movie. The fix is in again and, given the quality of what Presley has been given to perform, it's just as well. Provided what's at stake isn't exorbitant, Presley's character demonstrates he's just as capable of rejecting crass materialism as the next Ted Jackson. Ted's capitulation to Jo's plans for an arts center, followed by the conciliatory tune "I'll Take Love," seems a cinematic admission that the filmmakers are striving to insist on Presley's relevance despite widespread cultural change. Enthusiastic Presley movie blogger Alan Hanson observed that this became a growing problem for Presley's movies of the time.[21] Presley's screen roles from here on seem more oriented toward asserting his currency amid changing times and shifting cultural norms. They implicitly grapple with the problem of how to fill the hugely over-sized shoes of the mass hysteria his past popularity had endued him with. There's a place for the counterculture within the lexicon of popular culture, *Easy Come, Easy Go* suggests: the anti-materialism of the counterculture is to be subjected to open, unquestioned ridicule.

[21] Alan Hanson, *Elvis-History-Blog.com*.

THE PARANOID PRESLEY PERSPECTIVE

F amed surrealist artist Salvador Dalí formulated the theory
of the paranoid critical perspective. The paranoid critical
perspective is a strategy for creative expression whereby the
artist leads the audience to hallucinate. Compared to other,
fantastical elements of surrealism, Hollywood movies are often
concerned with making the hallucinatory credible. Decades
of having required darkened viewing auditoriums and with
a ready repertoire of special effects, much cinema emulates
the quality of dreams. Often, success in the movies is chiefly
gauged by how effectively the hallucinatory has been brought
to realization. As discussed in the critique of *Tickle Me,* the
Presley screen persona was among the last major stars to
manifest the surreal Hollywood singing identity, complete with
invisible vocal back-up singers doing back-up vocals, as well as
instrumentals from invisible back-up bands.

Dalí sought to deploy the paranoid critical perspective to
propagate art with two or more ambiguous images for the
purpose of increasing the possible interpretations. Presley's 1967
feature *Double Trouble* doesn't advance a surrealist method for
the purpose of advancing psychological emancipation. By 1967,
Presley and his movies tended to stay at the level of banality.

Occasional incursions into the surreal might bolster the audience's propensity to indulge in Presley-oriented fantasies. As per the advertising industry's recruitment of psychology for coercive, commercial purposes, *Double Trouble* appeals to the audience's capacity for paranoid ideation, ideation being the manner in which the mind structures its perception of reality. A thinly-sublimated climate of generalized anxiety among Cold War audiences, that is, nuclear-related anxieties, could have been what motivated this attempt to capitalize on mass paranoia as an entertainment axiom. As per the cognitive dualism of paranoid ideation itself, *Double Trouble* presents two distinct scenarios of paranoid ideation.

Psychologist Karl Menninger and others have argued persuasively that paranoia is a form of ego defense.[22] In *Double Trouble,* the assault on the egos of the movie's protagonists, Presley's Guy Lambert and his girlfriend Jill Conway (Annette Day), are brought on by a duality of crises. Unwitting dupes in a diamond-smuggling scheme on one front, trying to evade killers sent to eliminate Jill by her less-than-avuncular Uncle Gerald (John Williams), on another front. Without delving too deeply into the psycho-babble, a movie invoking the idea that Presley's ego, who he is, is under attack, mirrors the real-life diminishing of Presley and of his significance as a leading cultural figure. *Double Trouble* will bring about a happy resolution to each of these problems.

As if to prove that, when the going gets tough, the tough get fashionable, Presley goes to "mod London and swinging Europe."[23] The Presley protagonist is presented as a singer, except that, in this instance, he's without another leisure-oriented profession. However, he is engaged in the ultimate

[22] Karl A. Menninger M.D. *The Human Mind,* pp. 85-89, 94, 245-7, 267.
[23] *Double Trouble* promotional trailer.

youth activity of the day: bumming around in Europe. This "Mod London and swinging Europe" were in fact shot in Hollywood. Although possibly a production decision wrought from financial considerations, travel restrictions on Colonel Tom Parker due to his criminal record, likely played a part in where the film was shot. It also does much to accentuate the movie's qualities as an Elvis psychodrama. Breaking with Presley opening credits tradition, the movie commences with jazz instrumental music and multi-colored tinted photographs of hip, dancing youths. Presley's voice eventually joins in to sing the title track.

Guy chats up the gorgeous Claire Dunham (Yvonne Romain) at a nightclub. There he performs with his band, Georgie and the G-Men, "G-Men" being a 1930s gangster-era name for the F.B.I., who aren't listed in the movie credits. However, "G-Men" does suggest another appeal to paranoia as a surveillance-oriented law enforcement agency. Jill enters as Guy and his blokes perform the upbeat "Baby, If You'll Give Me All Your Love." Although tame by today's standards, the song lyrics and other elements in *Double Trouble* move in a noticeably more risqué direction than earlier Presley movies, elements indicating an acknowledgment that there's more to sex than kissing. The song contains the line "It ain't gonna be no one night stand," one of several instances in the movie where the theme of sexuality moves in an overtly adult direction. Afterward, when Guy is shown alone with Jill in his flat, he clearly wants to do more with her than just kiss, even providing his own make-out music as he warbles "Could I Fall in Love" to her.

Unable to get past kisses and sweet talk with Jill, she leaves him for the night. A moment later when he goes to answer a knock at the door, Guy is greeted by a punch in the face that knocks him unconscious until morning. His assailant, a generic cockney brute, checks the door number and says "B-six; I do believe I've made a mistake. Ah well, from the look of 'im, 'e probably deserved it anyway." This irrational incursion of violence corroborates paranoid ideation as legitimate. Even in the presumed safety of one's own domicile, the potential for harm is an ever-present reality. In such a world, proficiency in the use of deadly force, for the Presley protagonist, a proficiency in karate, is a necessity.

Guy is awakened by a phone call the following day from Jill's uncle Gerald, who arranges to have Guy drop by for a visit. Uncle Gerald snootily boasts that the painting on his study wall is a Constable. Affiliation with high culture is frequently a tip-off in popular culture that one is dealing with a villain. *Double Trouble* adheres to that formula. Associating quality artistic achievements and those who enjoy them with evil promotes a stereotype: that the wealthy, the culturally refined, are evil and deserve to be resented and envied.

Jill enters, confronting Guy in her schoolgirl's uniform. "I'll be eighteen in four days," she tries to reassure him. The significance of is telling. Demographically, she typifies Presley's earlier greatest fan base. Uncle Gerald dismisses Jill's wish to marry Guy. After Guy leaves, she argues the matter with her uncle until he tells her of his intention to send her to Belgium. She submits to her uncle's authority, knowing that that's where Guy and his band are also headed.

Coincidentally, Guy and Jill wind up on the same ship to the continent. Nearly plunging overboard when the railing he leans against swings open, Guy has an opportunity to attempt panicking comically. Enter the bumbling British diamond smugglers Archie Brown (Chips Rafferty) and Arthur Babcock (Norman Rossington) in search of an unlikely looking suitcase in which to stash their contraband jewels. When they choose Jill's suitcase, lovers Jill and Guy are unwittingly recruited into a criminal conspiracy, conspiracy being a dominant motif of paranoia. Before meeting Guy again, Jill meets another young man on the fog-shrouded ship. Morely (Michael Murphy) claims to be a graduate student on his way to research "certain European cities" for a history thesis. Morely tells Jill she can't get married at age eighteen in Belgium, but she can in Stockholm. Meanwhile, Guy enjoys copious eyefuls of other female passengers. He converses with his lead guitarist Georgie (Monty Landis), who attempts to affect a comical seasickness. As with most comedic efforts in Presley's movies, it's not funny.

Guy rallies his band to launch into a rocking, ship deck version of "Long-legged Woman with the Short Dress On." Again, innocuous by more contemporary standards, the title lyric is more salacious than standard Presley film music up to that time. The interlude alerts Jill to Guy's presence on the ship. The two are reunited in time for Guy to rescue her from being crushed by a falling trunk. When they arrive in customs, the scenario is repeated after an anonymous gloved hand unfastens a bolt holding a trailer full of luggage, sending it careening toward Jill. Again, Guy rescues her. Strangely coincidental too is the reappearance of the gorgeous Claire Dunham at a smoky Brussels nightclub wherein Guy performs "City by Night." "Why do I feel like I'm being followed?" he asks Georgie.

Jill arrives at the nightclub to have a spat with Guy over his questionable loyalty. They leave together and are nearly run down by a speeding motorist who Guy perceptively calls a "Crazy idiot!" as he exits a taxi with Jill. Increasingly metaphysical dimensions enhance the paranoiac dualism, the "double trouble." Forces of chance itself seemingly persecute them. "Don't you realize you're alone with a man in his hotel room?" Guy asks Jill. Despite Presley's disinterested delivery of the line, the suggestiveness resonates with the innuendo-laden quality of the movie. Linguistically, innuendo can, at times, reflect a paranoid irony, indicating that language can't be taken at face value, not always anyway. Could the world's leading male sex symbol of the day be showing signs of performance anxiety? As Guy and Jill kiss, he accidentally dumps his drink down her back. She changes clothes, putting on an alluring nightgown as saxophone music emphasizes the sexual potential of the situation, even the instrumental soundtrack is an innuendo. "Seventeen will get me twenty," he quips nervously, reiterating fear of punishment for sexual gratification. Meanwhile, the klutzy smugglers await outside the hotel room to retrieve their diamonds. An unidentified trench coat–clad man stands nearby in the shadows. It all confirms the legitimacy of Guy's apprehensions. Jill dissuades him from sending her back to Uncle Gerald, telling him she'd be beaten and locked up. Despite the dishonest manner in which he's told this, Guy takes her word for it.

They leave the hotel for Stockholm, but not before Guy expresses anxiety over possibly being tried for kidnapping. The migration is punctuated by a large flowerpot crashing in front of them, then their narrow escape from gunshots emanating from the darkness. Jill joins Guy on a familiar Presley movie conveyance, the back of a pickup truck, this one loaded with livestock. Guy treats Jill to a snappy rendition of "Old MacDonald." She joins in the chorus. Danger can be alleviated, temporarily at least, through regressing to the infantile. Yet the alleviation of their terrorized condition quickly resumes when they arrive in the masquerade world of Antwerp's version of Mardi Gras. A demoniacal-looking clown fires a play gun in Jill's face. In this anarchic world of an externalized unconscious, one populated by all manner of costume grotesques, Guy/ Presley is the only bastion of sanity. He leads his beleaguered, enthralled fan to safety, just as Mentor led Odysseus out of the Underworld and Virgil led Dante out of the Inferno. Guy orders Jill to stay in her hotel room during the festival as he goes off to exercise his musical male prerogative. He sings the sexist, kitsch standard "I Love Only One Girl (The One I've Got my Arms Around)" to a largely female crowd, a folk-ish celebration of polygamy. Encountering yet again the gorgeous Claire Dunham, she suggestively invites him to the studio of an artist who "makes nude ladies." Racy stuff for a Presley movie, but it also suggests a childish attitude toward sexuality.

Jill appears in a mask, tripping Guy and threatening to cut his throat. This is what isolates and identifies Guy, not Jill, as the protagonist. At least for that one moment, it's Guy who's clearly identified as the focal point of all that is conspiratorial in the movie. Fleeing into the crowd, Jill again meets alleged graduate student Morely, who lures her to an abandoned well to kill her. In true movie villain style, Morely explains the plot that's been hatching. Her Uncle Gerald had him, Morely, and his associate, "following [Jill's] every move." As with comedy, in movie rescues, timing is everything. Guy shows up at the critical moment between Morely's plot exegesis and the moment before the dry well is to be lined with Jill's guts. Guy gives Morely a free karate lesson, sending Morely crashing to his death, unless, perhaps, he is able to land on his head.

A reunited Guy and Jill book passage on an old scow, the S.S. Damocles. Unknown to them, the ship will be scuttled for insurance money by its captain (Stanley Adams) and the man the closing credits identify only as his "mate" (Walter Burke, in the only instance of a Presley movie ever hinting at anyone having a homosexual relationship). That Guy and Jill are unknowing of this additional plot, or that the jewel smugglers are still following them, indicates that they have dangers to overcome they don't know about, a literal, tangible unconscious.

Before their ship sails, Guy and Jill check into a hotel. Beside the hotel clerk is an ebulliently deranged fat woman named Gerda (Helene Winston). At first, she presumes Guy is her husband. The clerk explains that Gerda mistakes every man for her husband after losing her mind when her real husband deserted her. This possible lone representation of a mentally ill person in any Presley movie (Michele Carey's Bernice in

1968's *Live a Little, Love a Little* might be one more) is of dual significance. The weighty woman psychotic is both a purveyor of comic relief and a disturbing harbinger of the threat of mental imbalance underlying much of the movie.

A fully clothed Guy and Jill lie side by side, in daytime, on a hotel double bed. He tries brushing off her references to matrimony by singing "There's So Much World to See," a reassertion of his leading-man wandering ways. Despite his resistance to matrimony, he assents to accompanying Jill to Sweden, where she'll be of legal age to marry him. Evidently, he's all wanderlust without any idea of either where or why he's wandering.

The oafish smuggler Arthur goes to the hotel, resulting in his encountering the deranged Gerda. The gorgeous Claire Dunham advises Guy of Jill's whereabouts, presumably a precautionary measure. He's then arrested for kidnapping by three diminutive, trench coat–wearing detectives (the Wiere Brothers, here appearing as the woefully unfunny plagiarized spawn of Peter Sellers' Inspector Clouseau). Uncle Gerald meets Guy at the Belgian police station. By phoning Claire, Uncle Gerald gives her the signal to kill Jill, while giving himself an airtight alibi because he's at the police station. You'd think that his staying in England would have been an even better alibi.

After drugging Jill, Claire leaves her in a bedroom to asphyxiate from an open gas line. Gerda the comic mental case is shown pursuing comically dim-witted Arthur. Exiting the hotel, Arthur shows signs of having a post-Gerda afterglow. This is the first instance in a Presley of total strangers having sexual relations with each other, here both of whom are somehow mentally challenged. Sexual freedom is the alleged compensation for the loss of reason.

Discerning Uncle Gerald's scheme, Guy busts loose from the police station and leads the police on another zany 1960s chase sequence. Central to the gag is that the chase happens in Volkswagon police cars. Smashing a window of the gas-filled room, Guy rescues Jill from a gaseous demise. Irrationally enough, the police then show up with Uncle Gerald in tow. Claire spills the beans about how the old upper crust snob plotted to do away with Jill, gain her inheritance and keep Claire in the style to which he'd accustomed her.

Concluding the ordeal, Guy confesses his love for Jill in a hotel room. Checking his watch, as of midnight, Jill's of age to marry and they kiss. Guy spies out the other, mysterious trench coated stranger who'd been watching them. He's a Scotland Yard detective on the trail of Archie and Arthur to arrest them and retrieve the diamonds smuggled in Jill's suitcase. As the ongoing conflicts and crises reach their resolution as if in a dream, Guy and Jill have been under police surveillance throughout their time in "swingin' Europe," a resounding refutation that they've ever been in any real danger. As if in a dream, the entire episode was symbolic.

Together on the S.S. Damocles, Guy and Jill kiss. It's interrupted by the explosion of the ship as per the plan of the Captain and his mate to scuttle the ship. The ship's name is likely an allusion to the Greek myth pertaining to the precariousness of being a king, possibly as per the King of Rock & Roll. As this relates to the Military Industrial Elvis, in a famous, 1961 address by John F. Kennedy to the United Nations, Kennedy stated how "Every man [now] lives under a nuclear Sword of Damocles." Archie and Arthur are shown struggling to stay afloat as Guy and Jill stand miraculously unharmed atop a fragment of the frigate. "What a kiss!" she squeals.

As Guy Lambert, Presley has safely shepherded Jill through a succession of nightmarish scenarios, sustaining her thraldom to the explosive end, overcoming an onslaught of assaults to himself, his cultural relevance and his ideal fan. Symbolically, they've survived a nuclear attack and, vicariously, so too has the movie audience along with them. The quasi-utopian idea of being able to survive a nuclear holocaust from a safe distance appeared at the end of other Cold War cinema too. Examples include an overjoyed James Coburn surrounded by adoring, bikini-clad beauties watching an island of anti-American villains explode before them in *Our Man Flint* (1965), as well as Sean Connery's James Bond and his on-screen squeeze viewing arch-criminal Ernst Stavros Blofeld's island explode in *You Only Live Twice* (1967). French poststructural philosopher Jean Baudrillard went so far as to suggest the abstract expressionist painter Jackson Pollock's large-scale drip paintings did likewise.[24] Unlike most of Presley's movies, this one doesn't feature a closing song, suggesting, perhaps, that whereas the self might somehow survive such an apocalypse, music and possibly culture at large could not.

As an effort to renew Presley's exoticism, the revamping of his novelty status in *Double Trouble* has precedents in earlier vehicles set in Hawaii. In the Hawaiian productions, at least initially with 1961's *Blue Hawaii*, Presley seemed to command equal if not greater star status than his paradisiacal surroundings. By 1967, situating him in a simulacrum of mod London, as per the currency of the British Invasion in pop and rock music of the time, was a shrewd strategy to infuse him with the elusive quality of staying contemporary. The once most dominant figure of rock & roll was realigned with the remnant of a once-great empire, an empire which by then had by then been reduced to simply being fashionable.

---

[24]   From a lecture Baudrillard presented at *Hot Paint For Cold War,* in September, 1985 at the University of British Columbia,

THE
CLAMBAKE MANIFESTO

Easy Come, Easy Go presents the Presley protagonist as someone going from fortune hunter to "with it," non-materialistic idealist. By comparison, in *Clambake,* a movie of the same 1967 vintage, the counterculture is largely conspicuous by its absence. A few elements from that year are evident: women's hairdos, clothing fashions and dance steps, although the young men are still clean cut. Of particular interest is how *Clambake* addresses the theme of materialism. Disdained, perhaps, by a generation guided by such principles as "turn on, tune in and drop out," Presley offers his followers another cinematic agenda: "Clambake! We're gonna have a Clambake! Clambake! We're gonna have a Clambake ... Hey world, you're gonna know, I'm cuttin' loose, I'm lettin' go." The "we," the movie audience, are going to have a beach banquet–oriented celebration, seeing how much Presley, as the imperialist epicenter of pleasure, can enjoy himself. The central plot dynamic of *Clambake* has clearly been cribbed from Mark Twain's 1881 novel *The Prince and the Pauper;* the disparities between rich and poor, matters that Karl Marx and Friedrich Engels exploited so skillfully, will herein be resolved by that most pragmatic of methods: havin' a good time.

As Scott Heyward, Presley is the son of a wealthy oil tycoon with something to prove, both to himself and to his father, Duster Heyward (James Gregory). Scott isn't opposed to money in principle. Neither is he devoted to it. Nor does he want to involve himself with a woman who's mainly interested in him on a cash basis. In a variation on intergenerational conflict and opposition to parental authority, Scott resents Duster for having made his life too easy for him. While en route to a Florida shot in California, Scott meets affable hick Tom Wilson (Will Hutchins). Young Wilson casually comments on how much he'd like to trade places with Scott, enjoy his filthy lucre and the appeal to women that goes with it. Tom', off-the-cuff remark inspires Scott to do just that: set out on a path for his life based on an affable hick's off the cuff remark. Scott trades names, identities and his fancy convertible for Wilson's humbler but more fashionable motorcycle. It's a tellingly simplistic comment on America: exchanging motor vehicles signifies swapping identities. As each of them drives off in the other's conveyance, they sing the cornball duet, "Who Needs Money?" The newly blue-collared Scott sings, "Not me," along with citing the virtues of being unhampered by worldly riches, as Tom sings "I do," and musically lists the benefits of affluence.

Arriving at a posh Florida resort hotel, nouveau riche Tom identifies himself as Scott Heyward of Heyward Oil. The hotel staff snaps to attention upon hearing his name. After identifying himself as Tom Wilson, the doorman tells Scott to move on. In the hotel lobby, Tom spies millionaire J.J. Jamison (Bill Bixby) boasting to a cluster of young women about his speedboat racing exploits. As Tom Wilson, Scott checks into the hotel as the new water skiing instructor. Presley is again occupationally affiliated the leisure industry. In her third Presley movie, Shelley Fabares shows up as Dianne Carter, this time hoping the wealthy J.J. Jamison will marry her.

When speedboating champion Jamison declines joining Dianne for a cruise, she enlists Scott's aid to make Jamison jealous by giving her a water-skiing lesson. Once on the water with her, to Scott's surprise and in full view of Jamison, she expertly executes every water-skiing trick short of pulling Scott's trunks down with her teeth. Afterward, Jamison cavorts in the Middle Eastern harem–themed hotel bar, another appeal to polygamous fantasies. In his conversation with an inquisitive bartender, Jamison reveals he either made or inherited his fortune from Jamison Jammies, a line of women's nighties. He tries titillating the bartender with talk of commodifying women, discussing the new line of "Jammies," "so sheer that you can't tell where the 'Jammie' ends and the girl begins."

Contrasted against Presley's Scott Heyward, there's something intensely lascivious about J.J. Jamison. As opposed to having a fortune wrought from something as honorable and clean as the oil industry, Jamison's wealth was accrued through the female fetishism industry. He might be the ideal antagonist relative to the Presley protagonist. Freudian psychoanalysis contends that the fetish, to which Jamison owes his riches, is "'inhabited by a spirit' … clearly associated with a person without being one, and as having 'magical powers,' since its presence gives [fetishists] the potency they otherwise lack."[25] In short, everything attributable to the appeal of the commodity that Jamison has made his fortune by can also be deemed attributable to the disembodied recorded voice of the singing idol, what Presley made it big with. As such, Jamison's rivalry with Scott amounts to a contest between two competing forms of magic.

Tom Wilson enters the barroom and, lacking the proper sense of decorum suitable for a man with the kind of wealth he poses as having, he invites Jamison to join him and the two

---

[25] Charles Rycroft, *A Critical Dictionary of Psychoanalysis,* p. 51.

gold-digging chippies escorting him. As the common man given uncommon riches, Tom presents what might become of someone ordinary were he positioned to trade places with Presley and not be up to the responsibility. As the next decade would bear out, not even Presley was up to the responsibility of being Presley.

When on an evening motorbike ride with Scott, Dianne confesses to him that, contrary to appearances, she's not rich and has joined him in another effort to make Jamison jealous. Scott consoles her with the tin chestnut that "they tell me if you look deep enough into a flower, you can see the future." He then musically expounds on the notion that he can see her in a house that has everything, "Everything but Love"—that is, the kind of house that marrying Jamison would probably land her in. Presley's prophecy will seem to move toward fruition the nearer Dianne moves into a romantic direction with Jamison.

Following the cautionary seeing and singing into Dianne's future, while varnishing a water ski in the hotel workshop, Scott tells Sam Burton (Gary Merrill) his speedboat is "running too cool." Complimenting Scott on his discerning ear, Sam tells him how the boat crashed into the pylons at the previous year's Orange Bowl Regatta. Sam leaves as Dianne arrives, but he's established himself as a key plot device. As an idealized father figure and millionaire, Sam will provide Scott with a means of participating in the movie's climactic hullabaloo sequence.

Scott drives a motorboat with Dianne water-skiing in tow. From a distance, in swimsuits and looking as if they'd been wrestling each other in Vaseline instead of swimming, Jamison and Tom take notice of Dianne. Swimming towards the motorboat, Dianne loses her balance and her bikini top. Further underscoring his lewdness, Jamison recovers Dianne's bikini top from the water. He then blackmails her into having drinks with him at the hotel bar in exchange for her bikini top. It's in the unethical playboy nature of a J.J. Jamison to reduce women to prostitutes. Jamison isn't just the object of resentment, but envy. When, in defense of Dianne's interest in Jamison, Tom opines that, you "can't blame a chick for wanting the finer things in life," Scott responds by dumping Tom from the boat into the water.

On a playground full of children, Scott favors them, to their delight, with a tune about "Confidence," a performance sparked by a little girl's fear of going down a playground slide. The song is met with an extravagant exhibition of calculated choreography on behalf of all present. Lame and lengthy, the sequence once more exemplifies how Presley was being recast to appeal to a universal age demographic. He's teacher and friend to children through the magical application of his singing voice. As the universal age demographic of these movies caters more specifically to children, the more dumbed-down the movies become. From a music lesson on the virtues of confidence, the music digresses into a pastiche of the children's songs: "London Bridge," "Here We Go Gathering Nuts in May," "Frère Jacques," "Row, Row, Row Your Boat," a hoe-down and a game of cowboys and Indians. Receiving melodic assurance that all she needs is confidence, the little girl too timid to go down a slide is emboldened. She gleefully, and perhaps dangerously, suspends herself by one arm from a rapidly spinning merry-go-round. She then turns multiple pirouettes with the proficiency of a young Nureyev. The crashing idiocy of this interlude peaks with an ice cream vendor joining in to proclaim, "Ice cream for everybody!" Presley's musical charms are such that they move people to abandon concerns over their livelihoods. By co-mingling ideas of belief in self with childhood songs and games, "Confidence" is more instructive for what it doesn't say than for what it does say. Children and adults alike are musically instructed to neglect effort and hard work in order to develop talent and achieve personal aspirations. Talent and work are thereby held in contempt. It's the same contempt underlying how an otherwise undeserving but confident Jamison happens to be rich, while the wealthy Scott's magnanimity temporarily elevates an undeserving Tom Wilson to the status of a Heyward oilman.

Assuming Tom's identity is not without a down side for Scott. Jamison degrades him in front of Dianne by holding out a few bucks for him to fix his water-ski bindings. Scott declines the offer with disgust. Apparently, Scott hasn't grasped the concept of being working class, that it means you really do work for money. A conciliatory Tom accepts Jamison's money on Scott's behalf. Exeunt Jamison and Dianne. "How are you going to compete with all that money?" Tom asks Scott. The answer, according to the movie's materialist bias is, of course, that he can't. The only thing that can compete with money, we are given to understand, is more money. Scott momentarily considers aloud drawing on his family fortune. "Aren't you trying to prove something to yourself—without using your money?" Tom reminds him. Desperate measures are called for. The screenwriters equip Presley's character with an education in chemical engineering. This might not be as far-fetched as it sounds. After all, by 1967, Presley had been chemically engineering himself for years. But education alone will not suffice. He must rely on the patronage of the benevolent millionaire in the machine: the paternalistic Sam Burton. At the risk of appearing obvious, the inherent contradiction is that, to prove himself, Scott must do without relying on the fact that his father is the beneficiary of a gross inequity in the distribution of wealth. To do so, he finds it necessary to seek out another millionaire father figure. The question arises: can he really prove anything?

The hull and engine of Burton's boat need rebuilding. Burton's engineers have told him the boat is a lost cause, but Scott persuades Burton to let him try and he didn't even have to sing to do so. They agree to split the ten grand prize money in half should Scott win the Regatta. Scott advises Tom that they'd best get the boat in the shop before the clambake. "You just said the magic word!" rejoices Tom. Figurative speech becomes a literal world-changing pronouncement, particularly when proceeding from the lips of Elvis Presley.

Cut to a frenetically convulsing assembly of young adults, most noticeably, of young women in bikinis and a languishing close-up of a shapely, shaking woman's derriere, a favored shot in several Presley movies of the 1960s. This time the setting is a torch-lit bungalow community, complete with uniformed servants, a sumptuous buffet, and a swinging band featuring bongos and a lead guitar that sounds like an electric mosquito. Scott announces that the food is ready: lobster, clams, chicken, shrimp and a little something for the rest of them. Just kidding. But who appointed him, posing as a lowly water-skiing instructor, to preside over the events? This is where the movie gives the nod to another frequently occurring element in the Presley film formula: the presentation of Presley as unquestioned leader in both dangerous and non-dangerous situations. This is highly questionable. It's also ironic given the nature of his business relationship with Colonel Tom Parker. By this phase of his career, to what extent was Presley in control of his own life? As with the distribution of ice cream at the end of "Confidence," the question of who's paying for all this fancy chow would also seem a reasonable one. Having announced that the food is ready, Scott then mans an electric guitar and breaks out into a musical rendition of "the magical word," clambake, accompanied by an invisible horn section. Again, an inclusion of the infantile, this time in the title track, tells us that "Mammy's little baby loves clambake, clambake," and so on. As per the meaninglessness of the song "Singin' in the Rain," discussed above, the song has nothing to do with the screen narrative. A song about speedboat racing or the *Prince and the Pauper* framework of the movie would have made far more sense. Yet those would have been story-driven musical centerpieces. Central to this phase of Presley's career was that his movies be "Elvis-driven." An examination of the trailers and posters for these movies is revealing. What they manically stress over everything else is the most outstanding feature being promoted: ELVIS! Posters feature his name in letters twice the size or better of the titles of the movies he starred in. To be fair, however, these movies deliver exactly what the trailers and posters promise: lots of Elvis. Poor quality on every other front, but lots of Elvis.

Following the "Clambake" performance, the movie's built-in advertisement for itself in which rhythmically agitated young people dance on rooftops and leap through the air on mini-trampolines, Scott tells Jamison and Dianne of his plan to repair and race Burton's speedboat in the Regatta. Jamison dismissively advises Scott to stick to what he knows. "You mean stay where I belong," says a visibly offended Scott. While casting aspersions on Scott's abilities, the scene also reveals that Jamison is un-American in his unwillingness to concede to Scott his right to upward mobility. *Clambake* is but one more piece of an ongoing deluge of denials of what communist Theodor Dreiser, in his novel *An American Tragedy* (1926), identified as a covert caste system in America. Dreiser intimates that that system is every bit as active and oppressive as any old world caste system. Jamison and Dianne follow Tom and his female escort's example, leaving to euphemistically "search for buried treasure." Scott is left alone.

Scott adjourns to the hotel ski shop to work on Burton's speedboat. Burton arrives to be told by Scott that the hull gave way because its protective cover broke under pressure. Having studied and worked in a research lab, Scott helped develop "Goop," a hardener that he hopes will resolve the speedboat's problem. The problem with Goop is that it turns to jelly when it comes into contact with water. Perfecting Goop is Scott's challenge. The paternal Burton confesses to Scott that he used to miss never having had a son, but does no longer. This is followed by a montage of shots of Scott working alone in a lab, scanning books and diddling away on the speedboat. Tom is shown pitching in a bit.

Dianne enters the ski shop holding a rose. Could the rose be a signifier of her unconscious passion for Scott, or is she on her way to a transcendental meditation seminar? Scott asks how things are going between her and Jamison. Things are well, she says, but Jamison has yet to propose. A sage Scott advises her that Jamison will invite her to his room, where there will be soft music, pheasant under glass, wine and cherries jubilee for desert. She thanks him and leaves hesitantly, leaving the rose with Scott for all the Freudians in the audience to see. A contemplative Scott then sings the melancholic "You Don't Know Me," one of the stronger songs of Presley's whole 1960s movie career.

Burton tries to curb Scott's maniacal work ethic that has him giving water-skiing lessons all day and trying to perfect his Goop until after midnight each night. Is Scott driven by his work ethic or resentment of his father? Daytime arrives at the boat shop and, with it, a tardy Tom who claps and four bare mid-drifted young women who mysteriously become a half dozen come dancing in. "Your obedient servants!" he proclaims. This cues Scott to sing an inane pop work anthem, "Hey, Hey, Hey," a tribute to dancing labor as a mystified commodity. "We got a magic potion that will help us win, I don't know how to spell it but dig right in. Glacko-oxytonic phosphate, it's the latest scoop, but that's alright girls, you can call it Goop …We'll fall right down and have some fun, and I'm gonna kiss you all one by one," Scott waxes melodically. Then, with the job on the boat finished, the womanly girls line up and Scott proceeds to kiss each one of them. As he does, each one swoons. Despite his role-playing, here as Scott pretends to be Tom, that is, in a role within a role, he has not stopped being Elvis. Tom's enterprising last-minute solution to Scott's crisis, recruiting sexy women to function as a labor force, shows that he, Tom, has risen to demonstrate the most indispensable skill of a true capitalist. He's kept the whole rambling work functioning. In so doing, he has demonstrated his capacity to manage a crisis. All that required was to adjust the commodity status of women from decor to workers. Scott/Presley retains an awareness of himself as a commodity and his kisses as a valued service. At the core of this musical digression is the glorification of the commodity, the "magic potion," Goop, which Scott has spent so many late nights perfecting.

Burton has expressed his concern to Scott about Goop's effectiveness, but Scott replies that there isn't enough time before the big race to test it. Goop's efficacy will be tried out at the regatta. Scott informs Burton, as he told someone else the previous day, that he has to have confidence. By now that's a loaded term: the audience has been primed to accept the term "confidence" as having a magical aura, much like an advertising campaign endeavors to bestow an aura or presence on a brand name. In turn, Goop bears the imprint of Presley's aura, given the screen time and cinematic technique devoted to depicting the hard work his character has put into it. Ultimately, the "magic potion" on which the outcome of the climactic speedboat race and the propagation of democratically upward mobility depends is not rooted in labor, but belief in the magic word "confidence." This is popular culture's repudiation of Marxism. The power of the commodity does not, as Marx would have it, result from the spirit that the worker pours out of himself and into its production, but in the magic he divests into the commodity he produces. Marxism's advocacy of the primacy of labor as the basic foundation of all human undertaking is replaced by an advocacy of the primacy of language as an alleged magic. This primacy of language has a theological credibility for those who believe. Biblically, for example, "In the beginning was the Word [Christ] and the Word was with God and the Word was God. He was with God in the beginning"[26]: popular culture is engaged in a constant fragmenting of linguistic wholeness and subsequent breaking up of cognition. Instead of coherent verses such as the aforementioned, or a statement such as "The son [Christ] is the radiance of God's glory and the exact representation of his being, sustaining all things by his powerful word,"[27]. Rather than theological language, popular culture gives us mantras: "clambake," "confidence," "Goop," etc.

Free-spending capitalist tool Duster Heyward arrives at the hotel where he's surprised to learn that his son Scott has supposedly been living it up with women, drink and cigars. Of course, it's the behavior of the yahoo Tom Wilson pretending to be Scott that has caused the confusion. At the hotel bar, Sam Burton, realizing that a charade is going on, takes Duster aside to explain things to him. Scott arrives at the bar and, at Tom's request, joins his table, at which Jamison, Dianne and several other beautiful women are seated. Fulfilling Scott's prophecy, Jamison invites Dianne to his room for soft music, pheasant under glass, wine and cherries jubilee. Despite the transparency of Jamison's seduction, Dianne agrees to join him. On his way out of the bar, Burton, the rich dad in the machine, instructs Scott to check on his speedboat before going to bed. Scott complies, and it is in the shop that he comes face to face with his real father, Duster. This is the dramatic hub of the movie's conflict. Scott must now confront the cartoon whose loins he is the fruit of, the oil tycoon who has made life too easy for him by not letting him make his own mistakes. Presley emotes capably enough and is met by sympathetic bluster from Duster, who confesses to his immense new pride for his son upon learning

---

[26] John 1:1.
[27] Hebrews 1:3.

what Scott has been doing without his help. The scene is a total derailment of rock & roll from its origins: that its King should star in a movie wherein the real happy ending results from his receiving the approval of his father.

Although Jamison proposes to Dianne as he uses all the moves that Scott advised her he'd try to put on her, delivering what Dianne thought she'd been hoping for all along, she is uneasy at his advances. Scott's timing is impeccable. He arrives at Jamison's "sultan suite" with the skis Jamison gave him to repair, showing up just in time to afford Dianne with an escape at the crucial moment. Condemning Scott as a "born loser," Jamison readies himself to administer a beating to Scott. "I call karate!" announces Jamison as he assumes a mock kata stance. "Shut up," Scott says irritably and punches Jamison in the face without any martial artifice, literally knocking him for a loop. Having given Jamison a foretaste of his comeuppance, Scott takes a solitary nocturnal moonlit stroll to moan the morose melody "The Girl I Never Loved," his confession of love for Dianne. A sampling of the lyrics is instructive: "Oh the girl I never loved will never know I care, and all my dreams of her are dreams I'll never share. Oh I want her and I need her and I know it might have 'bin, but it ended long before it could begin." What on the face of it is just another sappy love song is a textbook lesson in the way an authoritarian authorship forges an irrational schism between language and meaning. The lyricist, presumably composing expressly for Presley, has him caring but not loving, has him keeping his dreams, that is, his unconscious to himself, which is probably just as well. But it's also a romantic affirmation of repression, needing and wanting "her" but never loving. "And I know it might have 'bin." The song has a melancholy quality comparable to "Everything But Love," as well as a comparable lack of substance as well.

Having eavesdropped on his lovelorn musical soliloquy, Dianne informs him that she's not going to marry Jamison. She plans to return to whatever water-skiing capital she's escaped from. The following day, she's in the stands to see the regatta. At great risk to his personal safety, given the not- fully-tested quality of the what's holding his boat together, with far more at risk than his competitors and still having something to prove, Scott goes up against three-time regatta champion Jamison. "If my boy says that Goop'll hold, it'll hold!" boasts Duster Heyward to surrogate dad Sam Burton. The gregarious Tom Wilson is embarrassed when he learns he's just tried to pass himself off to Duster as Scott. "Quick, get me some popcorn!" says the humiliated Tom as he returns to his seat next to his female escorts, realigning his identity with the anonymous movie audience. Running in the race under the name of Tom Wilson, Scott pushes the speedboat to nearly the breaking point, one supposes, and the audience is encouraged by way of reaction shots to wince along with the on-screen audience. Scott takes the lead away from Jamison and cruises to victory. The real mystery is how any thinking person might possibly have doubted this outcome. What alternative might there have been by this point? Scott proves to himself and others that he can be a loser on his own terms? Scott martyrs himself, but man's noble quest to perfect Goop lives on? Following Scott's win, Jamison isn't shown anymore. His true vanquishing occurred the previous night, when Scott ordered him to shut up and smashed him in the face. It's violence, not non-violent competition, that is upheld as the truest form of conflict resolution. Scott and Tom celebrate Scott's accomplishment over champagne before a celebratory hotel dinner. And let's not forget the true champion: the commodity. "Goop is going to be the hottest thing to hit the beach since the bikini!" crows Tom. While there are expectations, the guiding imperative for the leading man is that he must lead and he must win.

Rather than cast a critique of *Clambake* in terms of its being a Hollywood appropriation of a historical fiction vindicating capitalism, it also conceals a central truth about the significance of Marxism as a religion. Marx's *Das Kapital* (1867) has long been venerated by his devotees, with its detailed interpretations of such economic machinations of what he deemed the exploitation of labor, the nature of material production, the growth of wage labor and the banking system. In contradistinction to that which he called "the opiate of the masses," religion, Marx articulated his utopian workers' revolution within a framework he openly ripped off from the Bible. The realization of the communist revolution would be a day of reckoning in which the working class would function as the messianic agency. The evil oppressors, the bourgeoisie, would be brought low and the low, the proletariat, would be made high in a worldly materialist paradise where class struggle, what Marx and Engels presumptuously identified as synonymous with all history itself, would be completely resolved.

In his 1844 manuscript "Alienated Labour," alternatively translated as "Estranged Labour," Marx describes the conditions of material production as inclusive of the worker divesting his own spirit into the commodity he produces. The exploitative capitalist then seizes the spirit-holding commodity and sells it. The commodity then reappears, he claims, to confront the worker as a power he cannot comprehend. Despite Marx's dismissal of religion as "the opiate of the masses," it's by way of Marx's theory of alienated labor that he reveals the primitive-mindedness of his own materialist philosophy. The idea that commodities, physical objects, are inhabited by spirits is an updated re-articulation of stone-age religion of animism. As the commodity that saves the day in *Clambake*, "Goop" mirrors the magic-mindedness of Marx's version of animism, the theoretical, religious basis of modern communism.

Having defeated Jamison, winning the race and his father's approval, Scott is free to tie up the remaining loose end: propose to Dianne. Now that Dianne has proved she has no interest in

Scott's money, she can share in it. That's the necessary condition of the deal she must fulfill. She accepts Scott's marriage proposal and, once she's accepted, he drops the bomb on her. She's hit the jackpot. She's given assent to pairing off with the winning lottery ticket with Presley's face attached to it. Contrary to F. Scott Fitzgerald's observation, at least one of the very rich is like us. He just sings better and more often.

When she learns that, in reality, the shmoe she consented to marry has a huge yacht and acres of oil fields, she faints, cyclically leaving the movie to conclude with Scott trying to explain the narrative that commenced at the movie's beginning. The happy ending, a simultaneous coalescence of business and romance, emphasizes that economics and marriage can indeed be brought to a successful realization. Though idealistic, in that the movie champions the virtue of traditional marriage, despite its being less than classic cinema, *Clambake* ought not be looked on too disdainfully. Clearly dated by more contemporary secular moral standards, or the absence of them, this same championing defends civilization. In that the comparatively innocuous hedonism of *Clambake* finds its resolution in advocating for traditional marriage and, by implication, the civilizing qualities of that institution and covenant relationship, the movie isn't without merit for those distressed by the proliferation of present day sexual chaos, or possibly we can see in the movie its espousal of values deemed amusingly antiquated.

THE IGNOBLE SAVAGE

Presley's turn as a hard-loafin' Indigenous American hedonist is the focus of 1968's *Stay Away, Joe*. With fewer songs, though none the worse for that and more attempted comedy, again, not Presley's strong suit, *Stay Away, Joe* possesses another minor strand of biographical authenticity: a fictional extension of Presley's part-Cherokee heritage. As a portrayal of contemporary American Indians in the 1960s, the movie capitalizes on the fashionableness of Native Americans, people whose seemingly willful rejection of materialism neatly coalesced with tendencies of the counterculture of the day. As another disparaging representation of those who dropped out of conventional society to opt for living in communes, *Stay Away, Joe* could hardly be said to honor American Indigenous people. Heroically giving up, courageously dismissing any possibility of doing better, these are hardly complimentary or flattering characterizations of any people. While Presley's mother is played by the Latina Katy Jurado, the tribal majority are played by Caucasians. As such, *Stay Away Joe* is less an Indigenous person's comedy than a White person's racist fantasy about Indians.

The film's opening credits show aerial shots of the rocky peaks of the Arizona desert, accompanied by a voice-over of Presley singing "Where the Hills Don't Say Stay Away," sung to the tune of "Greensleeves." It's operatically kitsch, but Presley carries it off admirably. Joe Lightcloud (Presley) returns to his parents' place on the reservation in a flashy convertible. He's welcomed by his old pal Bronc (L.Q. Jones). The happy reunion includes their having a spontaneous wrestling match in Joe's car. Throughout *Stay Away, Joe,* it's repeatedly suggested that wrestling and outright brawling are preferred means for communicating and expressing affection between American Indian men. After jovially chasing down a herd of cattle with his car, Joe exhibits his laughably Indian inability to take proper care of material possessions by driving his convertible into a large pond of muddy water.

At Joe's folks' place on the rez, his eccentric father Charlie (Burgess Meredith) is shouting at a pack of barking dogs to shut them up while negotiating a deal with a visiting congressman. The congressman tells Charlie that, if he can get a government handout for free cattle, Charlie will "be an example to every other Indian in the territory." At first, Charlie responds to the proposition by struggling to catch a chicken while observing smoke signals on the horizon. Crotchety Grandpa (Thomas Gomez), a self-described direct descendant of great chiefs and mighty warriors, says the smoke signals say that Joe is coming home, and so they need to "get ready for a big whoop-up." Charlie rhapsodizes about being able, by way of tending cattle, "to prove that an Indian can be fine, hard-working American citizen and not a lazy bum, like some White men think." Charlie Lightcloud's mission is to contradict a negative stereotype. He's a man with a mission, as will be his son Joe.

Erratically driving the family jalopy, Joe's mother Annie Lightcloud (Katy Jurado) runs the congressman's car off the dirt road to her house. She dismisses the idea of Charlie becoming a cattleman, reminding him of his failed attempts at both oil well and golf course entrepreneurship. Despite her nay-saying, a truck delivers twenty heifers to the Lightclouds. Joe arrives on a bull to receive an ecstatic welcome from the tribe, but the bull soon becomes agitated and throws him off. One of the residents from the rez congratulates him, "You sure rode that bull, Joe!" while punching him in the face. Joe wrestles in the dirt with a half dozen other Indians as they exchange social niceties. He mentions trading off something for some "city fella's wife" during the fracas, how sleeping under a roof doesn't feel natural to him anymore, and how they don't make Cadillacs like they used to. Native women and children look on admiringly, both at Joe and the casual violence. Civilized, verbal communication coincides with physical violence, an abandonment of civilized communication.

As the rough-housing dissipates, Joe pulls out a hundred-dollar bill that his fellow Indians stare at in stunned amazement. Joe announces that they're going to have a party, one that "could last a week, or a month—however long the beer holds out." Exemplary of negative racial stereotyping, this, the lone instance of Presley's movie persona having inconsistent sobriety, seeks to make much comedic hay out of drunkenness and, specifically, drunken Indians. The very thought of a hundred 1968 dollars' worth of beer seems sufficient in itself for the men and women present to jump and frolic in another pond of muddy water. These people need no encouragement to spontaneously sacrifice personal hygiene.

The evening's beer bacchanalia features a jubilant country and western band. A grinning Charlie, none too vitally concerned with his noble savage dignity, crawls on all fours across a crowded dance floor. Meanwhile, wife Annie puffs on a cigar. Joe sings the title song, "Stay Away, Joe," including a reiteration of the Presley sexual smorgasbord creed: "love 'em and leave 'em." He then hugs and kisses various women as everyone claps along. Joe's younger sister Mary, having found employment at a bank, is referred to by a tribe member as "being city folk now." She joins the party with her clean-cut White boyfriend Lorne Hawkins (Angus Duncan). Lorne has bought out the local newspaper. He's starkly contrasted against the other party-goers as the only one there in suit and tie.

Taking notice of a nicely-proportioned young woman on the dance floor whose hindquarters are given repeated close-ups, Joe tells Bronc, "She can chew on my moccasins anytime." That is, Joe's attraction to her is such that he's prepared to subject her to ethnically specific forms of degraded intimacy. Bronc cautions Joe that the woman, Billy Jo, is girlfriend to imposing-looking Frank Hawk (Michael Lane) who "watches her like a hawk." Joe approaches Frank, hinting that the man dancing with his girlfriend is getting too familiar. Flying into a fit of violent jealousy, Frank attacks the man dancing with Billy Jo. Within moments, the men are all duking it out with each other. The women, or "squaws" as they're repeatedly referred to, continue dancing and, eventually, many of them join in the fighting. One woman joining in the ruckus smiles broadly as her head is pulled backwards by her hair and the band proverbially plays on. The audience need not care either. Presumably, this is just another example of how Indians have a good time. A bag of flour bursts into a dust cloud and, in another of many failed comedic moments, a group of dogs mutely looks on. Meanwhile, Joe, the true instigator of the riot, has sneaked outside with Billy Jo.

After the brawl has gone on for a quite a stretch, Joe returns to break it up, again identifying the Presley protagonist as leader and again demonstrating the readiness of those around him to submit to his authority. Frank Hawk asks Billy Jo, who has returned with Joe, if she is all right. "Uh-huhhh," she drawls with a heavy inflection of having just been sexually satisfied. This is the first time it's so strongly implied that a Presley protagonist, the G-rated sex symbol, has just had sexual intercourse with someone. As a moment in screen history, it's a development concurrent not only with the growing permissiveness in American cinema but also, tellingly, the representation of a Native American. Casual sex is the perfect companion to casual violence.

Mary, Joe's sister, works the title of the movie into the goings-on once more, asking Joe why he always returns to the reservation instead of "staying away and making something of [himself]." "Maybe it's because I wanna know that this place is still here if I need it," says Joe. In saying as much, the free-wheeling Joe integrates into his partying creed an acknowledgement of a dependency on White America to sustain his choice of lifestyle. The reservation, the crumb bequeathed to Native Americans out of governmental philanthropy, is a place offering no opportunities, but it's also a place that even the tribal best and brightest still need.

Meanwhile, Joe and Mary's mother Annie takes a bath in an outdoor tub in plain view of all present. The "Whoop-Up" continues as a side of beef roasts on a spit. More drinking, dancing and brawling goes on. Men haul away women caveman-style to secluded areas, presumably for the purposes of acquiring carnal knowledge. The typical American Indian social is represented as closely resembling a gathering of budding, alcoholic adolescents.

The following day, Charlie exits his shack with his face much darker than it previously appeared. The change of movie make-up might have been intended to communicate what a hungover Indian looks like. Yet he better resembles someone about to get down on one knee Jolson-style, breaking out into singing a chorus of "Mammy." Charlie, Joe and an apoplectic Annie discover that, during the previous night's revelry, Bronc was "so stoned" that he butchered their bull for the barbecue instead of a cow. Joe allays his parents' anxieties by telling them that he can obtain a 700-pound blue ribbon stud. Going to the roadside bar of an aged White woman named Glenda Callahan (Joan Blondell) to use her phone, Joe discovers that Glenda's mini-dress-wearing daughter, "Little" Mamie (Quentin Dean)—specializing in extemporaneous, sensuous writhing and squirming, has turned nineteen. Glenda comes on to Joe somewhere around the same time, telling him she's being watched by the police. They want to limit her sales to beer and wine. When Joe and Mamie get too friendly with each other, Glenda chases Joe off with a shotgun, birthing another unfunny running joke.

Expanding on his roguish ways, Joe wrangles a car salesman—whose lot sign boasts, "We Trade on Anything"—into swapping a new convertible for Joe's old nag. The sequence, silent apart from musical accompaniment, transpires in fast motion, a popular device in 1960s comedies that harked back to silent movies. As a mini-ideology play, the Indian is shown to have equal rights under the law to swindle someone out of something of significant value, a basic principle that the country was founded on. In another one of the movie's blunted allusions to Native mysticism, American Indian spirituality is reduced to the quality of sneakiness.

In town, as part of his scheme to do some wrestling with Mamie, Joe invites Deputy Sheriff Hank Matson (Brad Parker) over to Glenda's place for all the beer he can drink in ten minutes. Once more, beer is identified as a completely innocuous beverage. "Mamie, Mamie, lovely little Mamie," sings Joe to invisible orchestral accompaniment playing "Frère Jacques," another musical inclusion of the infantile as he recklessly drives off. "I'll see ya there, redskin!" the deputy affably yells at Joe. Since it was still the name of the Washington Redskins football team, the term "redskin" wasn't deemed bigoted.

Joe makes a pass at Glenda, arranging to meet her at Flagstaff, a ruse to get her away from her daughter Mamie. As soon as Glenda leaves in Joe's car, a logistical problem that leaves no way for Joe to get to Flagstaff, the deputy and Bronc arrive as Mamie drags Joe into her bedroom. Glenda returns to find a raucous party taking place in her establishment, a party wherein liberal use is made of her liquor and her daughter. Glenda lets the air out of all of Joe's tires, then chases him off with her shotgun for a second time. Presley's Joe Lightfoot has proven himself to be a true id-motivated idiot, indiscriminately conniving while courting sex, drunkenness and death, all the while seamlessly moving from generating one raucous party after another. Of all of his feature films, *Stay Away, Joe* is conspicuous for presenting Presley at his most hedonistic extreme.

Bronc arrives at Charlie and Annie's place with Dominic, an indifferent blue-ribbon bull. Joe gets Annie the money to fix up his parents' shack by selling parts from his new convertible. Manifesting another variation on the Presley screen identity as polygamous potentate, Joe cruises along in a partially stripped-down convertible with a carload of delighted young women. That's followed by the unfortunate musical ode to Dominic, the impotent stud bull. The song is presented in voice-over as an increasingly exhausted Joe chases two gradually disrobing, but never fully naked, young women. Joe continues financing the renovation of his parents' place by selling unseen government-supplied heifers alongside the ongoing joke of selling parts from his gradually dismantled convertible. The running gag concerning Joe's treatment of his cars is a double-edged indictment of the American Indian and the then-burgeoning counterculture. The American Indian is esteemed as comical because of his disregard for the idols of consumerism. Because he's too lazy to work, it's suggested, Joe lacks a proper appreciation for the value of manufactured goods. Attenuating this racist characterization, the American Indian demonstrates the laughable primitivism of an anti-materialist outlook.

New goods such as a television, an oven and, to a fanfare accompaniment, a toilet are shown streaming into Charlie and Annie's place. Dominic continues reluctantly performing his designated duty for the herd. Following the sale of the transmission and wheels from his car, Joe whimsically tosses the cash from the sale into the wind, the Indian's defiant refusal to be civilized. The destruction of currency made iconoclastic incursions into other movies of the era, including *Ocean's Eleven* (1960), *Who's Minding The Mint* (1967) and *The Magic Christian* (1969). Outside at night in a downpour, Joe tries getting comfortable in the remnant of his convertible. To the accompaniment of baying hounds, he simultaneously sings the lightly bluesy lament, "All I Needed was the Rain," a melodic meditation about a woman who left him when his liquor money ran out.

The following day, nothing if not resourceful, that is, capable, but unwilling to take his proper place in the melting pot and the labor force, Joe repairs an old motorbike, and then visits Mamie. His sister Mary is joined by her upright beau Lorne, a banally contemptible 1960s stereotype of the successful White male contributor to society. His mother Mrs. Hawkins, perhaps an oedipal referencing to her watching Lorne like a hawk, arrives to visit the Lightcloud's house. After Mrs. Hawkins comments on the niceness of the Lightcloud home, Lorne steps through a hole in the floor and, struggling to retain his balance, puts his arm through a section of the living room wall that's only wallpaper stretched across support beams. "Would either of you like to use the toilet?" Charlie asks Lorne and his mother to show his civility. That's followed by the collapse of a cheap chandelier.

Armed with a six-shooter and calling Joe a "no good, cradle-robbing, dirty bum," Glenda arrives to hunt down Joe for his suspected impropriety with Mamie. He avoids her by jumping through a bathroom wall that turns out to be just another screen of wallpaper. As he makes his escape on a motorbike, Joe pilfers another kiss from Mamie, leaving her to squat in a dirty pond, again to the sound of "Frère Jacques." "Looks like you and I weren't meant for each other, baby," he tells her. Mamie is another configuration of a typical Elvis fan. Now on the cusp of adulthood, but sexually unknowing, the virginal Mamie wants to be up-to-date in her mini-dress and eagerness for sexual initiation. However, Glenda, the prohibitive maternal force, prevents Mamie's realization of becoming the completely sexualized pleasure unit that is otherwise characteristic of her.

Joe visits Mary at her workplace, the bank. He apologizes for spoiling the family meeting with Lorne and his mother. She tells Joe she's written Lorne a good-bye letter. He urges her sternly to make a go of it with Lorne, calling her a phony, one who enjoys feeling sorry for herself. Presley again manifests his efficacy as pop therapist, code for being an expert at telling people off. Having tried to set his sister straight, Joe encounters Deputy Sheriff Hank Matson on the sidewalk, punching him in the face for giving him a bum steer about Dominic's capacity as a stud. "Just like old times!" chuckles Hank. The two then indulge in vigorous fisticuffs. "Dominic the twelfth ... just happens to be the best buckin' bull on the eastern circuit. He ain't never 'bin rode," says Hank. Joe takes Dominic "the virgin bull" to the rodeo where he wagers all the cowboys in attendance that no one except himself can stay on Dominic for eight seconds. Evidently, like his father, Joe has something to prove too. Dominic[28] then throws a succession of cowboys into the air in slow motion. Glenda arrives to coerce Joe into a shotgun marriage with Mamie. Four Indian toughs show up to settle the score with Joe for his having dallied with their girlfriends. Joe rides Dominic successfully as a crowd of bandaged cowboys look on dejectedly. This is not so much a statement on the Indian's superior rodeo prowess as it is a reiteration of the enchanted quality of the Presley protagonist. Even livestock aren't immune to his animal magnetism.

---

[28] This same cinematic device was pioneered by film maker Leni Riefenstahl in her notorious 1935 Nazi propaganda documentary *The Triumph of the Will*.

The congressman and the banker return to Charlie and Annie's, whereupon they reprimand Charlie for selling government cattle to the stockyard. Lorne tries to take a resistant Mary away with him. Joe repeats his triumphal entry to the reservation by returning with a bill of sale for 100 cattle that he's bought in his father Charlie's name. Charlie's government subsidy of cattle has been multiplied fivefold. The gleeful congressman commences planning for publicizing Charlie's and his own success. It's now official. Indians are not bums, as if any movie setting out to establish such a proposition deserved a hearing in the first place. Upon insisting to Glenda that all he and Mamie did was kiss, Glenda curbs her shotgun and admits she must have a talk about the birds and the bees with her dim bulb of a daughter. An impossibly long brawl breaks out between Joe and the jealous boyfriends. However, all ends happily and homelessly, as the brawl destroys every vestige of Charlie and Annie's facade of a respectable house. The place collapses into total wreckage as Mary and the persistent Lorne kiss. She's been assimilated. Joe is re-confirmed as a bachelor with the threat of a shotgun wedding now averted. "One helluva fight!" pronounces Joe as he, Charlie, Annie and all others present roar with laughter. The movie climaxes with the total annihilation of the idea that an American Indian couple might possibly succeed in emulating middle-class White people. The fighting has remained wholesomely bloodless and without bruising. In keeping with an observation made earlier in this book, that the Presley movies display violence as a form of pleasure in its own right, the combatants here display more resilience against registering pain than animated cartoon characters. The net result is the propagation of another surreal idea, that there exists a people capable of tirelessly engaging in a largely consequence-free violence.

Didactically, this is how the movie cleanses collective White consciences. American Indians are repeatedly shown enjoying being beaten down and are oblivious to pain and suffering. The display of a comingling of violence with every aspect of the Indian's life is White America's excuse for building a nation on genocide. How else does one reason with a people who, as shown here, laugh at their own homelessness? Violence is shown to be essential to the Indian's way of life, something stemming from a statically stereotypical warrior spirit. Violence, it's implied, is the only way the White man can get through to him. It's a matter of no small coincidence that, when America's faith in materialism was being questioned as never before, one of the world's supposedly least materialistic people groups should be targeted by such a mean-spirited cultural attack.

INTERNAL COMBUSTION
ENGINES: THE MUSICAL

Following the bizarre, bigoted faux-look at America's Indigenous underbelly in *Stay Away, Joe,* Presley returned to more predictable, familiar territory. As Steve Grayson in 1968's *Speedway,* Presley is again an accomplished race car driver, this time of stock cars. Concurrent with *Speedway's* presentation of stock car racing is the theme of debt. In its own way, *Speedway* is more single-minded about money than any other Presley movie. Due largely to bad management from his lifelong pal Kenny Donford (a reconfigured Bill Bixby from *Clambake*), Steve owes the government a lot more than the pledge of allegiance. The third leg of this stool is, inevitably, another romance. This time, the love interest is played by Nancy Sinatra. She's hyperbolically billed in the previews as "the queen of pop," presumably based on the strength of her one hit "These Boots are Made for Walkin'" (1966). The path to true love between her majesty and the King of Rock & Roll doesn't run smoothly for much of the movie. Propelling the narrative is another co-mingling of romance and commerce, though far more so than any comparable forerunner.

The up-tempo, Presley-sung, opening theme is significant only for being a song about the thrills of stock car racing, doing so without positing any analogies between stock car racing and making out with or objectifying women, all to a fat-sounding jazz orchestral accompaniment. *Speedway* commences familiarly with Presley, as Steve Grayson, driving up in a red convertible to the well-appointed mobile home he shares with pal Kenny. Kenny is introduced trying to force himself on Miss Charlotte Speedway (played by the real-life Miss Beverly Hills of the time). Steve pries Kenny off Miss Charlotte and gives him the bum's rush, leaving the room as he explains to her his business and friendship involvement with Kenny. Steve returns to her in racing overalls. He's openly costuming himself for how he's to be packaged for the ensuing narrative, the narrative clearly being secondary to the main focal point, Presley himself. He shares a passionate kiss with Miss Beverly Hills until Kenny returns to inform her that her appearance is required at a drivers' meeting. She leaves in a panic. Contextualizing Presley as a man introduced on the receiving end of an amorous welcome from a beauty queen also imbues him with superior sexual status.

Despite nearby fire from a nearby smoking tire, Steve successfully battles his way into winning another race. Awarded a trophy at a floral arch of roses, surrounded by dignitaries and photographers, he bestows kisses on Miss Charlotte Speedway. Internal Revenue Service agent Susan Jacks (Nancy Sinatra) phones her boss, Mr. Hepworth (Gale Gordon, Lucille Ball's stiff-necked banker boss on TV's *The Lucy Show* [1962–68]), informing him of Steve's 77-hundred-dollar win. North American mass audiences of the time would have readily accepted Gordon as a killjoy in charge of overseeing lots of money. Returning to his mobile home, he finds Susan waiting in his living room. "A pretty girl like you didn't come here to talk about money," he says, indifferent to the fact that his home is occupied by a total stranger. For no apparent reason, Kenny, shoved outside by Steve, frantically locks the two indoors together. When he then unlocks one of the doors moments later, Susan, having disappeared through the French doors like a phantom, has vanished.

At an evening hangout called The Hangout, Steve is coaxed into performing. He sings well too. Before a full house is seated in mock automobiles, he performs "Let Yourself Go," a series of lyrical instructions for the musically informed seduction of young women. Familiarly-clad in a red windbreaker, possibly his most often resorted to on-screen color, the attire recalls James Dean's Jim Stark in *Rebel Without a Cause* (1955). The idea of serving liquor to people in imitation automobiles suggests a cavalier attitude toward drinking and driving. Thematically, *Speedway* is a celebration of the automobile and American automobile culture. Driving real cars to a nightclub to sit and consume alcohol in fake cars is a bizarre symbolic equation, adults sitting in toy cars and drinking liquor.

Having paid musical tribute to the movie's other idol, the automobile, Steve finds Susan seated at one of the nightclub's "sedan booths." Producing a silver racing helmet, he pretends it's a crystal ball and tells Susan he sees a new man coming into her life. She's unimpressed as he makes a failed attempt to hypnotize her with a wristwatch that he accidentally drops into a drink. The Presley protagonist's magic charm has been scaled back, but his fortune-telling will eventually come to fruition. Nonplussed by Steve's advances, Susan leaves. In another "sedan-booth," Kenny puts the moves on a dumb blond (Gari Hardy, identified in the closing credits as "Dumb Blond"). When asked by a nightclub magician to help with one of his tricks, Kenny declines, saying, "I already have a trick of my own," to the blonde's approving giggle. It's a fairly risqué line, given that "a trick" is also slang for a liaison with a prostitute.

A little tyke is shown stealing a half dozen hot dogs from the nightclub concession stand. Steve picks up the tab for the red hots and soda, and then follows the tyke outdoors to a station wagon and her destitute dad, Abel Esterlake (William Schallert) and her five little sisters. It's another occasion demonstrating Presley's instantaneous rapport with children. We don't hear Esterlake's story, why he's single, has five little girls within a couple of years in age of one another, with none of them resembling him or each other. It's hinted at that his impoverishment resulted from a racing background in which he injured his leg. He's also the lone example of a homeless White man in a Presley movie. Yet in America, even those reduced to penury are not without a car of their own.

Steve returns to The Hangout where Susan sings the decidedly dated "'Till You Bring Your Groovy Self on Home to Me." It's all in a day's work for an IRS field agent. Whereas Presley's singing "Let Yourself Go" featured a seven-man rock band accompaniment rather than the ordinary four or five at most, Susan has an eight-man rock band accompaniment. The over-determined theatricality suggests that playing rock & roll is far more labor-intensive than might otherwise be supposed. In a generically-maternal way, she gives musical advice on what a young woman is to expect of the young man in her life, not talking to strangers on buses and things to that effect. That is, young women really ought not to expect much of the young men in their lives. Meanwhile, Kenny maneuvers Dumb Blond over to his mobile home where he scares her into staying with him, using a tape recording of wild animals to persuade her that they're just outside the door. Steve arrives to expose Kenny's ruse, whereupon Dumb Blond knocks Kenny unconscious with a swat from a club stuffed into her mink. The idea that man might need to take recourse to such gimmickry to win a woman's affection, though absurd, finds its more plausible correlative in the movie's promotion of the automobile, the ultimate gimmick, as fundamental to getting a woman.

The following day, Steve and Kenny visit Abel and his kids, this time with the free gift of a new station wagon filled with a month's worth of groceries. In America, there's no good reason for anyone to not have plenty of food and a working automobile. Popular culture makes a rough approximation of imitating life when Elvis gives away not a Cadillac, but a station wagon. Little Ellie Esterlake (Victoria Meyerink) tells Steve she wants to marry him. He responds by singing the quasi-children's song "Your Time hasn't Come Yet Baby." The song includes such lyrics as, "When it does your heart will know ... You got a few dreams to go." This lyrical instruction is commendable in that it promotes both marriage and a later age of consent.

Steve wins another race and 9,500 dollars. Susan dutifully reports it to Mr. Hepworth. Accompanied by another beautiful woman, Steve goes to a drive-in restaurant, one featuring the then-fashionable display of go-go dancers in cages. Caged go-go dancers raise several questions: is this just another manifestation of the commodity status of women? Does the caged go-go dancer suggest that a woman, by definition, is someone who must be punished? Or rather, is dancing identified here as a form of penitence? Are the cages there to keep the women in or to keep us out? It bespeaks an irrational promotion of the contradiction of woman in Western civilization, at once free and visibly bereft of freedom, wildly expressing both herself and her confinement, simultaneously manifesting her physicality and the prohibition against her doing so. Possibly too, it bespeaks the political position of American popular culture of the day toward the emerging women's rights movement, that it was deemed something that needed to be contained.

At the drive-in, Steve is served by a weepy waitress (Charlotte Considine) who relates a literal sob story to him about her boyfriend's not having enough money to complete his vocational training. Steve and Kenny, the two-man welfare state, strike again. The waitress and her boyfriend have their wedding financed by the magnanimous pair. Here an inexplicable plot point surfaces. Susan Jacks is present to see off the newlyweds. Either she's keeping far closer surveillance of Steve and Kenny than we've been shown, or they all inhabit the same, magical world where everyone knows what everyone else is doing. It's no slight coincidence that a downside of communal living, its potential for totalitarianism, is referred to through the inclusion of the I.R.S., one of the American government's most ruthless institutions. Steve and Kenny digress into one of the rankest of propaganda exhibitions for any Presley movie. A score of men in conservatively tailored dark suits, many of them conspicuously smoking cigarettes or cigars, sit in the waiting room to see Mr. Hepworth. Presley's Steve Grayson is distinguished by his suit of Nixon blue, as opposed to the more staid black and charcoal tones of the otherwise identically tailored suits. These are the official uniforms of the American taxpayer and politician alike. Steve confesses his worry to Kenny, then all those present to join his performance of "He's Your Uncle, Not Your Dad," which, by virtue of it's unmitigated jingoism, bears some spelling out, should the reader still doubt the significance of Presley's movies as ideological statements.

He's your uncle, not your dad,
He's the best friend you ever had,
So come on and dig, dig, dig 'till it hurts,
Just remember Pearl Harbor, the Alamo
When nothing could be worse,
He's your favorite relative,
And he needs a lot to live,
So just bring, bring, bring everything until you bleed,
And he'll send back what he don't need …
Just be thankful you don't live in Leningrad.

Every man present on screen joins in the dance, some of them providing backup harmony and lyrical flourishes. At times moving in tight, shoulder-to-shoulder formation, they perform a hybrid of the can-can and a burlesque on military marching while holding each other's hands. A startled Mr. Hepworth steps out into the waiting room and gets drawn into the dancing as if unwittingly swept up in a gay pride parade.

In discussing Freud, T.W. Adorno noted that Freud believed "that the bond which integrates individuals into a mass, is of a libidinal nature," and that Hitler "was well aware of the libidinal source of mass formation through surrender when he attributed specifically female, passive features to the participants of his meetings, and thus also hinted at the role of unconscious homosexuality in mass psychology."[29] Just as fascist oration relies on the formation of a latent homosexual link among audiences for its persuasiveness, things in this scene are more than a trifle festive. The choreography of "He's Your Uncle, Not Your Dad" is pretty blatant stuff hidden in plain sight. The only thing keeping the number beyond reproach is the audience's knowledge of Steve and Kenny's raging heterosexuality. Another irrational schism is posited as the manly, patriotic musicality is juxtaposed against a corresponding homosexual dance number. The appeal in the lyrics to wars both hot and cold: Pearl Harbor, the Alamo and Leningrad, suggest that more is being marshaled here than the transformation of Presley into another plastic establishment creep, as the vernacular of the day might have put it. This is in essence the 1968 equivalent to a pitch for war bonds to support the continuing U.S. invasion of Vietnam.

When the delirium subsides, Hepworth privately interviews Steve and Kenny over their jointly filed tax return. In part because of Kenny's bad management, in part because of Kenny's gambling (shades of 1961's *It Happened at the World's Fair*) and in part because of their illegitimate charitable expenses, Kenny and Steve owe the government $145,000. They are put on a

---

[29] T.W. Adorno, "Freudian Theory and the Pattern of Fascist Propaganda", pp. 121-22.

budget and, afterward, Susan shows up at their home where she phones Hepworth to inform him that Steve has just raced to another $7,500 victory. Susan falls back into an easy chair, thus inadvertently activating the play function on Steve and Kenny's tape recorder. The recording is of Steve uttering a hypnotic incantation. It is the second instance of a reference to hypnosis articulated by the Presley protagonist, the focal point of the spectacle. Here, it is as if the screenwriters were taking their cues directly from Adorno: "Socialized hypnosis breeds within itself the forces which will do away with the spook of regression through remote control, and in the end awaken those who keep their eyes shut though they are not asleep."[30] It is Susan who is thus far under the influence of "the spook of regression." How else are we to account for her capacity to resist Steve?

When Steve and Kenny return home again, completely unruffled by Susan's uninvited presence, she identifies herself as an IRS agent. Kenny leaves and Steve gets seductive (without even singing!) "Nothing personal," she tells him; "it's just my job." They have a spat and she leaves, only to tell the returning Kenny on her way off his lot that he'll only be getting half of what Steve will receive after Kenny further aggravates her. This smacks of something of a warning to the taxpayer-viewer. The I.R.S. agent is only doing her job one moment, yet may capriciously act in a punitive expression of power the next. "That iceberg!" Steve says to Kenny. As per Lili "The Iceberg" in 1960's *G.I. Blues* and Nurse Diane in *It Happened at the World's Fair,* for any woman to resist Presley is deemed abnormal.

There's another bit of business regarding Kenny's physical safety being threatened by his bookie, some back and forth between him and Susan, then between Steve and Susan. Without any exposition, the two friends have learned where

---

30   T.W. Adorno, 'Freudian Theory and the Pattern of Fascist Propaganda", p. 137.

her hotel is. Kenny watches a woman made to look seven feet tall drink herself into unconsciousness at Susan's hotel bar, one of the few presumed options for those outside the requisite physical requirements to play the sexual field. Kenny is threatened a second time by his bookie. The monotony of the plot machinations resonate with the tedium of the movie's central spectacle of stock car racing.

Abel and his brood of little girls, their car repossessed because Kenny's New Deal economics means paying for things with checks, show up at Steve and Kenny's place. Feuding between Steve and Susan escalates. She slaps his face and flees to her hotel room. More violence is added as Steve puts his fist through her hotel room door, knocking down a passing stranger in the process. He threatens to "knock the stubbornness out of her head" in a crowded elevator. Other passengers chime in with an endeared "Aww." He chases her into the hotel lobby where she's meeting Steve's racing rival Paul

Dado (Ross Hagen) shows up. Earlier he scorned Steve. Now, he's a prime target to have his clock cleaned. Steve takes two punches to the head before counter punching and sending Dado sliding all the way across the hotel lobby floor. Never mind that a blow of half that force would have taken Dado's head off, the gratuitous inclusion incorporates that other too-familiar-ingredient of Presley movies. Steve steers Susan into a closed area of the hotel where they continue telling each other off and, having verbally exhausted their mutual animosity, they kiss. By this point it appears as if Presley is sharing his prescriptions with his songwriters. He launches into the extra mushy "Just One Kiss would Tell us Who We Are," featuring the borderline psychotic question, "Are we really here or lost in time?"

On discovering that the IRS has repossessed his home, Steve puts up the extra-saccharine Esterlake kids into Susan's hotel bedroom. "They're adorable," says the maternally reconfigured I.R.S. agent. She calls Mr. Hepworth to advise him of Steve's threat, that, unless allowed to keep a portion of the prize money for "personal obligations," _____. Hepworth consents under protest. Steve blows his engine during a test run. Team Grayson is bust, but with Susan's bright idea that they borrow replacement parts and Esterlake volunteering knowledge of where to get some, Steve and his pit crew labor on his car all night, with entertainment value interjected through the depreciated levity of a couple of pit crew members.

Escalating tensions is the accidental presence of Abel Esterlake, who pops up in Steve's backseat during the race. He'd fallen asleep in the back of Steve's car during the lengthy repair session. Esterlake mugs comically, presumably to provide vicarious amplification of the thrill and danger of being in a stock car race. Steve wins third place, good enough to secure him enough prize money to temporarily alleviate his and Kenny's trouble with the I.R.S. As per so many other Presley features, *Speedway* concludes with Presley in a nightclub. Although his Steve Grayson character is still in debt to the I.R.S., he happily performs a duet with Susan, the situationally non-specific, "There ain't Nothing Like a Song," from a rotating, faux convertible, as per higher end automobile showrooms of that time. In a manner more than a trifle totalitarian, the hero has found true love with a prying I.R.S. who never respected his civil rights.

Above and beyond any other Presley feature, *Speedway* comments on economics, as well as the centrality of the automobile to American life. A subsidiary element in *Clambake,* in *Speedway,* the automobile is a theme in its own right. The movie engages three principle themes: first, there's the theme of tax debt feeding the story's basic conflict informing the hero's romance. That theme is echoed through second banana Kenny's gambling misadventures. Further filling out the threadbare plot is Steve and Kenny's philanthropy toward Esterlake and his daughters, as well as toward Lori, the overwrought drive-in waitress, all aligned with the forces of good. Steve's philanthropy is more incentive for the audience to be on his side. Third, prize money is how Steve and his crew receive an earthly blessing for their efforts. Yet effort, labor and even risking one's life are not sufficient to secure remuneration. Good luck or, theologically, grace or unmerited favor, are also necessary components for victory.

Stock car racing is analogous to the workings of a money-based economy. Uncannily replicating the workings of a capitalist economy, the dollar, historically the fundamental unit of American and Canadian currency, ranks among four categories. M-zero dollars are closely controlled by narrow monetary policy. M-three dollars are least closely controlled by monetary policy. In between are M-one dollars, those invested in the bank, and M-two dollars, those the bank lends out. Depending on the vitality of the economy at any given time, economists estimate that M-two dollars are loaned out at a rate of anywhere from six to twenty M-two dollars for every M-one dollar deposited in the bank. Much of the health of the economy and the dollar are largely determined by the velocity of the movement of M-two dollars. The movement of M-two dollars is integral to sustaining and growing the economy. That's how currency functioned when this Presley movie was filmed and did for some time afterward. In an economy based on the primacy of keeping currency moving at a brisk pace, rapidity of movement is glorified, even exalted, in various ways by popular culture. Stock car racing is an allegory for the economy, starring the internal combustion engine. Fetish elements of the automobile race, engine power, speed, competition and the falsified rarity of remuneration for labor (prize money) combine in an extravagant spectacle positing athletic heroism manifested through high-speed driving.

Although engaged in a dangerous profession, as race car driver Steve Grayson, Presley is again the focal point of the leisure industry. The threat of inflation is something John Kenneth Galbraith described conservatives as having always taken more seriously than unemployment, with its "persistent threat to social balance ... [which] requires that there be a substitute for production as a source of income—and that it be ample."[31] Meeting his duty as a taxpayer, Steve Grayson is rewarded by finding true love with his own personal agent of government surveillance. In today's era of digital and electronic capital, an era in which paper money is increasingly marginalized, a fairy tale in which much of the narrative relies on the primacy of intangibles might make for even better cinema.

---

[31] John Kenneth Galbraith, *The Affluent Society,* p. 246.

THE TAMING
OF THE PELVIS

B ased on a novel entitled *Kiss My Firm But Pliant Lips* (1965),[32]
Presley's next movie project, *Live a Little, Love a Little*
(1968), is a weird reflection on the counterculture of that time.
In his most permissive role, Presley unintentionally romances
a flighty young woman. Incorporating then-salacious allusions
to sex in advertising and sanitized pornography, the movie isn't
among Presley's more impressive cinematic accomplishments.
As photographer Greg Nolan, Presley is introduced driving
another motorized conveyance. Production designers assert
Presley's contemporaneity by displaying him in one of the most
up-to-the-minute late-1960s leisure accessories: a dune buggy.
With equal parts jubilation and recklessness, Presley plows
along the beach, musically accompanied by his own voice-over
singing the ultra-schmaltzy "(In This Wonderful, Wonderful,
Wonderful) Wonderful World."

Greg Nolan arrives at a vacant beach to fiddle with his
camera. He's interrupted by an attractive young woman in a
bathing suit. "Today I feel like Alice," she tells him. After citing

---

[32] By Dan Greenburg, who also shares the screenplay credit with
Michael A. Hoey.

several other aliases, she identifies herself as Bernice (Michele Carey). Within moments of meeting Greg, she propositions him for sex. A variation on the 1960s undiagnosed, free-spirited female flake, she's comparable to Julie Christie's starring role in *Petulia* (1968), Goldie Hawn's dancing bubble head on TV's *Laugh-In* (1968–73) or, to a lesser extent, Jo Symington (Dodie Marshall) of *Easy Come, Easy Go* (1967). At first, female roles identified with the emerging women's rights movement were often typified by Hollywood as kooky eccentrics. Part precursor to current, postmodern strains of disdain for the contributions of European men to civilization, these female eccentrics mocked male rationalism.

Greg kisses Bernice disinterestedly, then busies himself with military calisthenics. Upon being told by Greg that kissing her firm but pliant lips didn't cause him to feel anything, Bernice's Great Dane Albert chases him into the ocean until sunset. Fevered and exhausted after being forced by Bernice's dog to spend hours in the ocean, Greg spends the night at Bernice's beach house. Having been kept in the ocean at dog point for hours, he sleeps for three, possibly four full days and nights. In another attempt at contemporaneity, an evocation of Presley on hallucinogenic drugs, as Greg Nolan, he sings his way through a hallucinatory episode with "The Edge of Reality." Musically and in regard to the accompanying choreography, the tune suggests a re-appropriation of how television variety shows of the era used production styles of earlier Hollywood musicals. As such, the musical interlude glamorizes the use of psychedelic drugs in the later 1960s as fashionable, obfuscating the dangers of using them as well. Donning a pale blue satin suit, Presley remains stationary amid swirls of colored lights. A noticeably far less good-looking woman than Michelle Carey's Bernice steps in to do her dance moves for her. Elvis movie-makers resorted to this dialectic before: a stationary Presley surrounded by women dancers at the end of *G.I. Blues,* and harem dancers swarming Presley at the end of *Harum Scarum*. The dialectic enshrines Presley as an idyllic, doll-like figure, referencing how, for many of the young, female audience members, their interest in Presley wasn't that far removed from their playing with dolls.

Upon waking, Greg meets Bernice's milkman (Sterling Holloway), who refers to her as Betty. Bernice shares a bizarre tale of how she met her late husband and, as Greg shaves in the bathroom, tells him she loves watching men in the morning, a hint that she's been with a plurality of lovers. As his disinterest persists, so does the aggressiveness of her interest in him. Bernice's friend and sometime lover, Harry (Dick Sargent), whom she'd falsely identified as her late husband, shows up at the beach house to pick up his clothes. Perhaps he's among the men she enjoyed watching shaving.

Driving to the office that employs him as a newspaper photographer, random violence erupts to liven up meandering screen time. Barely audible over the noise of the presses, his boss fires him and then orders two pressroom stooges to throw him out. After a several minutes of trading punches to the head with the brutes, he prevails. In a moment of what might be called neo-Presley realism, he's sustained a hint of a bruise below one eye. In the life of the Presley protagonist, irrational violence can break out anywhere, anytime.

He then drives home, discovering that Bernice has rented it out to a hefty, hostile mother and her young son. Wearing only a slip, she accuses him of being a "sex maniac" and a "bluebeard." Declining Bernice's amorous interest for some time, Presley's Greg Nolan evokes characterizations of the artist as religious ascetic, as well as the artist as hero to the extent that, at least for a while, he opts for sexual purity. While this amalgam of historical, religious and symbolic associations aren't commonly found in Elvis Presley movies, whether knowingly appropriated or not, allusions to some typologies are heavily-laden with a wealth of possible, related meanings. These meanings extend well back into the traditions of fine art. They are also readily co-opted and applied to the modern photographer to bestow enhanced artistic credibility on him for anyone skeptical of the photographer's artistic legitimacy.

Returning to Bernice's bungalow in anger, Greg kicks out the milkman, and then profanely asks her, "Damn it Bernice! What do you want from me?" She deflects his anger by cleaning his clothes, informing him that she's paid off his back rent. Following a spirited argument, they agree he'll stay the night at her place again and, in a moment of peek-a-boo to Greg, but not the camera, she makes known to him that, beneath her fur coat, she's probably naked. "That's a dirty trick!" he snarls, somewhere between purity and prudishness.

The grocery delivery boy (Eddie Hodges) storms in, accidentally knocking Greg on his back, then helps himself to a beer from Bernice's fridge. Discounting Greg, each of the three other men in Bernice's life seem to demonstrate considerable familiarity toward her. It's unclear whether this suggests that she's promiscuous or that she enjoys cultivating platonic relationships with men. Greg approves of the sample taste of her cooking she gives him, until she tells him it's for her dog Albert.

Harry arrives in time to have the beef stew dinner with Bernice and Greg that she's cooked for them. Harry encourages Greg to look for work as an advertising photographer. The work is easy, the pay good, and the breasts of the office personnel are very large. Greg doesn't seem immediately interested. Harry furnishes Greg with some personal details about Bernice. He tells Greg how she's "scared of life, being alone, love," how "making love never works for her; she always stops short," and how he "think[s] she's hoping to find the man who can bring her the right kind of love." This is pretty vapid stuff at the level of both insight and dialogue. Poor Bernice is so lonely and afraid that she has to proposition total strangers for sex, threaten them with her Great Dane, and feed them dog food. Mysteriously, this "never quite works for her."

At the time of this movie's initial release, between the drug culture, the popularization of various kinds of Eastern mysticism, the advent of psychedelica, and the mental dead ends of philosophers such as Timothy Leary and Alan Watts, reality was a heavily contested territory in many quarters. The dream sequence showed that a movie protagonist breaking out into song with full orchestral accompaniment is a surreal occurrence. They pull out all the stops from their miserly budgetary considerations. Greg is sent tumbling down, in fetal position, by someone in a dog suit. He addresses whoever's in the dog costume as Albert. Decked out in a cheap-looking blue satin suit, a half dozen dancers in black body stockings undulate around him. A flurry of multiple-colored spotlights drift about. Bernice, Harry, the milkman and the delivery boy are all present to childishly taunt Greg about how he doesn't know Bernice's real name, among other red herrings. Trick photography is employed to have her transform herself into a comparably shaped but different woman. The reason for this transformation is obvious and pragmatic. Michele Carey, the actress playing Bernice, probably has two left feet. She couldn't pull off a drunken rendition of the Chicken Dance if her wedding night depended on it. Rather than exalt the supremacy of Greg's unconsciousness, victorious here is the power of the flaky woman: "On the edge of reality where she overpowers me with fears that I can't explain (?) the edge of reality she sits there tormenting me, the girl with the nameless name … She drove me to the point of madness, the brink of misery, if she's not real then I'm condemned to the edge of reality." While completely disjunctive from Greg Nolan's circumstances within the objective screen narrative, his musical confession is that the woman who has inexplicably and ineffably captivated his interest must be real, or his own understanding of reality is threatened.

Following a night of uneasy dreams, while en route to apply for work at an ad agency, Greg stumbles across the office of *Classic Cat*, a *Playboy*-style magazine in the same building. Something caught his eye, possibly the cutout billboard of the model with an impossibly huge bust. "Nolan is here with the truth," he enigmatically tells the receptionist. He meets the Hugh Hefner-style magazine patriarch Mike Lansdown (Don Porter), who is being massaged by three young women in feline-themed attire. "The truth is I need a job," Greg says to their amusement. His opening promise of profundity is followed up by a weak joke. Lansdown tells Greg of his magazine's creed: "Truth is beauty, and the highest expression of beauty is the relationship between a man and a woman." Lansdown continues, "it is to the glorification of this relationship that Lansdown Enterprises is dedicated." Erotic pleasure is exalted without any moral qualifications as to whether or not there might possibly be something dubious about pornography. As newly-hired photographer for *Classic Cat,* Greg lands a voyeur's dream job, being paid to do something many men would do for free.

As Lansdown converses with Greg, he enjoys accoutrements of the good life as promoted by the likes of *Playboy* magazine: surrounded by beautiful young women less than half his age, receiving massages from multiple female masseuses, presiding over a party at his mansion, drinking health food shakes and taking steam baths, presumably to keep up with his sexual workload. It's what Christopher Lasch in *The Culture of Narcissism* (1979) identified as giving the ordinary man a taste for the extraordinary.[33] Without incurring allegiances to what American humorist James Thurber satirically commented

---

[33]   Also mentioned in the discussion of *Blue Hawaii* on p. 16.

on in his essay "The Psychosemanticist Will See You Now, Mr. Thurber" (1955) that is, without incurring allegiances to "creeping socialism", the notion that everyone has the same opportunities to accrue what materialism posits as synonymous with the good life could seem questionable.

Greg goes from the office of *Classic Cat* to the office of Creative Advertising, where he again introduces himself as "Nolan with the truth" to get his foot in the door. There he meets chief executive Louis Penlow (Rudy Vallée). Penlow tells Greg, "advertising is the art of attracting attention." In turn, Greg explains to Penlow, that "the secret of good photography is not to get fooled by what you see. Get to know your subjects. Find the truth in them, and photograph that." If advertising really encouraged people toward the contemplative, most advertising agencies would likely go bankrupt in short order. After Greg and Penlow share pontificating, Penlow hires him. Greg phones Bernice to tell her of his two new jobs. He'll soon be positioned to pay back the money she loaned to him. Momentarily, at the movie's opening, it's shown that Bernice might earn her livelihood as a painter, but it's never made explicit. As Greg becomes more well-disposed toward Bernice in his new home, Harry shows up to join them for a housewarming with flat champagne and his favorite meal of hot dogs and egg rolls. Angered by evening's end, Greg demands of Bernice, "how long do you think this ridiculous situation can last?"

At work the following day, Greg goes back and forth between shooting cheesecake pictures for Lansdown and ad layouts for Penlow. In another overused cinematic effect of the period, fast motion photography, Greg rapidly changes clothes back and forth, suit and tie for his advertising gig and a more casual look for his work with *Classic Cat,* in accordance with the wishes of his two bosses. As comedy, it follows prescriptively from philosopher Henri Bergson's claim that something or someone becomes funny at the point it commences resembling the mechanical.

At an advertising shoot, a caricatured intellectual-type tries to discuss how Greg plans to approach the photo shoot using high-flown art-speak. Oblivious to the intellectual, Greg proceeds with the shoot his way. We can all see who the real man is in the situation. His approach must therefore be the superior one. This characterization is dismissive of the flamboyant heterosexuality of multitudes of accomplished artists throughout history, as well as the genuine labor that goes into making most quality works of art.

Greg's relationship to his work, work that his indebtedness to Bernice forced him take on, requires that he affect more than one personality. Typical of the Presley movie formula of the 1960s, Presley rarely wears the same clothes twice. Again, the idea of Presley as doll is suggested.

Greg arrives at Bernice's place to find her arm in arm with Harry. By this time, Greg is sufficiently emotionally invested in Bernice to react by punching Harry. Then, after persuading Lansdown to give him a six-month salary advance, Greg returns to his own home in a Cadillac convertible. Bernice and Albert turn up at Greg's place too. She sobs because the beach house she lives in is in Harry's and he's decided to sell it. Greg boldly escorts her and Albert out of his home. Simultaneously, another side of Bernice's femininity is evoked, that of woman as helpless maiden in need of rescue.

Greg attends a party at Lansdown's mansion where he again encounters Bernice. "We have nothing in common: never did, never will," he tells her flatly. Lansdown tells him there's a ratio of five women to every man at his parties. Greg commences flirting with a beautiful blond named Ellen (Celeste Yarnall). Within moments of meeting, they're kissing. The scene glamorizes the emerging sexual revolution. With Ellen's clichéd astrological inquiry, "what's your sign?", as the conversational garnish, a reference to the occult is also introduced. He sings, "A Little Less Conversation (A Little More Action)." The song would be posthumously remixed and re-released to become a minor hit decades later, in 2002. Yet in its initial screen presentation, lyrically, the song suggests that language can be completely disregarded between man and woman, that sexual attraction is all that matters. For Presley's Greg Nolan, who has just dumped Bernice because they have no shared interests, he doesn't appear to have much to chat about with Ellen either. Not only is linguistically-based attraction of no consequence, linguistic deception, cheating verbally, is of no consequence.

Greg brings Ellen to his home where they're interrupted by Bernice's vacuuming. Greg and Ellen opt to go to Ellen's place, whereupon Bernice faints, or pretends to, sending a vase crashing to the floor. Ellen leaves by taxi, leaving Greg to pay a doctor for a house call. Bernice has a bump on her head, the doctor says, and needs a couple of days bed rest. "Oh, ommm, oh …" she alternately moans and chants from the bedroom.

The next day Greg is nearly caught working for both Penlow and Lansdown, inadvertently getting on an elevator with the two men. Arriving home from work, while she flips through a fashion magazine, it's revealed that Bernice is faking her injury. Presley and his co-star don't need to act in this scene to convey that they're genuinely enjoying themselves. While he's in the shower, Bernice reaches over the shower door to wash Greg's back with a scrub brush. Kissing of firm but pliant lips aside, the scene presents lovemaking at its most hygienic.

The next day, a sleep-deprived Greg rushes from a public aquarium girlie-mag shoot of a mermaid to an advertisement shoot. The wimpy art director tells an oblivious Greg that he's "trying to develop an intrinsic, multi-layered symmetry between animate and inanimate objects." Though not total babble, it's the kind of verbose art talk that art students can invest years of study in learning how to speak, comprehend and cause to further proliferate. Greg's irritation at the comment prompts him to back the suit-and-tie-clad art director into a fountain. It's an enactment of hostility simultaneous with an anti-intellectual and hostile attitude toward understanding art. As enacted by the Preslyan protagonist, it's shown to be an acceptable form of philistinism, the scorning of privilege associated with cultural sophistication and advanced reasoning.

Hurrying between photo shoots in his Cadillac, Greg commandeers police motorcycle escorts, then waves them off in a friendly fashion. This friendliness would have been significantly counter to the popular attitude toward police authority in 1968 America. Just as the rebellious times were thought to warrant Richard Nixon as the law-and-order president, had Elvis Presley become the law-and-order rock star? Greg's two professions, photographer of advertising and soft porn, reflect author Dan Greenburg's observation that there's a continuum between the worlds of advertising and pornography, and that they're not so very different from each other. Indeed, the distinctions have become routinely blurred in the years since this 1968 feature was made. Otherwise socially responsible, Presley's Greg Nolan is a cleaned-up version of another then-emerging typology: the swinger.

After dinner, Greg again warms up to Bernice. She plays the acoustic guitar as he sings the samba-like "I'm Almost on Love Tonight." "And here in the spell of evening, I long to hold you near. Heaven is here tonight,; why wait for tomorrow? I'm almost in love tonight"—this is pretty much the entirety of the song's lyrics, repeated several times, a mysticism again invoking to the occult, the hereafter and a live-it-up-for-the-moment mentality regarding romantic intimacy. Bernice is the more emotionally flighty of the two of them, but Greg's something of a yo-yo himself. They do some slow dancing, share a bed that Bernice virtuously divides between them with a pillow. "For safety," she says. Albert respectfully covers his eyes with his paws. Bernice gives Greg what she calls a "sisterly" kiss on the ear from behind her side of the dividing pillow.

The following day, both Penlow and Lansdown fire Greg upon their mutual discovery that both of them are employing him. Returning to his home, Greg discovers that Bernice has printed a message in lipstick for him on his bedroom mirror: "Bernice is very confused. Please don't look for her. Thank you, darling, for making me a woman." Apparently he really burned her house down. Racing to her beach bungalow, he encounters Harry again. He tells Harry that "maybe [he's] in love with her and maybe [he] want[s] to marry her." Harry lies, telling Greg that Bernice asked him, Harry, to take her back. He punches Greg in the head, but then recovers his civility by apologizing and cowering. Possibly too focused on wanting to find Bernice, Greg opts against hitting back and proceeds to the beach. Seated together there are Bernice and Albert.

Greg and Bernice exchange confessions of love for one another. In a reversal of the movie's opening, after they kiss, she says it didn't make her feel anything, and so Albert then chases *her* into the ocean instead of Greg. Greg and Bernice embrace and kiss each other. The movie concludes with Albert looking on from the shore. His masculine authority repeatedly undermined by Bernice's antics, a measure of equanimity is suggested by the turnabout in their circumstances.

Live a Little, Love a Little is an exception to the usual love theme played out in Presley movies. Ordinarily, the woman that Presley's character is interested in is resistant to him. It's a theme explored in some Shakespearean plays, the *discordia concors,* "the discord behind the concord"[34] or war between men and women. It's on "the edge of reality' that Presley's Greg Nolan finds himself on the edge of endangerment to

---

[34] Nathalie Vienne-Guerrin, "'The noise they make' in *A Midsummer Night's Dream* on Screen." *Shakespeare on Screen,* p

more traditional man-to-woman relations. Ordinarily, in that arrangement, the man chases the woman until she catches him. As the eccentrically multi-faceted, flaky woman, Bernice is a trickster figure with a difference. Sexually confused herself, she stirs up much interest among men. That her affiliation with a woman who holds séances is only another passing detail of her character's eccentricities suggests that those responsible for *Live a Little, Love a Little* were either naïve about the evils of occult involvement, thought it a fashionable inclusion, or were knowingly complicit with those evils. While the main focus of the movie is on Presley's Greg Nolan, despite everything identifying her with kooky, 1960s contemporaneity, Bernice is driven by a basic imperative: to get the man she desires by any means necessary.

The Good, the Bad and the King of Rock & Roll

Not to be confused with the voluptuous Latino woman Charo, *Charro!* (1969) is the lone instance of Presley in a totally non-musical role. Only in voice-over format during the opening credits, featuring 1960s spaghetti western production-style, is it that Presley's voice-over sings metaphysically lines about the role of Charro: "You've lived and died and come to life again, and now you're standing at the crossroads of your mind." What Presley sings of the character he plays is also true of genre he stars in here. Etymologically, the term "Charro" is of Spanish origin, and refers to someone thought to be despicable, whereas the term "Charo" is common parlance for a horseman from Mexico. The notion that someone other than Christ has been resurrected is evoked, an grossly conflated estimation of Elvis Presley, even on his best day.

As reformed outlaw Jess Wade, Presley is only referred to a few times as "Charro" by a Mexican cantina proprietor in the movie's opening scene. An element of his rock & roll status still intact, the Presley protagonist is in the process of reformation from a rebellious past. He's moved on from a criminal career with the Hackett bunch. Screen narrative action soon commences when Jess is ambushed in the cantina for reasons not made immediately clear. "You all know I'm gonna make a move for that door!" Jess shouts from behind an overturned card table, at once a warning and an announcement of his predictability. Successfully negotiating his way outside and past three bad dudes, he's halted by three more just outside the cantina doors. Alone and out-gunned, Jess submits to being taken captive and is brought into the desert by the desperadoes. Rubbing Jess's nose in his momentary defeat is the maniacal laughter of Billy Roy Hackett (Solomon Sturgess), younger brother of heinous head honcho Vince Hackett (Victor French). Before the next 90 minutes have elapsed, Sturgess and French are going to do some aggressively scenery-chewing.

Vince reads a Mexican "wanted" poster for Jess, accusing him of stealing Mexico's Victory Gun, a solid gold-coated cannon that Vince and his henchman have stolen. Jess is identified as having a scar on his neck. The scar had belonged to another member of Vince's gang who succumbed to a neck wound, not Jess. Vince and his band of fiends frame Jess for stealing the cannon by giving him the neck wound. As several of Vince's men pin Jess to the ground, Vince brands his neck with a red-hot iron. To the astonishment of Vince and his gang, Jess stands up immediately afterward. Adding injury to injury, Vince's men hold Jess's arms back as Billy Roy uses Jess's torso as a heavy bag. Lest anyone think Vince is unfeeling, he admits to his reason for framing Jess. "Nobody leaves me," Vince says bitterly; "if I live to be a hundred, I'll never get over it. Somebody left me: you!" Further aggravating to Vince, Jess also took his girlfriend, Miss Tracy. He seems far more upset at the thought of Jess leaving. American cinema trod this terrain earlier, at least as far back as Gore Vidal's homoerotic subtext in his account of Billy the Kid in *The Left Handed Gun* (1958), and, a year previous to *Charro!*, with Andy Warhol's *Lonesome Cowboys* (1968). This is the perverse irony of the representation of masculinity in the Old West: the men are so manly that they have no need of women.

After the brutality, Vince considerately states, "Alright, that's enough. Make him comfortable." Vince's men then prop Jess up using his saddle as a pillow for his back. Jess is then abandoned by the Hackett bunch to make his way alone through the wilderness with only the clothes on his back, the hat on his head, a saddle in one hand and a rope in the other. Clint Eastwood received comparable movie treatment three years earlier in Sergio Leone's *The Good, The Bad and the Ugly* (1966). Jess spies a herd of wild horses and, in a true Charro manner, his stunt double lassos and breaks one in for him. Jess wanders into a small town to visit the sheriff, Dan Ramsey (James Almanzar), an old friend who believes that Jess is innocent of the crimes that the wanted poster ascribes to him.

At the local saloon, Jess spies on the showgirls dancing the can-can. He then snoops in a hotel room where he is reunited with Miss Tracy (Ina Balin). She left Vince for him, and Jess later left her. Getting out of her bath, she's accompanied by dainty-sounding background music, accentuating her femininity. They kiss and she incongruously tells him, "You're worse than [Vince] ever was. At least he never made himself out to be anything but a crook and a killer!" Despite her contradictory hostility following their kiss, she restores to him his six-shooter and gun belt, accouterments often deemed necessary for the American man of action.

Billy Roy Hackett arrives at the saloon in time to proposition a blond showgirl named Marcie (Lynn Kellogg). He tries to woo her by showing her a lewd illustration of a naked woman on his gun holster. When Marcie hesitates, Billy Roy quickly retracts his offer: "You missed your chance, Marcie girlie. I take what's warm and close." Reading Billy Roy like a book, Jess has situated himself at the far end of the bar, anticipating Billy

Roy's actions. Evidently Vince and the rest of his men are on the wagon for the evening—quite possibly an actual wagon.

When Billy Roy protests being denied service by the barkeep, Jess steps away from the bar in a typical, Hollywood quick-draw posture. "Outside," he says somberly. Sheriff Dan enters the saloon, and Billy Roy grabs Miss Tracy to take her hostage. Billy Roy shoots Sheriff Dan and is then momentarily punched into unconsciousness by Jess. That Jess would want to protect Miss Tracy from Billy Roy is understandable. Resorting to non-lethal means to do so also helps fill 97 minutes of screen time. Questionable is the readiness with which Jess dutifully takes on the responsibilities of lawman. Once jailed, Billy Roy lets out a big, over-the-top belly laugh. The audience is being primed to see Billy Roy meet with a gratuitously grisly ending.

Jess helps Sheriff Dan down a glass of whiskey, Old West anesthesia to dull the pain as Dan has the two bullets inflicted by Billy Roy removed. "I've spent twelve years getting this town safe to live in," Dan tells Jess; "you've got to keep it that way, Jess, until I get back on my feet."

"I'm no lawman, Dan," replies Jess, but he is sworn in as deputy by the ailing Dan nevertheless. Therein is presented another familiar stereotype of popular culture. The trope goes back at least as far early as the Biblical reference to the reluctance of Moses to be God's lawgiver for the people of Israel.

Jess tells Billy Roy that, if Sheriff Dan dies, he'll hang for it. Billy Roy lets loose with more maniacally hearty laughter, shouting from his cell window, "Ya hear that Vince? They're fixin' to hang yer little brother!" Jess reminds several of the men of the town of their business interests. After dispensing shotguns to each of them, he advises them to protect those interests. It's an intriguing cinematic precedent for the legitimacy of the National Rifle Association: evil is that which might interfere with business.

The next day, a visibly distraught Vince is upset that his men didn't tell him that Billy Roy hadn't returned from town. "Because I didn't want to wake you!" shouts one of them. Despite much shouting at each other, these are sensitive desperadoes. Vince whimsically belts a couple of his men in their faces, but then apologizes for doing so. "Billy Roy's my fault," he says humbly.

At the town barbershop, barber and doctor Opie Keetch (Paul Brinegar) optimistically opines to Jess that the Sheriff will probably fully recover. Miss Tracy scolds Jess for leaving prisoner Billy Roy unguarded. She tells Jess he ought to have armed men on the rooftops. She then leaves to be greeted by a succession of armed locals on the rooftops as her dainty background music accompanies her. When she returns to her saloon, she sees that Jess is escorting Billy Roy back to jail. Jess has proven he has everything it takes to be a front line worker in a frontier police state. Vince and a fellow Hackett Bunch member ride into town, entering the saloon where a drink is instantaneously poured for him. For unspecified reasons, the "no Hacketts allowed" rule has been suspended. Vince and Miss Tracy do some catching up in the saloon. While talking about Jess, she informs him that Billy Roy shot Sheriff Dan, and that Jess arrested Billy Roy for it. A distraught Vince visits his jailed brother Billy Roy. Vince issues Jess an ultimatum: unless he releases Billy Roy by sundown, there'll be trouble. Jess escorts Vince onto the street where gunmen on rooftops identify themselves by cocking their rifles. An identical scene was played out between Karl Malden and Marlon Brando in *One-Eyed Jacks* (1961), only Malden was the bad sheriff to Brando's anti-hero outlaw.

A Mexican army rides into town searching for their prized stolen cannon. In *Charro!*, the cannon is a variation on what Alfred Hitchcock called the "MacGuffin": a plot device propelling the storyline, usually in thrillers. In crime dramas, the MacGuffin is often a piece of jewelry, stolen diamonds, or something to that effect. In spy stories, it's often classified information, microfilm in the olden days of technology. It's what most of the screen characters either chase to acquire or fight to hold on to, but is usually not the focal point of the storyline. In *Charro!*, the MacGuffin is manifested in a more destructive and utilitarian way. At gunpoint in jail, Vince agrees to not tell the Mexican army about the scar on Jess's neck in exchange for Jess not telling them about Vince's theft of the cannon. It's a modification on the western genre that glorified men of action, those reputed to resort to the six-gun as the most expedient route to justice. Considering Vince's extensive criminality, Jess has allotted him much leeway.

Riding off with the Mexican army detachment, Vince tips his own gang to return to camp, and then unleashes the cannon's firepower on the town. Vince values his younger brother Billy Roy's freedom over acquiring the reward money for Jess. Visiting a convalescing Sheriff Dan, Jess tells him he's going to release Billy Roy to save the town. Dan insists that he mustn't do that; it would amount to an admission of guilt on Jess's behalf. "You can't give in to 'em! You let a handful of filth scare us, there'll be nothing left," Dan cautions Jess, equivocating law and order with hygiene. Jess agrees, despite the histrionics of the sheriff's wife Sara and her shrill protestations. "I'm sorry," says Jess, apologetic that duty will take precedence over her objections.

The Mexican troops are led by Vince to a passage of a shallow river, whereupon they're wiped out by cannon-loads of dynamite. Vince guns down the lone surviving soldier, the only one given a line of dialogue. Since it's the Mexican government offering the reward for Jess and the cannon, killing the Mexican soldiers makes no financial sense. One of Vince's gang then rejects as too risky the plan to see Billy Roy freed from jail by sundown or else pick the town apart by cannon fire. The malcontent then fatally loses a quick draw competition to his more family values–oriented leader. It's an inclusion of gratuitous violence to liven up a lethargic storyline. Alternatively, perhaps it's illustrative of philosopher Alfred North-Whitehead's altruistic claim that evil eventually collapses due to the stress of its own internal contradictions. Maybe it was just time for something to go boom.

When Vince rides back into town, Jess looks eager for another mythological quick-draw competition. The modifier of 'mythological' is added in deference to the expertise of Louis L'Amour, highly accomplished writer of western novels and a stickler for authenticity. In an interview on CBS's *Sixty Minutes*, L'Amour stated, among other interesting facts about the Old West, that there were no known instances of quick draw competitions ever having happened there. "You know me, Jess," Vince says mockingly. "I'm not a man of violence. I don't approve of violence." As the words leave his mouth, a church steeple in the background explodes. Language and what actually happens are again violently pitted against each other. Sheriff Dan's house is fired on, killing Sheriff Dan and causing his wife Sara to emote strenuously. She goes to the jail, fetches Jess's wanted poster and informs the townsfolk of his being a wanted man. Much grumbling ensues until Jess, also a ready public speaker with a keen apprehension of doomsday strategy, tells those assembled that "Vince will blast [them] off the face of the earth no matter what." Even in the midst of a crisis threatening the whole town, Jess still resorts to referring to the menacing desperado on a friendly first-name basis.

Miss Tracy apologizes profusely to Jess. "You're all that you said you'd be … for whatever I thought, I was wrong," she confesses. They embrace, but refrain from kissing. As Jess then releases Billy Roy from jail, he crudely asks, "You lockin' us up so we can be cozy?" Reacting as do the other townspeople to Jess releasing Billy Roy from jail, the newly widowed Mrs.

Ramsey accuses Jess of colluding with Vince's gang. However, the continuing cannon fire indicates that Billy Roy didn't return to Vince.

A businessman-looking type tells the townsfolk to leave the streets and hide in their cellars. It's an Old West version of bomb shelter living and an evocation of nuclear age anxieties for 1969 audiences. When night falls, Scorched Earth Policy Vince orders his men, "Everything goes except the jail." Jess's counter-move is to make it known that, unless Vince gives him custody of the cannon, Billy Roy will die. "Maybe you've got me where you want me and maybe you haven't. Anything wrong with talking about it?" Vince diplomatically asks into the darkness. Vince is soon to become more strategically disadvantaged and sensing it. Jess guns down Vince's associate. The cannon rolls down from the hill, crushing Billy Roy to death with all the grizzly goriness of an updated Elizabethan revenge play. The emotionless face of Presley's Jess might suggest various things: stoicism in the face of horror, Clint Eastwood-like lack of affect, satisfaction, or masculine emotional restraint. "Billy Roy!" Vince cries out, Stanley Kowalski–style. He then randomly shoots his remaining bullets into the darkness. Jess tells Vince what he's going to do next: take him and the cannon to Mexico.

No further details of Vince's arrest are shown, only Jess and Vince on a horse-drawn wagon pulling along the cannon the next day. Vince doesn't even appear to be handcuffed. The implausibility of his passive surrender, particularly considering what may lay ahead of him in Mexico, seems inconsistent with Vince's character. Either he's not an entirely static character and has learned from his malfeasance, or his role has been written to be compliant with the feature's estimated running time.

In a harking back to old radio and TV episodes of *The Lone Ranger,* the townsfolk gather to thank Jess for his heroism. Oddly, and unlike most other Presley movies, absent from this representation of the town's populace are any children. The widow Ramsey kisses Jess's cheek. As he rides away, he tells Miss Tracy that he won't be back that way, but will soon send for her. Although in an entirely different genre and in much more violent fashion, the Presley protagonist here is not just victorious respective to the resolution of a central conflict. He's steamrolled over all resistance from everyone who doesn't love him. Even the mentally deficient Billy Roy Hackett, prior to his being crushed by a loose cannon, confessed to Presley's Jess that he "always liked and respected" him. Jess was the only one to successfully walk out on his brother Vince, Billy Roy observed.

Although lacking a bearded, non-singing Presley, the Clint Eastwood western *Hang 'Em High* (1969) also focuses on a deputized cowboy who survives the homicidal intentions of an ornery lynch mob. Comparable to Presley's Jess, Wade, Eastwood's lawman with a rope burn on his neck, embarks on a campaign of retribution. Both westerns exalt not simply justice but revenge as a human need. As such, it's possible they present an embittered depiction of human nature.

It would not be for another three years later until the torch of the leading movie genre would pass from the western to the gangster movie. In *The Godfather* (1972), revenge as entertainment would no longer express itself in the guise of justice, law and order. Possibly most intriguing about *Charro!* is its revamping of Hollywood clichés about bands of marauders shooting up a town. That cliché goes back to another Hollywood myth from the silent film era, running right up to being definitively parodied in 1974's *Blazing Saddles*. As Louis L'Amour observed, there's no way that an armed frontier populace would sit still for such an attack. The appropriation of a cannon and dynamite to accomplish the same ends suggests a plausible, hypothetical alternative to inflicting catastrophic damage on a town in the Old West and terrorizing its citizens. It's a variation on a scenario that Jewish immigrants who left the Old World and its barbaric pogroms would embellish in their heavy influence on early western movie mythology. Cinematically dramatizing their experiences of such perils to seem a threat to an entire, ethnically non-specific populace, early Jewish-American movie-makers promoted empathy by conveying to mass audiences a sense of what it feels like to belong to a persecuted community. Whereas *Charro!* is indebted to the same narrative tradition, simultaneously, the characters featured in Presley's reworking of that old saw are situated in a metaphorical Old West approximation of nuclear-related anxieties of the Cold War era. With movie advertisements boasting of "A new kind of western, a new kind of man," the centrality of that ideological relevance called for a new kind of Elvis Presley—one who doesn't sing.

HOME SICKNESS

Regarding nostalgia, something American popular culture began capitalizing on in the early 1970s, Presley's starring in *The Trouble with Girls* (1969) was slightly ahead of its time. The cultural proliferation of nostalgia was, quite possibly, undertaken for the purposes of retarding the wealth of 1960s cultural agitations. Set in the mythical, small town of Radford Center, Iowa, in the summer of 1927, Presley, as Walter Hale, presides over an American cultural phenomena called a Chautauqua, a traveling recreation and educational medicine show. Despite allusions to a previous era, Presley is again affiliated with a recreation industry. That he initially came to public attention by way of his performing at county fairs, a successor to the Chautauqua, he's again cast in a familiar context. Whereas neither love of country nor propaganda are invariably bad, when they engender unnatural affections of move people toward doing things they wouldn't normally do, such cultural processes merit questioning. A year following John Wayne's disastrous bid at filmed patriotism with *The Green Berets* (1968), Presley would take his turn at expressing love of country by sneaking it in through old-time Americana. It's not until the conclusion of *The Trouble with Girls* that the audience is gently alerted to the fact that they've just been spoon-fed a healthy dose of patriotism, what Samuel Johnson called "the last refuge of a scoundrel."

For a few moments, a crowded city square full of people fanning themselves in the heat is shown in black and white. As the train carrying the Chautauqua arrives and Presley disembarks, the scene switches to full color. A narrator's voice tells us that, with the arrival of the Chautauqua, "the whole town came alive." A big parade, something once indivisible from patriotism for Americans, sweeps the town. Presley is given another celebratory, ceremonial, cinematic introduction.

Presley is immaculately dressed in an all-white suit and hat, a hearty rebuke of the sloppy deportment of 1969 American youth. It's unclear until the closing credits that Presley's character has a name other than "Hale" His older, hefty second-in-command is Johnny (Edward Andrews). Various glimpses of promotional signs and inquiries from patrons reveal that the Chautauqua features a group of "Collegian Madrigal Singers," lessons on "The Kitchen and You" by a French chef, and talks on cannibalism. A group of small children rehearse the playing of "God Bless America," with an uneven collective buzz of kazoos playing along. Patriotism is presented as sentimental and cute.

The Chautauqua's new shop steward, the emancipated 1920s career woman Charlene (Marlyn Mason) aggressively approaches Hale. In his new role within management, he's expected to be anti-union. An aggressive woman, Charlene is often referred to by her masculine nickname of "Charlie." There's a passing reference to Hale and Charlene having been previously romantically involved with each other. "Don't you bedroom-eye me, boss man!" she yells at him, seemingly immune to his charm. "I'm not anti-union," he tries to counter. "We're on opposite sides of the bargaining table, Buster!" she says. Predictably, her resistance gives way when he turns on the charm; that charm reemerges when the transparency of his business motives assert themselves.

In the tent of the kiddies' kazoo orchestra, other children audition for the Chautauqua pageant (though this is pageant never shown). Following a bland rendition of "Toot-Toot-Tootsie" by the mayor's daughter, Lily-Jeanne Gilchrist (Linda Sue Risk), a little waif named Carol Bix (Anissa Jones) and her Black male sidekick Willy (Pepe Brown) do a far livelier song and dance. Presley's appeal to children is again referenced. Following the audition scene, the movie audience is introduced to drugstore proprietor Harrison Wilby (Dabney Coleman). He's working up a steam with Carol's mother, *Miss* Nita Bix (Sheree North). She exits before the activity exceeds G-rated behavior. The sexually frustrated Harrison takes out his hostilities on his employee. Wilby threatens the soda jerk for helping himself to too much drugstore food. When the soda jerk asks if he can take go to the Chautauqua, Wilby angrily profanes the traveling fair.

Juxtaposed against this menacing moment, action shifts to the fairground. A succession of shots is then presented: snow cone making, hot dog eating, dogs playing and the making of cotton candy. It's a quick visual summation of fairground life, complete with its hucksters and junk food. Charlene chooses little Carol Bix to lead the pageant. More of the Chautauqua is shown: Metropolitan Opera stars, a Russian ballet, gospel singers and a performance by a Gilbert and Sullivan troupe. A lecture on morality by Mr. Morality (Vincent Price) is presented. American pragmatist philosopher and psychologist William James made passing reference to such activity in *The Varieties of Religious Experience* (1902), in which he describes the formation of so-called ethical societies, organizations of people seeking to be good without having God in their lives, perhaps among the spiritual repercussions of those who accepted too unquestioningly the speculations of Darwin. Casting Vincent Price, Hollywood's most enduring horror movie actor, as an expert on morality suggests a consistency with the positioning of rock & roll's orientation toward conventional morality.

Infatuated with and distracted by the sight of Hale, a dizzy innkeeper's daughter named Betty (Nicole Jaffe) stumbles and falls over a tent peg. Her main cinematic purpose seems to be to remind the audience that Presley is still as desirable as ever to any healthy American teenage girl. Mayor Gilchrist (Bill Zuckert) tells Hale how progressive the town is: it has no Ku Klux Klan affiliations, a few Catholic families and even one Hebrew family living among them. Carol Bix and Willy take in an impromptu sidewalk performance by a local bluegrass band. They then go to Wilby's drugstore to spend a silver dollar they've inexplicably obtained. Wilby cagily unloads a box of otherwise unsaleable fireworks on the children, warning them against mentioning where they got the illegal post-fourth-of-July merchandise. As they stash their contraband, the anxious pair bumps into Mr. Morality, who spits out more aphorisms than a fortune cookie factory. In a span of under two minutes he quotes Nietzsche, Confucius, Jonson and Shakespeare at length, probably not among those authors most familiar to Willy and Carol.

Carol and Willy wander onto the wrong side of Hale's impromptu football game. Fleeing from the playing field, they inadvertently go in the same direction as the flow of the game. Hale tells Johnny that they played to a superhuman 110 to 97 point lead. Johnny nervously shows Hale that the Russian ballet is being performed before an empty tent, explaining that's due to trouble stirred up by "Miss American Labor Shop Steward" Charlene. He's anxiety-ridden because the lead vocalist of the Bible Singers has laryngitis. Presley fills in for the absent singer with a rousing lead vocal on an upbeat gospel song, "I've Got a Home on the Other Side." It's a pleasant reminder that, even amid such a hum-drum material, Presley could still shine musically with the right material.

The gospel song is followed by the displaced spirituality of a lecture from Mr. Morality. Mr. Morality proclaims: "What you have been is of little significance. What you are is the essence," undoubtedly refreshing words to a single mother in 1927, among others. "There is no such thing as immorality once you yourself have become a moral force!" Even in parody, philosophy dismissive of God inexorably gravitates toward self-deification or, in this case, a component of *Star Wars*.

Hale approaches Charlene to have the mayor's daughter lead the pageant, despite her lack of ability. Charlene insists that the part will go to Carol Bix. Charlene angrily cites labor regulations to Hale as he laughs in her face. Threatening to quit if she doesn't get her way, Charlene storms out. Hale's enthralled admirer, Betty, enters with the laundry. Her demonstrative affection suggests that, despite his roguishness, he's still lovable. She jumps at the opportunity to voluntarily take over Charlene's position as the Chautauqua pianist. Charlene and Hale meet alone to discuss labor negotiations. She has him toss away his lit cigar, saying, "it makes you look too much like a caricature of a capitalist." Her pejorative use of the term "capitalist" identifies her as a pinko, if not a full-blown red. Hale emphasizes double-entendres as he slowly starts putting the moves on her. "Business interests can sometimes be better solved by what is called 'getting into bed with each other.'" His discarded cigar then ignites the fireworks that Carol and Willy stashed behind a nearby tent. Startled by the sudden pyrotechnics, Charlene hops into Hale's arms. A storm of Roman candles, pinwheels and other fireworks light up the night sky as Carol and Willy look on in wonder. The display disrupts a nearby blackjack game between Harrison Wilby and a slick Chautauqua card sharp named Clarence (Anthony Teague). When Charlene and Hale kiss, she's aligned with the role of potential prostitute as commerce and carnality co-mingle. As they press lips, Hale exposes his business motive, telling Charlene to "use the mayor's daughter [to lead the Chautauqua pageant]." She angrily tries to hit him, misses and leaves.

Charlene visits Wilby's drugstore. She hears him in the back room trying to pressure Nita Bix into having sex with him. Wilby threatens to tell Nita's daughter Carol about their affair if she doesn't comply. After she threatens to kill him if he carries out his threat, he offers her money for sex. A loud slap is then heard. Emerging from the back room chastened but undeterred, Wilby salaciously asks Charlene, also the Chautauqua's story lady, to tell him a traveling-salesman story. In 1920s parlance, Wilby is a masher. What Charlene overheard from the drugstore backroom will not be lost on her or on later plot developments. After hearing little Carol Bix perform, Hale is convinced she should lead the pageant. Wilby loses to Clarence the card shark again, tries to overpower him and is clobbered. When an agitated Betty approaches Hale to help her leave town, he assigns her to accompany Chautauqua long-distance swimming champion Maude (Joyce Van Patten) on a swim at a nearby lake. Moments after entering the water, Maude discovers the dead body of Harrison Wilby. In keeping with the typical murder mystery, the victim was constructed to appear completely deserving. The murderer is presented in a manner to elicit more audience sympathy than the victim. As is often the case in such narratives, the wrong man, Clarence the card sharp, is the first character jailed for the crime.

A familiar storyline—the possible cancellation of the big show, in this instance the Chautauqua, emerges on various fronts. The townspeople don't want the Chautauqua back because of the murder scandal. A senator booked to speak at the Chautauqua is unable to attend. Charlene tips Hale about the dispute between Nita Bix and Wilby. Hale then realizes what's happened and how to make a buck from it. He approaches a weepy Nita Bix who now disparages the teaching of Mr. Morality with his claims that "you could make a fresh start [because] you can't!" That is, she's balking at the American Dream. Hale observes that, if Wilby's killing was self-defense, the killer could get off and make a bundle of money. It's the icing on the utilitarian cake. As often happens in detective stories, murder turns out to be for the betterment of more sympathetic characters and a societal improvement. In a world that hates inefficiency, even crime has societal usefulness. Hale takes the situation to its next logical phase: exonerating the murderer and getting paid for doing so.

After Hale's business proposal to Nita, the town is besieged by advertisements for the unnamed murderer's confession to be heard at the Chautauqua. Angered by what she perceives as Hale's latest unethical ploy to draw crowds, simultaneously boasting that her economics education that included six months of studying law, Charlene threatens Hale and Johnny with having them sent to prison as accessories to murder. Calling Hale "a lying, conniving charlatan," she again storms off. That night, a drunken Nita Bix attends the Chautauqua. Several musical distractions are presented as the audience awaits an admission of guilt from Wilby's real murderer. Two anachronisms are included: a Donald Duck impression by one of the Chautauqua's collegians (Frank Welker), and Presley, as Hale, singing a good but too contemporary-sounding blues number, "Clean Up Your Own Backyard." In the only instance of Presley taking recourse to violence in the movie, he slaps Nita in the face to sober her up. He then encourages his staff to "keep belting her; it might work." Returning to the stage, he performs two songs with Charlene, who breathes enraged whispers at him as they sing and dance together. As Hale is about to concede failure and return the audience's money, a bedraggled-looking Nita, soaked from a bucket of water that was thrown on her to sober her up, takes to the stage and confesses to having killed Harrison Wilby in self-defense.

With Wilby's murder mystery solved and Clarence exonerated, the Chautauqua has secured a guarantee to return to Radford Center the following year. Hale boards an outbound train. Still angry, Charlene continues ranting against Hale until she overhears him sing another too contemporary-sounding tune, a torch song, "We Almost Went All the Way." He tries talking Charlene into staying with the show, explaining that his strategy was the only way Nita Bix could get a fair trial. Now Nita and her daughter Carol have the means to leave town and make a fresh start. The American Dream is alive and well. Charlene insists she's not going to stay with the Chautauqua. Stating that her contract stipulates Hale is to pay her own fare and that of her replacement's, he gives her 300 dollars. Yet another Presley movie concludes on the theme of successful bargaining. Playing up another sneaky angle, Hale secretly advises the local policeman (Med Flory) that a single woman is going to be loose in his town with 300 dollars. The cop picks up Charlene bodily and, despite her protests, forcibly puts her on the train with the rest of the Chautauqua as it leaves town. The last shot of the movie shows Charlene flailing wildly, held back while trying in vain to jump from the caboose.

Slightly comparable to unscrupulous newspaper editor Walter Burns (Cary Grant) in *His Girl Friday* (1940), Walter Hale isn't above resorting to any chicanery necessary to hold on to his most useful female employee. However, whereas *His Girl Friday* is a brilliant comedy, *The Trouble with Girls* doesn't clearly belong to a specific genre aside from being an Elvis Presley movie. Moderately a musical, part unfunny comedy, part un-mysterious murder mystery, tinted with and tainted by nostalgia, as with its distant predecessor, *The Trouble with Girls* concludes on the theme of how to keep an emancipated modern woman from disrupting the status quo. These are two very different movies, but they have one thing in common: showing how a cunning man successfully holds on to a talented woman to suit his own purposes. Both movies acknowledge the reality of sexism and the comical acquiesce to it. The disturbing nature of sexism was and is such that it's treated through the candied gauze of comedy. The cunning but unprincipled man recognizes his need for a skillful woman. He expresses his dominance by prohibiting her from expressing independence and enforcing her subservience to him. As such, *The Trouble with Girls* reflects discomfort respective to the women's movement emerging near the time of the movie's production. As per Homer's Odysseus, who uses cunning to overcome mythical forces, Hale uses his cunning to keep down woman and unionized labor. But he's not simply oppressing women and unionization: he's defeating ideologies unpopular with the values of the makers of late-1960s popular culture.

The narrator concludes by saying that the Chautauqua would cease by 1934 because of radio, talking pictures, the Model A, hard roads and sophistication. The Great Depression probably figured somewhere in there too. "In its time, [Chautauqua] was the most American thing about America," were words uttered by none other than Theodore Roosevelt, declares the narrator. As per the children's kazoo chorus version of "God Bless America," such information is rooted in patriotism snuck in through nostalgia, nostalgia for a North American sexism in which men could douse women with water, slap them around and even kidnap them with impunity. Provided they didn't express their power over woman by being too sinister, as did Harrison Wilby, there was much disparity in the rights of men over women. Wilby's murder isn't shown. That might have undermined Nita's femininity. Only a reference to Nita's threatening to kill Wilby, if he revealed their affair to her daughter, receives on screen attention. Wilby doesn't seem to have made a literal attempt on Nita Bix's life, only on her reputation in the eyes of her daughter. Nita and Carol Bix not only give new life to the American Dream. They'll also endeavor to partake of another American pastime: reinventing themselves.

Ominously undergirding the self-reinvention phenomenon is another unofficial American institution: vigilantism. Unlike Charlene, the caricature of the intellectual woman leftist, Nita Bix earns her emancipation the old-fashioned way: she kills for it. Also unlike Charlene, she has a last name. Unfortunately, the same unofficial American institution that's the justification for Nita Bix's transgression, vigilantism, also persisted as the means by which racist Whites continued to lynch countless Blacks well into the twentieth century. What, if anything, the disappearance of Carol Bix's African-American playmate, Willy, has to do with that isn't clear.

Aside from his voice-over singing of the movie's opening theme, we are presented with a totally non-musical Elvis Presley in *Charro! The Trouble with Girls* could be said to be presenting a milder approximation of a failed revenge comedy for women. Just as movie musicals were of little interest to movie audiences by the late 1960s, Presley's fan base was such that all that an Elvis Presley movie required to insure its commercial success was that it focus on the appearance of Elvis Presley. In that this, Presley's second-to-last screen narrative, *The Trouble with Girls* was bold enough to champion single mothers. It can only be lamented that the production failed in virtually every substantive respect to realize its objectives.

THE PAPAL PRESLEY

I n his final non-documentary screen role, 1969's *Change of Habit*, Presley plays a doctor. As someone without much formal education, he was definitely cast against type. Though still youthful-looking, his career and image had both traversed a considerable arc. In previous features such as *G.I. Blues, It Happened at the World's Fair* and *Speedway,* his love interests were, at first, hyper-resistant to him. Presley's fictive cinematic swan song would constitute an even bigger challenge: romancing a nun (Mary Tyler Moore). Disguised as a regular career woman, Sister Michelle lives in the same locale as Presley's character's medical practice: an inner city ghetto. This is the basic stuff of Presley's last movie role. As was true of the more widespread political activism of the time, much American popular culture was less directly escapist in nature. Engagement with the social turmoil of the day was far more common. Issues such as urban blight, interracial tensions and the increase of drug abuse, however candy-coated, were often favored in socially-conscious movies and television of that era. Further expanding on the conscience of *Change of Habit*'s social conscience is the glossily-generic inclusion of Roman Catholicism.

The movie commences with a Catholic priest's partial paraphrase of Christ's Great Commission[35] to His followers: "It is written, go out into all the world and proclaim the good news to all creation." The priest continues, "Let us pray now for three members of our order who leave us today to carry on this work beyond these walls", he's referring to Tyler Moore and her sister nuns. Those uncomfortable with references to the Bible will have little to feel distressed about from this movie. Presley's voice-over sings the title song as the opening credits are displayed, and the trio of nuns tastefully change out of their nun's habits into civilian garb.

With his pork chop sideburns in full bloom, Presley's character, Dr. John Carpenter, is introduced playing a jaunty ode to girl-watching, "Rubberneckin'." In a small apartment, Dr. Carpenter is instrumentally accompanied by over a dozen young adults. This is an Elvis Presley still in touch with the younger generation. Outside the compact living room, it sounds like a horn section is hidden in the bathroom. The covert nuns arrive at Dr. Carpenter's office. In the case of mutual misunderstanding, the nuns say he doesn't look like a doctor. He mistakenly thinks they've showed up to procure abortions, something he tells them he doesn't do. Without divulging their identities as nuns, Sister Michelle tells Dr. Carpenter that she's a psychiatric social worker with a degree in speech therapy. Sister Barbara (Jane Elliot) is a laboratory technician and Sister Irene (Barbara McNair) is a registered nurse with a degree in public health. "Great, just great," grumbles Dr. Carpenter, "I ask for hard-nosed nurses and they send me Park Avenue debutants."

"Which end of Park Avenue do you figure I'm from?" asks the Sister Irene, the lone Black woman among them. Ignoring the question, Dr. Carpenter warns them, "The last two nurses sent were raped, one of them even against her will",

---

[35] Matthew 28:18–20, Mark 16:15–18, Luke 24:47.

an unpleasant witticism that falls flat. He warns them that, in the neighborhood where his practice is located, "diplomacy starts and ends at the edge of a switchblade knife." After they leave, Dr. Carpenter comments, "Weirdos man, weirdos." His use of the day's vernacular is yet another sign of his hipness. The nuns are verbally harassed by a half-dozen prostitutes who caution them, "Washington Street is our turf!" Undeterred, the sisters march to their local accommodations, a rundown basement suite provided by the local parish. Their arrival is overseen by two unnamed old ladies who, along with the local priest, reflect the older-style Catholic church.

"Talk about the wages of sin! Would you look at the duds on them!" says one of the seniors in response to the sisters' comparatively high-end attire. "Look who's coming into church," she says, prejudicially instructing her friend to tell the priest that "one's as black as the ace of spades!"

Upon entering the ravaged suite, the pathologically perky Sister Michelle states, "Let's get this place next to godliness," a scriptural-sounding truism not found in scripture. The determined trio visits the garish parish, finding it locked at seven p.m. They're met by crusty old Father Gibbons[36] (as in the Gibbon ape). Gibbons makes it clear he doesn't approve of "secret agents … underground nuns who wear bobbed hair and silk stockings." The church is locked to keep out thieves, he explains. Sister Michelle suggests that he "put away the candlesticks and whatever else can be stolen, and open the doors for those who'd like to pray to our Lord." In a movie steeped in religiosity, that's the singular reference to Lord, Christ or God.

"Flapper skirts I've been ordered to countenance, but I warn you, Sister, that I'll have none of your arrogant lip," the elderly priest growls. This too bespeaks older-style religion, as well as

---

[36] "And do not call anyone on earth 'father,' for you have one Father, and he is in heaven," Matthew 23:9.

the kind of Pharisee-ism that Christ Himself didn't demonstrate. It's unclear whether the priest's sexism is exceptional, typical for an older man of that time, or meant to characterize an aged Roman Catholic priest of that time.

Dr. Carpenter happily gives a clean bill of health to a pregnant woman. He enlists Sister Michelle to help him in the office, and sends Sister Irene to do house calls. He states that there's a shortage of drugs because they don't want anyone getting mugged for narcotics. Sister Irene replies that she "was born in a place like this [and knows] where it's at." After she leaves, Dr. Carpenter asks Michelle why Irene's there, "because she sure doesn't look like she enjoys it." "Because it's her duty," replies Sister Michelle, as if the question was too obvious to bear asking. Dr. Carpenter opines that Sister Irene "should raise a whole bunch of kids. Turn your hang-ups into something worthwhile. I prescribe that for all three of you." For some women, this might not seem the most desirable of possible options. Yet the doctor's partiality to fecundity certainly places him on side with Roman Catholic values.

Dr. Carpenter then introduces Sister Michelle to the reality of drug abuse in the slums as they administer aid to a junkie. Unable to get Sister Michelle's help to move the nun's furniture, Sister Barbara tarts herself up for the attention of the Latino porch-sitting men who volunteer their assistance. One of the anonymous aged women neighbors, the voice of old-school Catholicism, covertly calls Sister Barbara a "hussy." From the back of a nearby limousine, a morbidly obese man wearing sunglasses, known only as "The Banker" (Robert Emhardt) puts the squeeze on one of the locals for exorbitant interest on loans. Even in this, Presley's last movie, the figure of the gangster will figure significantly as was the case in *King Creole, Follow That Dream, Kid Galahad, It Happened at the World's Fair* and *Girl Happy*. Such references to gangsters further explains why the Presleyan protagonist is well-schooled in physical altercations.

Yet whereas gangsterism is largely a phenomenon of capitalism, other political perspectives, fascism and socialism, for instance, and a range of special interest groups can show themselves as every bit as capable of demonstrating gangster-like ethics and gangster-like behavior.

A little girl named Amanda (Lorena Kirk) is brought to the clinic. The astute Sister Michelle suspects that Amanda is autistic. The plainclothes nun explains to Amanda's aunt Miss Parks (Virginia Vincent; there are no single mothers in this ghetto), "sometimes when a child is rejected very early in life they crawl inside themselves and shut out the whole world as if they're trying to punish the rest of us along with themselves." For those whose sensibilities have been directly or indirectly informed by a Freudian paradigm, the nun's explanation might sound credible. Contextually, it's also an explanation that would play well to a 1960s youth culture audience, one that lays the blame on parental authority.

Dr. Carpenter and Sisters Michelle and Irene pay a house call to an elderly Black woman. Upon learning that the senior citizen has been restored to breathing on her own and is going to survive, the nuns kneel at her bedside to pray. The doctor and Sister Michelle compliment each other afterward on successfully treating their patient, and he invites her out for dinner and a drink. She nervously declines. In the rigidity of her religious observance, she's missing legitimate enjoyments in life. Whereas believers ought to count themselves "dead to sin,"[37] Christ also came that we "may have life, and have it to the full."[38] How Sister Michelle experiences that fullness is possibly alluded to later in the movie.

Amanda is brought back to the clinic. Dr. Carpenter confirms Sister Michelle's intuition that the little girl is autistic.

---

[37] "count yourselves dead to sin," Romans 6:11.
[38] John 10:10.

He suggests using the new "rage reduction" method, to which the kinder, gentler Sister Michelle counters that she'd prefer trying patience and love. Their exchange is interrupted when Julio, the troubled stutterer, appears for his speech therapy session.

Sister Barbara, the most practical of the nuns and, therefore not surprisingly, the one most likely to leave the order, contends against the surly local grocer (an uncredited Timothy Carey) trying to shortchange a Latina customer. The grocer's is where the Washington Street Community's upcoming feast of San Juan de Chequez is celebrated, the Caribbean patron saint of fishermen and, apparently, land-locked slum-dwellers.

That night, Sister Barbara tells Sister Michelle she should have taken up Dr. Carpenter on his dinner offer, telling her he's "cute and groovy." Her sister nuns respond in unison by commanding her to say 25 Hail Marys. With all due respect to Roman Catholics, and there might be those who attempt comparable criticisms of Protestantism, such practices are inconsistent with biblical Christianity. Whereas examples of ritual in observances of faith can be seen in Old and New Testaments, Christ specifically instructs His followers, "And when you pray, do not use vain repetitions as the heathen *do*. For they think they will be heard for their many words" (Matthew 6:7). Among other theological questions to those in agreement with the non-biblical doctrine of the deification of the Virgin Mary, when she states in Luke 1:47, "And my spirit has rejoiced in God my savior." That is, she too acknowledged her need for a Saviour.

Dr. Carpenter brings a group of locals over to the nuns' apartment to paint it, but afterward he's the only one who stays for a dinner of Sister Barbara's noodle ring. Even playing a man of advanced learning, Presley ducks a question that might draw him out intellectually. "Tell me," asks Sister Barbara, "As a doctor, would you diagnose what's happening today, the riots, the student unrest, as not really the death throes of an old order, but the birth pains of a new one?" Dr. Carpenter quips in reply, "I didn't know I was makin' a house call." Pretentious though it might sound, Sister Barbara's question is the only instance of dialog in a Presley movie of a specific reference to the politics of the day, and is something he responds to apolitically. Insofar as advocating for the Western world ideology of pleasure, however, that doesn't mean that the Presley movies are exempt from demonstrating political tendencies.

"Don't we all in our own way have to man the barricades?" persists the aspiring activist nun. "At the Ajax Market?" retorts the playfully cynical Dr. Carpenter. It's unclear whether this reply is another instance of the superficially apolitical, or a still normalized sexism that preferred to ignore a woman's politics. Presley's Dr. Carpenter casually dismisses as petty and peevish the concerns over injustice to consumers—*in a ghetto!* Sister Barbara will later exemplify the film maker's perspective that there's a kind of pathos about political activism for people of normal intelligence. This was among the more socially-destabilizing tendencies amid liberal democracies in the late 1960s and early 1970s. From the perspective of the makers of *Change of Habit,* as exemplified by Sister Barbara, it's not a tendency they favor either.

A member of the apartment-painting party forgot his guitar in the nun's apartment. Do Latinos do their house-painting with guitars? Dr. Carpenter snuggles up to Sister Michelle as he teaches her a few guitar chords. As Dr. Carpenter, Presley then plays the piano and Sister Michelle strums the guitar. The stiff-necked old Catholic women complain to Father Gibbons by phone about debauchery occurring in the home of their new neighbors. Alone in the kitchen together, Dr. Carpenter tries to put the moves on Sister Michelle. "I get the feeling there's somebody else," he says. "You could say that," she replies. It's hinted that Dr. Carpenter, a.k.a. Elvis Presley, is in competition with God for a woman's affections. Moore's capacity to evince nervous virtuousness works well with her playing Sister Michelle, a woman seemingly frightened by her own sexuality. "Message received. Goodnight Michelle," says a gracious Dr. Carpenter. As he leaves the apartment, Julio the stutterer lurks in the shadows. He too wants something from Sister Michelle.

Autistic Amanda returns to the clinic the next day with her aunt, Miss Parks. Having seen Sister Michelle fail to accomplish anything with kindness, Dr. Carpenter treats the child with the controversial "rage reduction" method. The opening credits of *Change of Habit* ascribe supervision of the rage reduction sequence to a Dr. Robert Zaslow. The method was based on the mistaken belief that autism resulted from a failure to bond between a mother and her newborn. Proceeding from that mistaken belief, the adult treating the autistic child would vigorously restrain the child, sometimes even lay on top of the child, all the while maintaining eye contact with the child. This was meant to evoke rage in the child. It was thought that the rage would turn to despair, thus breaking down the child's resistances, thereby bringing about a bonding with the adult administering the treatment. Within two years of the release of *Change of Habit,* after inflicting serious injuries on many helpless autistic children and at least six deaths resulting from "rage reduction" therapy, Dr. Zaslow's license to practice psychology was suspended.[39]

While there remains no known cure for autism, Dr. Carpenter and Sister Michelle achieve miraculous results with Amanda. Several minutes of screen time are edited to suggest the passing of hours of Elvis Presley out-wrestling a little girl. He goads her to get her angrier as Sister Michelle helps pin the girl to his lap. "We love you Amanda," they chant in repetitious

---

[39] *Wickipedia*: Attachment Therapy, September 18, 2010.

unison. After persisting with this for most of the day, Amanda starts speaking pigeon English, telling the doctor and the nun that she loves them. "You did it!" chirps the nun. "We did it," replies the doctor. It just goes to show that one man's victory is another man's spending the day wrestling with a mute little girl.

After treating a badly beaten Latino unable to make good on a loan repayment to The Banker, Sister Irene is confronted by two Black Panther types. "We've got to know where you stand," says one of the militants.

"I'm a nurse. That's where I stand," she replies. From that point, the verbal conflict between Sister Irene and the Black Panther types escalates. While such a conflict might not be impossible, as with some men of almost any ethnicity, this derogatory, as-if-typical characterization of Black men in *Change of Habit* as clannish, bullying and misogynistic is clearly racist. Despite Sister Irene's protestation that she's done her share in the struggle for racial equality (as if the battle for it had been completely won this world by then), she's suspected of being an Aunt Tom. It's another telling aspect of the movie's reactionary outlook that Sister Irene, in several ways the most devout of the three nuns, identifies herself as a Negro instead of being Black.

Playing on opposing teams, Dr. Carpenter and Sister Michelle have a friendly game of football in the park with some of the locals. Ever the leader, Presley's Dr. Carpenter calls the plays for his side, informing one of his Latino players that using a knife in the game is prohibited. Sister Michelle, her youth accentuated by her donning pigtails, throws a successful touchdown pass. Moments later she's tackled by Dr. Carpenter, but the game, like the movie itself, plays to an indeterminate ending.

Dr. Carpenter springs for ice cream cones for himself, Sister Michelle and, mysteriously, the formerly autistic Amanda, who's materialized as if beamed down by the Starship Enterprise. He explains that practicing medicine in the Washington Street slum is his way of showing gratitude to his former army Sargent. The Sargent had lived there, saved his life, but then died on the other side of the world. At a time in popular culture history when Vietnam veterans were usually either unrepresented or shown to be dangerously unhinged criminals, Presley's Dr. Carpenter has seen the Viet Cong face-to-face in combat and has lived to talk about it. A triple function is served thereby. Presley's character is reestablished as a man of action, one who eventually, inevitably, takes recourse to violence. It also recycles Presley's former army affiliation, again implicitly, without extensively advocating for American militarism. Possibly extensively commenting on the Vietnam War would load more socio-political content than a Presley movie could sustain. Additionally, the brutality of war is downplayed by showing Dr. Carpenter as someone who did a tour of duty in Vietnam without experiencing any psychological repercussions beyond an admiration of his Sargent.

Dr. Carpenter, Sister Michelle and Amanda, ice cream cones in hand, go for a merry-go-round ride. When Amanda resists Presley's ability to charm children by refusing to smile for him, his identity as a figure of enchantment is reasserted. "This calls for a special kind of magic," he says in response to Amanda's recalcitrance. He launches into "Have a Happy (Warm Smiling Face)," complete with invisible orchestration. It's a song that might have made it onto *Sesame Street* episode and does bring a smile to Amanda's face. Presley's musically irresistible magnetism to children is restated. Sister Michelle is more demonstrably jubilant in her response to the song.

Following the song, the creepy Julio is seen retreating from the park. "It's his stuttering," says Sister Michelle, "[it] makes him feel inadequate."

"You take away his stuttering, you're gonna find a deeper problem. I don't think you wanna part of that," cautions Dr. Carpenter.

"Maybe you're wrong about Julio," says the nun. "You were wrong about Amanda [thinking she was deaf]."

"I hope so," says the doctor. He adds, "The other night when I put my arms around you, it wasn't an accident. You didn't quite level with me. There isn't anyone else." It's an odd bit of verbal irony. Is Dr. Carpenter's comment related to his romantic interest in her, or is he covertly disputing the existence of God? At night on Washington Street, Sister Barbara sees a man being beaten and abducted, an example of the savage logic of how business can be conducted in the slums. A weary Sister Barbara says, "Me for the sack." "Me for the sackcloth and ashes,"[40] replies Sister Michelle, a possible expression of regret over having had fun that day. Before the two nuns part company that night, they're confronted by the draconian Father Gibbons. He chews them out for wearing jeans and sweatshirts, telling them he wants them out of his parish.

The next day, The Banker shows up at the clinic to warn Dr. Carpenter to keep his staff from interfering with the grocer at the Ajax Market. Dr. Carpenter puffs on a long, slender cigarillo. The tobacco industry might have financed the entire movie to show Presley smoking. There's some true-to-life authenticity therein too. Presley liked to smoke thin German cigars, a taste he might have acquired while stationed in Germany for military duty. The cigarillo brings out his inner Groucho as he quips, "I can't help you, Banker. I'm a doctor, not a veterinarian."

---

[40] Aside from the movie's opening allusion to The Great Commission, this is the movie's only other direct verbal reference to scripture, "So I turned to the Lord God and pleaded with him in prayer and petition, in fasting, and in sackcloth and ashes," *Daniel 9:3.* "Woe to you, Korazin! Woe to you, Bethsaida! If the miracles that were performed in you had been performed in Tyre and Sidon, they would have repented long ago in sackcloth and ashes," *Matthew 11:21.* The opening line of the closing song performed by Presley in this movie is close, but no cookie.

Whereas Groucho might have made the line funny, Presley only sounds openly contemptuous.

Sister Irene has borrowed 100 dollars from The Banker for the community feast of San Juan de Chequez. Concealing her identity as a nun, she confesses to Dr. Carpenter that she's used her vocation to run away from things all her life. Dr. Carpenter empathizes, telling her that he too knows what it is to be hungry, frightened and poor. Again, Presley's biography sneaks into his movie role. Sister Irene tops Dr. Carpenter by dropping the n-bomb, telling him of her experiences growing up in the ghetto, how she prayed she could be somebody other than "just another [n_____] in the streets."

In the office of Bishop Finley (Richard Carlson), Father Gibbons complains about the unconventional attire of Sisters Michelle, Irene and Barbara. "Inexperienced people who get emotionally involved can do more harm than good," the Bishop advises the nuns. "Among our first lessons is the importance of discipline and order." The philosophical clergyman's statement is another instance of verbal irony as it relates to the flailing romance between Sister Michelle and Dr. Carpenter. The priest then suggests a compromise between Gibbons and the nuns. The Feast of San Juan de Chequez will proceed as planned, but the nuns will have to wear their habits. The change of habit was a short-lived one. "But there's so much we haven't accomplished as women!" says a crestfallen Sister Michelle, as if nuns are not women.

As the re-habited sisters somberly stride back into the Washington Street slum, one of the anonymous old woman neighbors comments to the other, "wild parties, pagan music, men at all hours, whatever they've done, they must have had good cause!" Sister Barbara, a mock proponent of what Christian philosopher Dallas Willard identified as "The Gospel on the

Left"[41], that is, an expression of Christian faith through social and political activism, pickets the Ajax Market. "Ajax Market Unfair to Consumers," states her placard. In an era of epidemics of civil unrest, Sister Barbara's placard caricatures the placard-carrying protester as a petty malcontent.[42] Her proclamation to her Catholic sisters that she's "being willfully disobedient" suggests a toothless reformism. Viewers are implicitly urged to rightly think of themselves as being above engaging in such futile exercises. Sister Barbara then takes allowing for this glimpse of her radicalism one step further when she reveals herself to Dr. Carpenter as a nun in a nun's habit to his astonishment.

"I couldn't," she says. "It was an experiment." Therein resides something insightful about the movie's vintage. An era of experimentation brought with it its own new rules and orthodoxies, whether stated or not. What was looked on as one of the most trustworthy and tradition-oriented of institutions, the Roman Catholic Church, is the movie's authoritative reference point indicting the dangers of experimentation, sensibly in some respects, perhaps, grossly closed-minded in other respects.

Dr. Carpenter is called to the Ajax Market where Sister Barbara is staging her one-nun demonstration. Arriving on the scene is local cop Lieutenant Moretti (Ed Asner), the picture of calm. "I don't employ obsolete tactics to deal with a contemporary situation," says the Lieutenant as he helps himself to a banana. As Sister Barbara announces that she wants to be dragged out by her heels, the Lieutenant tells her, "If you come by the station house, we might discuss environmental

---

[41]   Dallas Willard, *The Divine Conspiracy.*
[42]   This is the third instance of a belittling representation of a protester in a Presley movie. Fans might recall Shelley Fabares brandishing a picket in *Girl Happy* that stated "I'm Evil," as well as the anonymous picketer at Jo Symington's Happening in *Easy Come, Easy Go,* whose placard reads "I Protest."

social pressures and how they affect present-day society." The completely unperturbed tone of his diction suggests several things at once. First, he reads her immediately and completely. To him, she's a relatively benign nuisance interfering with local business transactions. Contrary to stereotypes of the cop of the inner city slum, Moretti is implacable when facing verbal hostility. He intuits unerringly that he's dealing with someone who regards herself as an intellectual, so then proceeds to show her that he can speak as a better intellectual. As a nun, a woman and an intellectual, Sister Barbara is no real threat to Lieutenant Moretti. To him, being an intellectual is merely a strategic pose. "Police brutality!" she shouts out of exasperation at not being taken seriously.

That evening, the stuttering Julio is shown stealing a modestly-sized statue of Christ and two other figures helping carry His cross. Julio is trying to "get religion." On Washington Street, the Feast of San Juan de Chequez is in full swing. As a band plays and a crowd of Blacks and Latinos dance jubilantly, Dr. Carpenter arrives in a black suit and black shirt. Except for the absence of a cleric's collar, he looks as if he joined the priesthood. Sisters Michelle and Barbara serve hot dogs to the multitudes as membership of the local chapter of Black militants, all two of them, look on stoically. Lieutenant Moretti and his men search for Julio Hernandez to apprehend him for the theft of the church statue.

"I can feel the lid rattling," Dr. Carpenter says of the celebration to Sister Michelle. "When it blows, you're going to need a doctor," he adds. The nuns are shocked to discover that someone is distributing free liquor. Sister Michelle introduces her Mother Superior, Mother Joseph (Leora Dana), to the formerly autistic Amanda. The little girl mimics Sister Irene's mini-soliloquy on growing up in the ghetto, rank offensiveness of the n-word included.

Sister Irene refuses to reimburse The Banker for the money she borrowed. It's his "donation," she tells him. Stoked by her own defiance, she announces that a moratorium has been put into effect on all debts to The Banker. "You'd better cool it, Irene," says a prudent Dr. Carpenter. Sister Irene boils over and tears a few verbal strips off The Banker. He responds by hitting her. Dr. Carpenter then administers fist therapy to the faces of The Banker and several of his torpedoes. As Lieutenant Moretti and his men move in, order is quickly restored by the doctor's actions and the intimidating presence of the two Black militants. One of the militants gives the Lieutenant his "triple-bonded, gilt-edged guarantee [that] there ain't no trouble." "I'll settle for that," says the Lieutenant, then takes The Banker away.

Why the police restore order this way isn't clear. However, it's another Presleyan utopian conclusion, the magnitude of which hasn't been seen since the ending of *Paradise, Hawaiian Style*. Momentarily anyway, evil is banished from the neighborhood. The Kingdom has symbolically arrived on Washington Street. All debts, sin being a debt in theological terms, have been canceled, as proclaimed by a nun. The violent, racially-divided environment of the slum has successfully policed itself with only modest help from the real police. Black militants and police are of one accord.

When Sister Michelle returns to the nuns' apartment, she finds Sister Barbara dressed in her civvies. Frustrated by the limitations of being a nun, Barbara opines, "I may be giving up the religious life, but I'm not giving up the fight. I've organized a political advancement committee right here in the neighborhood, and we have our first meeting tomorrow morning. Look, we've scored two victories already, the Ajax Market and The Banker, and now is no time to stop."

Subsequently, Julio interrupts Sister Michelle as she's changing into her nightgown. She orders him to put down the knife he's brandishing, to no avail. "No, knife make me big man," he stammers in Tarzan-style elocution. She wants to help him, she says, and urges him to turn himself in. Stating that she "make a fool of [him]," he commences groping her. As Sister Michelle is being assaulted, Sister Irene and Dr. Carpenter discuss a foreshadowing of the movie's conclusion. "I come from a long line of people who believe in getting married, having kids," he says.

"Our church believes in that too," replies Sister Irene.

Sister Michelle is overheard screaming. Dr. Carpenter expediently thwarts her attacker. Sensing that Dr. Carpenter can readily handle Julio, Sister Michelle cries, "John, don't hurt him!" The slum-dwelling assailant runs away. "I tried! I tried!" sobs the nun in Dr. Carpenter's welcoming arms.

Back at the convent with her eyes open, Sister Michelle is shown contemplating. Mother Joseph enters, telling Sister Michelle she's "got to choose the kind of love [she] want[s]: physical love or the kind of love [she] can only find through prayer. From my own experience I can tell you that nothing is more painful than no decision." Mother Joseph recommends an "outside stimulus." Dr. Carpenter arrives, heightening the contrast of whether the nun will choose to live her faith or marry, her conflict possibly precipitated by her belief devout prayer life necessitates staying single.

The frustrated lovers meet in the convent hallway. A significant passage of time has elapsed since they last met. Informing her that the austere Father Gibbons "is coming out of the Middle Ages" and isn't going to press charges against Julio for theft, Dr. Carpenter says the troubled youth will soon be released from a psychiatric hospital, but he'll still be in need of a speech therapist. He then asks her directly, "Would you be committing a sin if you were to leave and get married?" She replies: "in marriage you love God through one person. As a nun, I made a commitment to love God through all people." As Christ commands, the greatest commandments are to love the Lord our God with all our hearts and minds and strength and to love our neighbors as ourselves.

Sister Michelle and Dr. Carpenter confess their love for each other. Yet she says she doesn't know if she can give him an answer. In self-martyring fashion, she walks away to occupy what Mother Joseph told her was the most painful of positions, that of failing to make a decision.

Sister Michelle and Sister Irene read a letter from the former Sister Barbara, who's continuing with her political activism. "What's an 'infrastructural sphere of mechanistic behaviorism'?" Sister Michelle asks while reading. Barbara has progressed in her capacity to use intellectually obscure terminology as well. A delightedly puzzled Sister Irene shakes her head.

"You think she's a communist?" asks Sister Michelle.

Sister Irene chuckles, "Oh no, no!", recognizing that confusing rhetoric is not the exclusive province of radical left-wing politics.

Sister Michelle comments, "whatever it is, she seems to be happy with it. You seem happy too."

"Peace, Sister, It's wonderful," says Sister Irene, in a manner akin to issuing a commercial endorsement. "You are never going to be able to fish or cut bait until you see that young man again," she adds.

The nuns return to the Washington Street parish. In between the pews, a more pious Dr. Carpenter leads a band singing a pop-sounding hymn, "Come Praise the Lord for He is Good." It's a good tune, too, though as per the rest of the feature, Christ isn't mentioned by name. That could be a discrepancy between Catholicism and Protestantism.

The movie's conclusion is a little perplexing. Sister Michelle smiles restrainedly. Her smile changes into something more melancholic as the camera slowly zooms in on her face. Her gaze, and the audience's gaze with it, shifts to a statue of an androgynous-looking Saint John the Apostle, then to a statue

---

of the Virgin Mary holding the Christ child, then back to the musically performing Dr. Carpenter, and then to a statue of the crucified Christ. An emotionally-pained look registers on the nun's face and she shuts her eyes. There's a cut to a shot of the entire interior of the parish sanctuary as the closing credits commence rolling. This ending might seem utterly ambiguous at first. It isn't, really. The final close-up of shows her, eyes closed, possibly in silent prayer or meditation. She may have lost Dr. John Carpenter as a husband, but she still has him as a brother parishioner.

EPILOGUE

R easons of financial exploitation aside, Elvis Presley's career as a movie star, in its totality, suggests, among other things, that Hollywood never really knew what to do with him. It's self-evident that the majority of Presley's movies, those of the 1960s, at least, have the cheap, hurried quality of poorly-made mass-produced goods. Nevertheless, he was the highest-grossing movie star throughout that decade. Feeling ill-at-ease with rock & roll's prospects for longevity played no small part in the shoddiness of the resulting cultural products. Producer Hal B. Wallis boasted that, in Presley's profitability, he had "the only sure thing in Hollywood." Presley's talent as an entertainer clearly took precedence over the flimsiness of most of the film projects he performed in, just as Colonel Parker cautioned at least one of Presley's directors that he wasn't interested in winning any Academy Awards. Though weary of the screen vehicles he was plugged into by the 1960s, Presley himself never challenged either Parker or the studios over the dreck he had to star in.

The implicit and problematic cultural question of "What is Elvis Presley?" was also financially advantageous. He could readily be made to fit various guises: delinquent Elvis, westerner Elvis, Elvis the soldier, Elvis the Hawaiian tour guide and so on. To observe that popular culture is an industry and Hollywood has always been in the business of making money is one thing.

Yet Presley's cachet among audiences was such that those responsible for the crafting and lack of craftsmanship in most of his movies got away with a lot. What they didn't succeed at, and their star was often resentfully well-aware of it, was leaving his fans with a few movies that were of any real quality. As noted in an earlier citing of Steve Pond's discussion on Elvis and the movies, for someone to establish himself as a singing star and then embark on a movie career wasn't a novelty. Rudy Vallée, Bing Crosby and Frank Sinatra had each trod that road before Presley. As previously discussed in this book, however, there were at least two distinctly different contingencies rooted in one commonality that set Presley's movies apart. They were at once advertisements not just for the star, but also for rock & roll. As such, they were Cold War propaganda weapons as well. While Presley's migration into filmdom was accompanied by a cooling down of his vocal and bodily hysterics, for young movie audiences, he continued to be the sound, the look and the embodiment of contemporary young America. Rock & roll first emerged, in part, as a less-than-completely-innocuous rebellion against authority, parental and otherwise. The 1953 production of *The Wild One* had a jazz soundtrack. Nevertheless, Marlon Brando's character of Johnny, the leader of a biker gang, spoke on behalf of an emerging rock & roll generation. When asked, "Hey Johnny, what are you rebelling against?" Brando famously replies "What have you got?" Youth and adolescent rebellion were interwoven with the zeitgeist. That popular culture would increasingly find ways to profit on that situation was inevitable.

Many of the Presley movies of the 1960s, with exceptions, presented a milder Presley, someone at a distant reserve from the rock & roll he'd done much to pioneer. As mentioned and attributed to Peter Guralnick's *Last Train to Memphis* (1995), Presley, Colonel Parker and various other prominent persona involved in the rock & roll industry were anxious and skeptical about the potential longevity of the new music.

Those insecurities fed well into the fast buck mentality and a let's-get-this-over-with approach to filmmaking starring Presley.

Pairing the leading figure of rock & roll music with motion pictures was implicitly, if not overtly, a marketing and a political decision. That the commencement of Presley's film career closely coincided with the end of McCarthyism's ideological pillaging of Hollywood meant that Presley the movie star wouldn't be hauling any politics into what he starred in, not too overtly anyway. The most comprehensive label for the majority of Presley's movies, as a genre, might be to call them capitalist fairy tales. Unfortunately, it's difficult, if not impossible, to discuss the political leanings of Presley's superficially apolitical film legacy without invoking variations of what American humourist James Thurber sardonically termed "creeping socialism."

In real life, or as near as Presley could get to it, by submitting to being drafted into the army, he could have hardly made a more overt expression of obedience to authority. As discussed previously, the movies Presley made after his military service seemed oriented toward the forgetting of Presley's rock & roll past and, to some extent, of Presley himself in terms of his first claim to fame. Producer Hal Wallis, Colonel Tom Parker and, to some extent, Presley himself, were going to take Presley's image to the race track and take some big chances with rock & roll's golden goose. While not entirely trash, the Presley movies of the 1960s, in their totality, they seem exemplary of a kind of contest. That Presley survived making 27 of them from 1960 to 1969 is a tribute to his endurance. The resulting products were a rarely remitting indictment of someone who'd made plain that he was capable of incomparably better things.

Presley-the-singing-actor of the 1960s acted in the servitude of erasing his own musical history. Following a series of passably entertaining features centered on the construct of the rock & roll rebel, the big screen Presley's rehabilitation was dragged out through banal melodrama, bland musicals and mirthless comedies. The same mentality that made a movie star of Audie Murphy, the most decorated American veteran of World War II, also seems to have been behind turning Presley into a movie star. Yet whereas Audie Murphy perished in a plane crash, Elvis Presley became a plane crash. Nevertheless, popular culture as a business recognizes the profitable mutability of celebrity. That a famous singer or war veteran can be turned into a major movie star indicates that celebrity carries with it a kind of authority. That same authority can be translated into various other cultural and marketing stratagems. It's the same principle by which star athletes can become trustworthy commercial pitchmen for products or services for which they have no logical basis to have any expertise about.

By way of a sustained application of the Freudian theory of thraldom, I sought to posit a possible explanation for the rampant mass adulation of Presley. I'm not a devotee of Freud's ideas, nor most any of the other thinkers whose ideas I've applied to Presley's movies. Often, however, strands of legitimate insight can be found in otherwise significantly flawed conceptual tapestries, as well as effectively illuminate other, specific phenomena.

To those who have read this book in its entirety, my opening claim, that Presley's movies champion the superiority of liberal democracy because it's the most fun, ought to hardly require further elaboration. The implied prohibitions on other pleasures, specifically pleasures related to the life of the mind, can readily be summarized in one name: Brentwood Van Durgenfeld (see "I need a girl to make my life worth livin'"). The rank hostility to the enjoyments of the life of the mind reflects how these movies, and perhaps even Presley himself as a movie star, cannot withstand critical scrutiny. By the same standard, in the opening to his lengthy tome *The Varieties of Religious Experience* (1902),

William James notes how we tend to recoil from seeing objects of our affection handled by the cold, dispassionate intellect.

Since Presley officially left the army in 1960, there has been an explosion in the growth of leisure and recreation industries in the Western world, something author and pastor Tim Keller has taken note of respective to other matters. Presley as swinging troubadour for recreation and leisure is central, both to his propagandizing for the supremacy of Western world forms of political organization, as well as his prescriptivism toward how the mass audience would do well to kill time.

Philosopher Max Horkheimer asserted that the primary role of the media, what now would be called mainstream media, is to normalize violence. While Horkheimer's assertion was an overstatement in that media functions, as is common in much American popular culture, nearly every Presley movie includes displays of violence. As per rock & roll's liberalizing of sexuality and sexuality among youth in particular, in addition to its appeal as entertainment, violence in Presley's movies is presented as something natural and normal. Typically in Presley movies, violence eventually and invariably results in justice being done, rather than being an injustice in its own right. Violence is generally venerated as a reasonable way to settle conflicts, rather than something likely to escalate a conflict or perpetuate an injustice. Also reflecting the normalization of violence in Presley's movies is the casualness with which it's regarded, that it's rarely ever even commented on by any of the screen actors. They appear to accept violence as something that just happens.

Explicitly identified by psychologist Diana St. Clair in *Spinout* as "the ideal American male," Presley's capacity for violence isn't separable from all else that makes him attractive to women. It's consistent what *Kissin' Cousins* expounded on as an unbroken continuum between the martial and the sexual. The quality of violence in these movies is in agreement with the sanctioning of polygamy. Stanley Kubrick's *Dr. Strangelove; or, How I Learned to Stop Worrying and Love the Bomb* (1963) satirized the idea of U.S. government bomb shelters, deploying them as places where beautiful women would sexually cater to the male power elite; in contract, Presley the Dionysian Cold Warrior of 1960s repeatedly engaged in comparable situations without a trace of satire or irony. Nuclear age polygamy reflects a primitivism within the military-industrial mentality. Affirming violence as a form of pleasure, the Presley protagonist's love-'em-and-leave-'em smorgasboard approach to women suggests not just something casually sadistic about his screen persona, but an element of cruelty inherent in the kind of relationships advocated by the sexual revolution.

The schism between words and action in the Presley movies, probably most evident in *Stay Away, Joe,* manifests another example of popular culture's contempt toward linguistic clarity. The result is not only a depreciated communication between individuals, but degraded cognition as well. Especially by the 1960s, as Presley's move song lyrics will attest, language can be trotted out as a kind of empty aesthetic. With a melody, a mood imposed on circumstances through plot developments and little else, language is reduced to a powder puff confection largely, if not completely void of content.

Hawaiian natives in *Blue Hawaii* and *Paradise, Hawaiian Style;* Mexicans in *Fun in Acapulco;* and Lunarkanians (Lunarkarkasses?) in *Harum Scarum* all provide occasions for non-White people to idolize Presley, doing so with as much or more zeal as adolescent American girls in the 1950s. Though relatively simplistic narratives, those movies also exhibit how easily idolatry, sexism and militarism can coalesce with each other. Exalting heterosexual coupling, while often disdaining monogamy, was one way of lessening the ongoing threat of mushroom-cloud-related anxieties. Exhortations to be promiscuous were expedient for other reasons. Affronts to political stability were vulnerable to unrestrained libidinal activity. The efficacy of this strategy was such that it was further capitalized on in the 1970s through the proliferation of so-called TV jiggle shows, disco culture and booming growth of the pornography industry in the 1970s. The guiding yet seriously flawed reasoning equates an ever-increasing removal of prohibitions and inhibitions as synonymous with progress. That any society can proceed on the basis of such presumptions ought to readily and rightly be seen as serious error.

Most often in the 1960s cycle of Presley movies, his character is overtly or implicitly in some form of leadership. Even as an army private in *G.I. Blues*, his soldier pals take their cues from him, calling on him to save their betting scheme. As a troubled youth in *Wild in the Country*, it's Presley who rescues his therapist. Elvis Presley, the most natural of Americans, is also the most natural of leaders. In other Presley movies of the 1960s, if a plan is needed, he's usually presented as having one. Having led the hedonistic charge as chief provider and partaker in fun, his latter movies display him being male-privileged, G-rated brand of sexual revolution. The results of that revolution are very much with us today. Regarding the legacy of that revolution and in light of the devastation it's wrought upon marriage, the conventional family, and the health and wellbeing of the individual is simply this: is society really any more free as a result of that revolution?

Presley's Charlie Rogers in *Roustabout* has a distinctly different lady love interest than Michele Carey's character of Bernice in *Live a Little, Love a Little*. While in *Roustabout*, Presley still possesses vestiges of his 1950s youth rebel persona, in the latter production he's a career man juggling catering to his self-interest. Both movies suggest there's something potentially socially destabilizing about Presley. Both narratives relate how to tame what's potentially socially destabilizing about him. Women, even a woman a flaky as Michelle Cary's Bernice, are necessary to reel him in from the threat he poses to society. The dance of going back and forth with his lady love interests until he's been romantically ensnared is still Presley's playing out an adolescent identity. If he doesn't know who he is, how can he know what or who he wants?

Frankie and Johnny, the closest thing to a historical movie that Presley ever made, recounts events in such a way that what was a murder turns out to not have been a murder at all. In keeping with the amnesia process of the culture industry, in *Frankie and Johnny,* history never happened. As with *Roustabout* and *Live a Little, Love a Little, Frankie and Johnny* appears to proceed from the same sensibility: when in doubt, have Presley sing about what a wonderful, wonderful, wonderful, wonderful world this is, albeit to different melodies each time. Indeed, this world as God created it is to be for our enjoyment and can be a wonderful place. The world in terms of its collective humanity, the world that God so loved that he gave his only begotten Son so that whosoever believes in Him would not perish but have everlasting life[43] is also wonderful. Yet it's also a broken, fallen world in desperate need of redemption. Is Presley a little too affirmative at times, a little too forgetful?

Following from the discussion of *Spinout,* the question of why rock & roll never gave rise to a concurrent cultural achievement anywhere else in the arts persists. Either the frenzy that rock & roll gave rise to was somehow inauthentic, or Nietzsche was wrong (it certainly wouldn't be the only time). Nor do the shortcomings of the great thinkers stop there. Marx and his followers understood ideology as the embellishment and glorification of a contradiction, a definition wrought from his attack on Christianity in an essay by Ludwig Fuerbach. Yet as seen in *Easy Come, Easy Go,* the exceptionally potent agglomeration of militarism, capitalism, sexism and rock & roll

---

[43]   John 3:16.

need not present a contradiction. In fact, these agencies can be made to appear to compliment and promote each other. As with using Presley to disparage the anti-materialism of the 1960s counterculture demonstrates, he could readily be utilized for a variety of political purposes.

Variations on what I've called the Triumph of the Deal, a theme that originated in *Blue Hawaii* and recurred through several later Presley features, including *Easy Come, Easy Go*, reflects how drenched in commerce these movies are. Many of these movies wrought so nakedly from business negotiations that they often intertwine business negotiations into their aesthetic structure. A theme presented in both *Blue Hawaii* and *Clambake* is that those born into great material wealth will, if circumstances require, demonstrate how deserving they are by accumulating that wealth all over again. Willfully forgetting the origins of rock & roll, they present the contradiction of the protagonist as someone who establishes himself as self-made man, but is simultaneously motivated by a desire to earn parental approval, something decidedly apart from the initial rock & roll ethos. Therein resides a part of the hypocrisy of rock & roll, the rebellion against parents coinciding with coveting their respectful opinion, though the truly self-made can't have parents.

The Presley movies of the 1960s weren't just advertisements for the superiority of the American way of life due to its abundance of pleasure. Comparable to advertising, they promoted social stability through the advocacy of constant leisure as a normal state of existence. Following a career of 31 narrative motion pictures, Elvis Presley returned to performing before live audiences. Two concert documentaries, *Elvis: That's the Way It Is* (1970) and *Elvis on Tour* (1972), provide glimpses of Elvis Presley doing he did best as a show business phenomenon. For some viewers it might be difficult to watch these highly entertaining concert films without experiencing feeling melancholy over the rapidness of his subsequent dissipation. Most of the 31 movies he acted in allow for little more than glimpses of ruthlessly exploited potential. With few exceptions, his 31 movie legacy plays out like a legacy of waste. Concomitantly, an old French proverb asserts that societies reveal themselves away. It is hoped for that this exegesis of movies with largely throwaway qualities has revealed matters of interest and value. For devout Presley fans, there's always his audio recordings.

"Little children, keep yourselves from idols. Amen."
1 John 5:21

CPSIA information can be obtained
at www.ICGtesting.com
Printed in the USA
BVHW062015120720
583532BV00008B/138